The Complete Photo Guide to

CROCHET

Creative Publishing international

Copyright © 2010
Creative Publishing international, Inc.
400 First Avenue North Suite 300
Minneapolis, Minnesota 55401
1-800-328-3895
www.creativepub.com

All rights reserved.

Printed in China
10 9 8 7 6 5 4 3 2 1

Library of Congress Cataloging-in-Publication Data

Hubert, Margaret.
    The complete photo guide to crochet / Margaret Hubert.
        p. cm.
    Summary: "Reference for crocheters; includes instructions and dia-
grams for 200 stitch patterns, basic information about how to crochet,
plus 20 patterns"–Provided by publisher.
    ISBN-13: 978-1-58923-472-7 (soft cover)
    ISBN-10: 1-58923-472-3 (soft cover)
    1. Crocheting. 2. Crocheting–Pictorial works. I. Title.

    TT820.H8325 2010
    746.43'4–dc22

2009031798

President/CEO: Ken Fund
Vice President/Sales & Marketing: Kevin Hamric
Publisher: Winnie Prentiss
Acquisition Editor: Linda Neubauer
Production Managers: Laura Hokkanen, Linda Halls
Creative Director: Michele Lanci-Altomare
Art Directors: Jon Simpson, Brad Springer, James Kegley
Lead Photographer: Joel Schnell
Photographer: Corean Komarec
Photo Coordinator: Joanne Wawra
Cover & Book Design: Kim Winscher
Page Layout: Danielle Smith

Visit www.Craftside.Typepad.com for a behind-the-scenes peek at our
crafty world!

Dedication

For my family, my children, grandchildren, and new
great-grandchild; they are the sunshine of my life.

Acknowledgments

I have a long list of people to thank for their help in putting this book
together.

I would like to thank Tahki Stacy Charles, Inc. for donating all of the
yarn used for the stitch samples and for several of the projects in the
book. I would also like to thank the company for its generosity and
continued support for designers everywhere.

Thanks to Aussie Yarns, Blue Heron Yarns, Knitting Fever, Lion Brand
Yarn, Patons, and Plymouth Yarn Company, Inc. for their continued
support in donating yarn for some of the special projects.

Thanks to Julia Bryant, Jennifer Hansen, Melody MacDuffee, Prudence
Mapstone, Pam Shore, Tatyana Mirer, Pauline Turner, and Myra Wood
for sharing their expertise in special crochet techniques and for allowing
us to photograph some of their very special items for this book.

Thanks to Jules Kliot and Nancy Nehring for sharing their knowledge
of the history of crochet.

Thanks to Jeannine Buehler, Dee Stanziano, and Paula Alexander for
helping me to make many of the samples in the book.

Last, but by no means least, is a very big "thank you" to my editor,
Linda Neubauer. Easy to work with, never ruffled, always pleasant,
ever helpful; without Linda, there would be no book.

The Complete Photo Guide to
CROCHET

Creative Publishing
international

CONTENTS

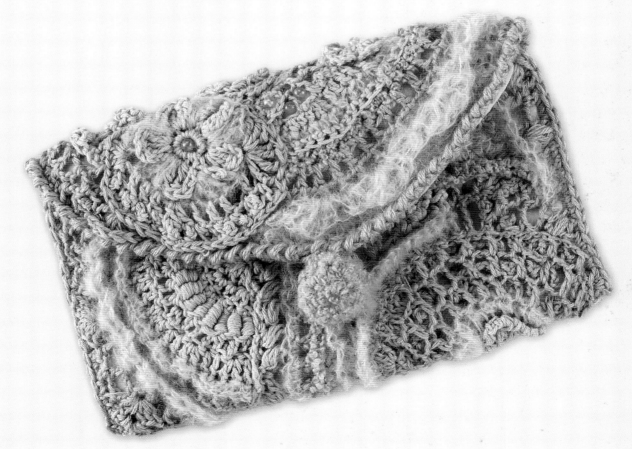

Introduction to Crochet

Crochet is such a wonderful craft. There are so many facets and variations to explore with a hook and some yarn. The creative possibilities are endless.

Crocheters do not just use yarn; they crochet with every imaginable form of fiber. I have seen items made with kite string, fishing line, wire, rag strips, and paper strips. I'm sure there are some fibers used for crocheting that I have yet to see.

In this book, I have included an extensive collection of stitches, from the very basic to more intricate techniques. Delicate lacy openwork to heavier textures like bobbles, bullions, limpets, basket weave, and double-sided crochet, edgings, and motifs are all included.

Detailed, step-by-step instructions, charts, and photographs accompany each stitch. Every stitch is ranked by level of difficulty to help you try your hand at progressively complex stitches, and there are sample projects throughout the book that showcase at least one of the stitches used in each group.

In addition to the stitch section, there is a specialty crochet methods section. In this section, I have included methods such as freeform crochet, intermeshing crochet, and crocheting raglans from the top down.

I have asked fellow designers, who are experts in their fields, to contribute a project in their area of expertise to the specialty crochet methods section. Contributors and their projects include: Pauline Turner, Polish Star; Melody MacDuffee, Overlay Crochet; Julia Bryant, Tapestry Tunision; Jennifer Hansen, Hairpin Lace and Broomstick Lace; and Tatyana Mirer, Bruges Lace. Fellow freeform crocheters Prudence Mapstone, Myra Wood, and Pam Shore have graciously allowed me to show photographs of some of their garments in the Freeform Crochet chapter.

Nancy Nehring explores the history of crochet, and her article is accompanied by an exquisite example of antique crochet.

Jules Kliot, who along with his wife, Kaethe, founded the Lacis Museum of Lace and Textiles in Berkeley, California, has allowed us to use photographs depicting special pieces from the museum.

I have tried to include something for everyone, so please enjoy!

Margaret Hubert

Crochet: Developing a Craft

by Nancy Nehring

Modern crochet dates to the early 1800s, which makes it a relative newcomer to the realm of needle arts when compared to other handwork pastimes, such as knitting or embroidery.

The history of crochet is well documented by Lis Paludan.[1] She found no extant pieces that dated earlier than 1800 after an extensive search in the collections of European museums and churches. Likewise, she found no written references to needlework that can be positively identified as crochet existing before the same time period. A reference to shepherd's knitting (slip-stitch crochet) in *The Memoirs of a Highland Lady* by Elizabeth Grant dates to 1812. The earliest known instructions are in an article in an 1824 *Penelope* magazine (Dutch) discussing the new technique.

Crochet started out as only one stitch, the slip stitch (single crochet in British terminology). Slip stitch with wool was used in the colder northern climates from Scotland through Scandinavia and into Eastern Europe, turning southward through Estonia and down into Bosnia. It was used to make warm, weatherproof clothing from wool. Mittens, underwear, and vests were most common. For mittens, the wool was often "fulled," or vigorously rubbed, to make them waterproof. The same materials and methods are still used today in a few places to make some of these same items. There wasn't much incentive in these areas to produce items with decorative lacy stitches when warm clothing made from thick, solid fabrics was required.

During the early 1800s, slip stitch was used to create personal accessories, such as miser bags, purses, and tobacco pouches, in the warmer southern areas of France, the Netherlands, and Germany. Though warmth was not required, a solid fabric was needed so items would not fall from the bags. Early miser bags, purses, and tobacco pouches were worked in multiple colors and either worked in rows or in the round in the back loop only. When working in rows, the work always had to be done from the right side so the yarn had to be broken at the end of each row. Crocheters could not turn the work in slip stitch because the pattern in the color work would get lost. Working in the round was borrowed from knitting and was done as a tube, again with crocheters working on the right side only. The open end was either gathered or folded in half and sewn.

Within 10 years of the earliest published miser bag patterns (1835), patterns for collars and babies' and women's caps were also being published in German and Dutch.

The chain stitch and the single crochet stitch had been added to make these accessories more decorative. This allowed more variety in shape and pattern; crochet was no longer limited to solid tubes and straight pieces. The chain stitch allowed chain meshes and corners to be made. Chain meshes are flexible, and collar patterns without increases in the body became popular as the mesh would curve around the neck. But these collars were simple, consisting of mesh stitches for the body and chain "ladders" (chain a few, then single crochet in the single crochet below) for the edging. Caps were equally simple. Single crochet, which had some height relative to slip stitch, was used to make a flat circle for the crown by increasing the number of stitches in each round (a technique borrowed from knitting). Increases were not possible with slip stitch alone. For the brim—a rectangular section worked on the right side only with yarn broken at the end of each row—crocheters used the same technique as slip stitch crochet except they made brims with chains and single crochet stitches.

The next major innovation came 10 years later, when in 1846 and 1847 Mlle. Riego de la Branchardiere published patterns in England to reproduce raised Spanish needle lace. Not only was the lace three-dimensional, it was worked forward and backward, included taller stitches, and was worked through both of the top loops. A complete foundation for crochet as we know it today was in place.

So how did we get from simple slip stitch to complex three-dimensional crocheted laces such as Irish crochet in 30 years? Four factors were involved: material, tools, education of women, and travel, all of which were the result of the Industrial Revolution.

Before the Industrial Revolution, lace making was a professional skill done by individual workers; all lace was handmade. During the Industrial Revolution, machines were invented that could make huge quantities of good-quality lace quickly. Commercial lace-making was taken over by machines and, for the most part, creating handmade lace became a hobby. Crochet lace was the last to succumb to modernization (and in fact, did not really get a good start until the advent of the Industrial Revolution). It was the only lace that could not be duplicated by machines and, in relation

Photo: Nancy Nehring

to other types of lace, could be made quickly. Elegant Irish crochet became the expensive handmade lace chosen by the wealthy; these crocheted dresses commanded prices equal to about $20,000 in today's currency.

Once humans' basic needs are met, their leisure time is used to create art and luxury. Upper-class women had long pursued needlework as both a required skill and leisure activity. But the Industrial Revolution gave working middle-class women free time to use as they pleased; typically, a working woman could claim a half day on Saturday and all day Sunday as leisure time, while a homemaker would find a few spare minutes somewhere in the day. Crochet became a hobby of choice for upper- and working-class women because stitches were fast and easy to learn and crocheting only required an inexpensive crochet hook and yarn/thread. Combining that with women's desire to be fashion conscious, crochet took off.

Materials for crochet, a hooked needle and yarn/thread, weren't always cheap. Before 1855, when the Bessemer process for large-batch steelmaking was patented, consistently good-quality needles were hard to make and expensive. The needle was made from wrought iron, which was softer than steel and easier to work. Iron wire was cut to length, pointed, and an eye was punched in one end. For a crochet needle, one side of the eye was also removed by the punch. The iron needles were then packed into crucibles surrounded by charcoal, heated white hot in pits in the ground, and then cooled slowly using the insulating quality of the soil. Carbon from the charcoal infused into the iron, which resulted in low-grade steel. But, the needles weren't finished yet. A hard scale formed on the surface of the needles during heating and cooling and had to be polished off. Then, the crochet needle was fitted into a handle for use.

By 1868, a single piece crochet hook (needle plus handle) was being made from tempered steel rod (U.S. patent 76916) in a matter of a few hours. Hooks were now cheap and readily available.

The manufacture of yarn and thread underwent its own changes. Most bobbin and needle lace had been made with linen thread. Before the invention of the cotton gin in 1793, cotton thread was as or more expensive than linen, and not as strong because the fibers were shorter. During the first half of the 1800s, England developed a huge textile industry based on spinning and weaving cotton so cotton thread became cheap. But, the thread wasn't useful for making lace until mercerization was invented in 1844. Mercerization made cotton thread stronger, lustrous, resistant to mold, and more like linen.

Education of women, specifically teaching women to read, was critical in the development of crochet. Professional crochet lace makers were illiterate people who crocheted small, simple items from memory. French crocheted buttons and Irish crochet motifs were learned by watching another person. Professional crocheters then specialized in a particular technique, making hundreds of identical buttons or motifs. In Irish crochet, the various motifs were combined into a single accessory or garment by others who specialized in creating grounds.

But as a hobbyist, the crocheter needed to complete an entire accessory or garment herself. The product was more complex than a single motif and a written pattern became necessary. The crocheter needed to be able to read. Most upper-class women had received at least basic education for nearly a century, but it was the concentration of women in factories with free time afforded by the Industrial Revolution that created the opportunity for many working-class women to obtain basic education. From 1850 to 1900, there was an increasing number of publications directed toward women, including periodicals such as *Godey's Lady's Book* (1830) and *Harper's Bazaar* (1867), and books such as *DMC Guide to Needlework* (1886).

Like today's crocheters, nineteenth-century crocheters wanted a never-ending supply of new and different patterns. It wasn't until the 1840s that crochet pattern books were first produced. One of the most influential crochet designers of this period was Mlle. Riego de la Branchardiere of London. She did much to popularize crochet by producing new designs and well-written patterns that she sold as a series of inexpensive booklets beginning in 1846.[2] She was skilled in many types of needlework and taught "point, lacet, crochet, tatting, embroidery, lace work, knitting, netting, tambour, etc." Her crochet designs were innovative and often borrowed ideas and design elements from other types of needlework. The designs published in her book, *The Crochet Book, First Series*, show that she has already experimented with reproducing point laces (needle laces) in crochet. In her *Second Series*, she reproduces raised Spanish needle lace in crochet and claims that it is the origin of Irish crochet. Whether her claim of inventing Irish crochet is true or not (and it may be), her work is important because her books were widely used and popularized such innovations as turning the work, stitches taller than a single crochet, and raised (padded) work.

As crochet continued to gain in popularity, the demand for materials and patterns kept growing. Thread companies such as DMC, Coats, and Clark (Coats and Clark were separate companies at the time) viewed publishing patterns as a great marketing tool to increase thread sales. One source of gridded patterns was an array of existing pattern books that dealt with filet (darned net) and other types of needlework.

Photo: Nancy Nehring

The pattern series *Grand Album de Modeles*[3] was heavily borrowed against.

In addition to using already-published patterns, thread companies hired women to travel around Europe to study local needlework and then produce pattern books based on these needlework techniques. Often the work was translated into crochet, which was easy, fast, and familiar to the target audience. In addition to the Spanish needle lace already mentioned, laces such as Cluny lace (bobbin lace), reticella (needle lace), Armenian lace (knotted lace), torchon lace (bobbin lace), princess lace (needle lace), and tatting (knotted lace) were imitated in crochet.

Thanks to cross-continental travelers, materials and patterns were quickly distributed around the world. The British Empire extended its reach around the world and many emigrating British women craved the luxuries they had left at home. Crochet was an easy addition to their new lives, and these transplanted women further promoted crochet by teaching it to local women.

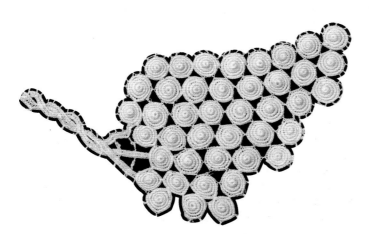

[1] Lis Paludan, *Crochet History and Technique*, 1995, Interweave Press, Inc., Loveland, CO.

[2] Mlle. Riego de la Branchardiere, *The First Twelve Crochet Books of Mlle. Riego de la Branchardiere 1847–1852*, 2007, Lacis Publications, Berkeley, CA.

[3] Boucherit, Edouard, editor, *Nos. 1–10 Grand Album de Modeles pour Filet*, circa 1880, Paris, France.

The Lacis Story

Tucked away in Berkeley California is a little jewel in the crown of the textile community known as the Lacis Museum of Lace and Textiles.

In 1965, Kaethe and Jules Kliot founded Lacis, a store like no other. Lacis was operated by Kaethe, until her untimely passing in 2002, as a haven for the textile community, a place where she provided support, encouragement, and knowledge to all. In 2004, the museum was established as an outgrowth and merging of the Lacis store and Kaethe and Jules' extensive collection of laces and textiles. Jules kindly allowed us to include photos of pieces in the museum's collection in this book.

One day, I received an e-mail from Jules Kliot asking me if I would like to participate in an exhibit that he was mounting in the museum. Jules had seen my work at a trade show and was interested in comparing modern-day crochet work with the gorgeous examples of antique laces showcased in the museum. I was very excited to take part in this endeavor. The exhibit he planned grew to include many modern-day examples, with contributors from all over the world, and was

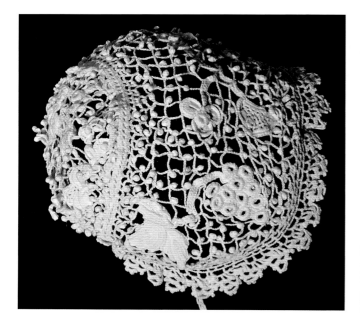

a huge success. You can still see this collection online at their website www.lacis.com.

The Kliots' collection of laces and textiles represents 40 years of dedication to the preservation of the finest human handiwork. The collection includes thousands of specimens from pre-Columbian Peru, the finest seventeenth-century works from European courts, and examples of machine-made laces from the nineteenth-century Industrial Revolution. An extensive library, focusing on lace, textiles, and costume, includes more than 10,000 books, patterns, articles, and ephemera. Related textile tools include those used for making all varieties of lace. The museum also houses an extensive collection of sewing machines.

As a statement of purpose, the Lacis Museum of Lace and Textiles will work:

- to preserve the spirit of Lacis as created by Kaethe Kliot as a place of support, knowledge, and encouragement for every person involved in any aspect of textile arts.

- to preserve and maintain the lace and textile collections of Jules and Kaethe Kliot.

- to preserve lace and textiles of all cultures from all periods, including the patterns and tools of creation, the objects of their purpose, and the literature associated with these objects.

- to provide a resource center for research and documentation of these objects.

- to educate and disseminate knowledge of lace and textiles.

- to provide and maintain a sales facility for generating financial support.

- to encourage interest in lace and textiles by providing professional services for conservation and restoration, as well as design and consultation services for costume and accessories as appropriate for period re-enactments and bridal occasions.

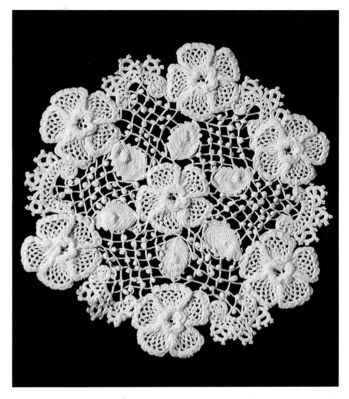

All photos: Lacis Museum of Lace and Textiles

CROCHET BASICS

In this section, you will find all the information you need to get you started. If you are new to crochet, use these pages to learn the basic techniques and terminology of crochet. If you are a seasoned crocheter, you will still refer to this section often for guidance on abbreviations, hook sizes, and more.

Crochet Hooks and Other Tools

Crochet hooks come in a large range of sizes and types. There are very fine steel hooks for fine cotton crochet, and aluminum, wood, and plastic hooks for heavier wools and synthetic yarns.

The diameter of the hook shaft determines the size of the hook and, ultimately, the size of the stitches the hook will make. Hook sizes range from a tiny A hook to a large Q and everything in between. There are many manufacturers of hooks, and it is very possible that two hooks with the same number or letter can vary from manufacturer to manufacturer. This enforces the need to take the time to check your gauge (see page 33) before starting a project.

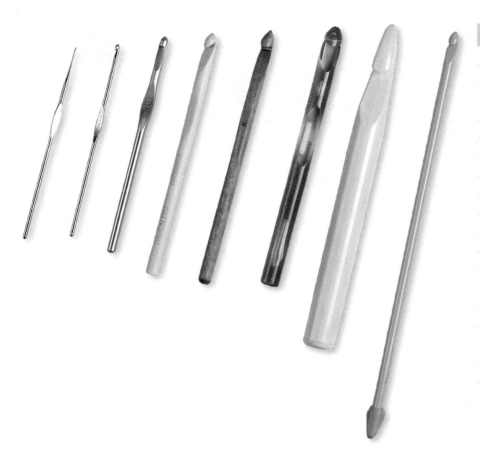

CROCHET HOOK SIZES

Metric Size	U. S. Size
2.25 mm	B/1
2.75 mm	C/2
3.25 mm	D/3
3.5 mm	E/4
3.75 mm	F/5
4 mm	G/6
4.5 mm	7
5 mm	H/8
5.5 mm	I/9
6 mm	J/10
6.5 mm	K/10½
8 mm	L/11
9 mm	M/N/13
10 mm	N/P/15
15 mm	P/Q
16 mm	Q
19 mm	S

Note: Steel hooks are sized differently than regular hooks: the higher the number, the smaller the hook. They range from the smallest #14 or .9 mm to the largest of #00 or 2.7 mm.

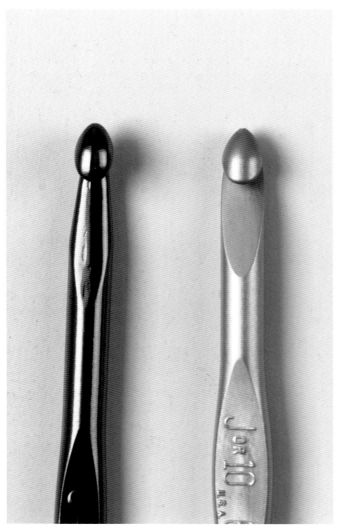

Tapered hook vs inline hook

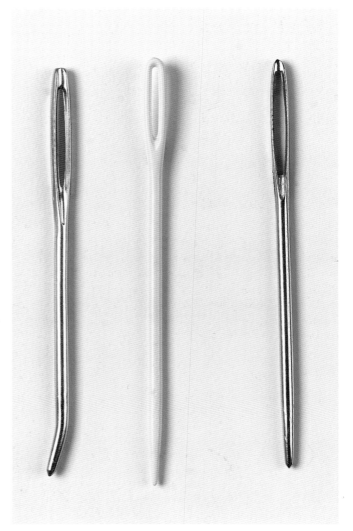

Yarn needles

For crochet hooks, there are two main categories in head shape; the inline hook and the tapered hook. On an inline hook, the neck just below the hook is the same diameter as the shaft of the hook. The neck below the hook on the tapered style is narrower than the rest of the shaft. You might find one style easier to use than the other, or you may notice no difference in how they work—it is strictly a personal preference.

In addition to hooks, a crochet kit should have a tape measure, sharp scissors, stitch markers, and a variety of tapestry or yarn needles. The bent-end yarn needles are particularly helpful in sewing seams in crocheted projects.

You can purchase yarn in different textures, styles, and thicknesses, which will affect your choice of crochet hook.

Generally, projects that require very thick yarns will require larger hooks. Projects crocheted with very fine yarn will require a smaller hook. Crochet patterns will recommend a yarn type and weight as well as the size hook to use. You can substitute the yarn used providing you check your gauge (page 33).

The variety of yarn available to crocheters is overwhelming. In addition to wool, cotton, linen, silk, and acrylics, choices include bamboo, corn, and sugar cane fibers. You can crochet with any yarn, but you'll find that some yarns will be more difficult to crochet with. When crocheting with very highly textured yarns—ribbon, eyelash, bumps, and bobbles—it is more difficult to see the stitches, but you can produce some wonderful results.

Techniques

These are the techniques used for crochet. Beginners can use this section to learn the skills they will need to tackle a crochet project. Refer to them whenever you need to brush up on stitches and maneuvers you have already learned. The instructions are written out completely, making them easier to understand.

BASIC SKILLS

Slip Knot and Chain

All crochet begins with a chain, into which is worked the foundation row for your piece. To make a chain, start with a slip knot. To make a slip knot, make a loop several inches from the end of the yarn, insert the hook through the loop, and catch the tail with the end **(1)**. Draw the yarn through the loop on the hook **(2)**. After the slip knot, start your chain. Wrap the yarn over the hook (yarn over) and catch it with the hook. Draw the yarn through the loop on the hook. You have now made 1 chain. Repeat the process to make a row of chains. When counting chains, do not count the slip knot at the beginning or the loop that is on the hook **(3)**.

Slip Stitch

The slip stitch is a very short stitch, which is mainly used to join 2 pieces of crochet together when working in rounds. To make a slip stitch, insert the hook into the specified stitch, wrap the yarn over the hook **(1)**, and then draw the yarn through the stitch and the loop already on the hook **(2)**.

Single Crochet

Insert the hook into the specified stitch, wrap the yarn over the hook, and draw the yarn through the stitch so there are 2 loops on the hook **(1)**. Wrap the yarn over the hook again and draw the yarn through both loops **(2)**. When working in single crochet, always insert the hook through both top loops of the next stitch, unless the directions specify front loop or back loop only.

Half Double Crochet

Wrap the yarn over the hook, insert the hook into the specified stitch, and wrap the yarn over the hook again **(1)**. Draw the yarn through the stitch so there are 3 loops on the hook. Wrap the yarn over the hook and draw it through all 3 loops at once **(2)**.

Double Crochet

Wrap the yarn over the hook, insert the hook into the specified stitch, and wrap the yarn over the hook again. Draw the yarn through the stitch so there are 3 loops on the hook **(1)**. Wrap the yarn over the hook again and draw it through 2 of the loops so there are now 2 loops on the hook **(2)**. Wrap the yarn over the hook again and draw it through the last 2 loops **(3)**.

Triple Crochet

Wrap the yarn over the hook twice, insert the hook into the specified stitch, and wrap the yarn over the hook again. Draw the yarn through the stitch so there are 4 loops on the hook. Wrap the yarn over the hook again **(1)** and draw it through 2 of the loops so there are now 3 loops on the hook **(2)**. Wrap the yarn over the hook again and draw it through 2 of the loops so there are now 2 loops on the hook **(3)**. Wrap the yarn over the hook again and draw it through the last 2 loops **(4)**.

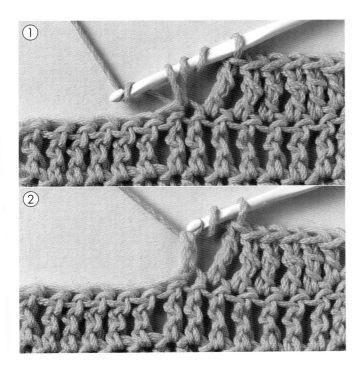

Double Triple Crochet

Wrap the yarn over the hook 3 times, insert the hook into the specified stitch, and wrap the yarn over the hook again. Draw the yarn through the stitch so there are 5 loops on the hook. Wrap the yarn over the hook again and draw it through 2 of the loops so there are now 4 loops on the hook. Wrap the yarn over the hook again and draw it through 2 of the loops so there are now 3 loops on the hook. Wrap the yarn over the hook again and draw it through 2 of the loops so there are now 2 loops on the hook. Wrap the yarn over the hook again and draw it through the last 2 loops.

Working Through the Back Loop

This creates a distinct ridge on the side facing you. Insert the hook through the back loop only of each stitch, rather than under both loops of the stitch. Complete the stitch as usual.

Increasing and Decreasing

To shape your work, you will often increase or decrease stitches as directed by the pattern. To increase in a row or round, you crochet twice into the same stitch, thereby increasing the stitch count by 1. To increase at the end of a row, you chain extra stitches, then turn and work into those stitches, thereby increasing the stitch count.

To decrease in a row or round, you crochet 2 (or more) stitches together as directed, thereby decreasing the stitch count. The technique varies depending on which crochet stitch you are using.

Single Crochet Two Stitches Together

This decreases the number of stitches in a row or round by 1. Insert the hook into the specified stitch, wrap the yarn over the hook, and draw the yarn through the stitch so there are 2 loops on the hook **(1)**. Insert the hook through the next stitch, wrap the yarn over the hook, and draw the yarn through the stitch so there are 3 loops on the hook **(2)**. Wrap the yarn over the hook again and draw the yarn through all the loops at once.

Double Crochet Two Stitches Together

This decreases the number of stitches in a row or round by 1. Wrap the yarn over the hook, insert the hook into the specified stitch, and wrap the yarn over the hook again. Draw the yarn through the stitch so there are 3 loops on the hook. Wrap the yarn over the hook again and draw it through 2 of the loops so there are now 2 loops on the hook. Wrap the yarn over the hook and pick up a loop in the next stitch, so there are now 4 loops on the hook. Wrap the yarn over the hook and draw through 2 loops. Wrap yarn over and draw through 3 loops to complete the stitch.

INTERESTING TWISTS TO BASIC STITCHES

No-Chain Foundation

The no-chain foundation is an alternate way to start a crochet project. This method is especially useful if your beginning chain and foundation row tends to be too tight. Using the no chain method eliminates this problem as you are making your chain and the first row at the same time. Because you don't start with a lengthy chain, this method is also very useful when making a large project, such as an afghan.

No-Chain Single Crochet

Chain 2. Insert the hook under the top 2 loops of the 2nd chain, yarn over hook, and pull loop through the chain (2 loops on hook), yarn over, pull through 1 loop (2 loops on hook) (**1**). Yarn over hook, pull through both loops on hook (one loop left on hook), first stitch completed (**2**). * Insert hook under both strands of the foundation chain of the stitch just made (**3**). Yarn over, pull loop through chain, yarn over, pull through 1 loop (**4**). Yarn over, pull through both loops on hook (1 loop on hook), second stitch completed (**5**). Repeat from * for desired length (**6**). Turn and work the first row after the foundation (**7**).

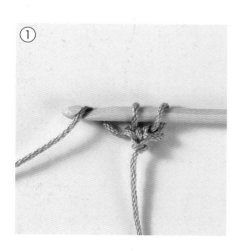

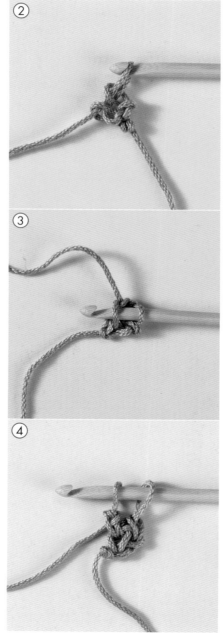

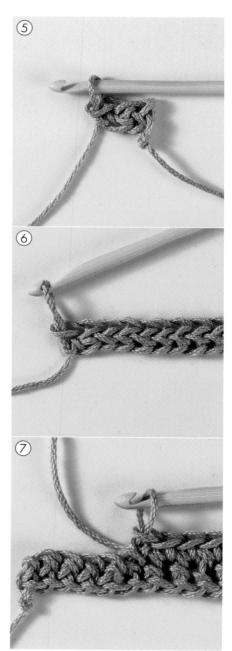

No-Chain Double Crochet

Chain 3, yarn over, insert hook under 2 strands of 3rd chain from hook, yarn over, pull up a loop, yarn over, pull loop through 1 loop (3 loops on hook) **(1)**. Complete stitch as a normal double crochet (yarn over, pull through 2 loops) twice **(2)**. First stitch made.

* Yarn over, insert hook under 2 strands of first chain made **(3)**. Yarn over, pull loop through chain, yarn over, pull loop through 1 loop (3 loops on hook) **(4)**. Complete stitch as a normal double crochet (yarn over, pull through 2 loops) twice. Second stitch made **(5)**. Repeat from * for each stitch for desired length **(6)**. Continue rows as regular double crochet **(7)**.

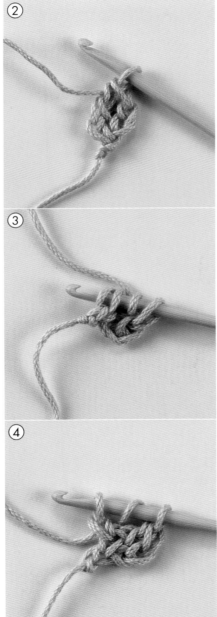

Front Post Double Crochet

This stitch follows a row of double crochet. Chain 3 to turn. Wrap the yarn over the hook. Working from the front, insert the hook from right to left (left to right for left-handed crocheters) under the post of the first double crochet from the previous row and pick up a loop (shown). Wrap the yarn over the hook and complete the stitch as a double crochet.

Back Post Double Crochet

This stitch follows a row of double crochet. Chain 3 to turn. Wrap the yarn over the hook. Working from the back, insert the hook from right to left (left to right for left-handed crocheters) over the post of the first double crochet from the previous row (shown) and pick up a loop. Wrap the yarn over the hook and complete the stitch as a double crochet.

Front Post Triple Crochet

Wrap the yarn over the hook twice. Working from the front, insert the hook from right to left (left to right for left-handed crocheters) under the post of the indicated stitch in the row below (shown) and pick up a loop. Wrap the yarn over the hook and complete the triple crochet stitch as usual.

Reverse Single Crochet

This stitch is usually used to create a border. At the end of a row, chain 1 but do not turn. Working backward, insert the hook into the previous stitch (**1**), wrap the yarn over the hook, and draw the yarn through the stitch so there are 2 loops on the hook. Wrap the yarn over the hook again and draw the yarn through both loops. Continue working in the reverse direction (**2**).

Cross Stitch

Skip 1 stitch and double crochet in the next stitch. Then double crochet in the skipped stitch by crossing the yarn in front of the stitch just made.

Shell

There are many types of shell stitches (page 53). Here is one example.

Make 2 double crochets, chain 1, and then work 2 more double crochets in the same stitch (shown). This is often called a cluster. In the following row, work the same cluster into the space created by the chain stitch. Other versions of the shell stitch may have more than 2 double crochets and more than 1 chain stitch between them.

Bobble

Bobbles, also called popcorns, are decorative bumps that can be created in various ways. Here are two examples. For more examples, see page 69.

(Worked from the wrong side.) Wrap the yarn over the hook and pick up a loop in the next stitch. Wrap the yarn over the hook again and pull it through 2 of the stitches on the hook. Repeat this 5 times in the same stitch. Then wrap the yarn over the hook and pull it through all 6 loops on the hook. The bobble stitch is worked from the wrong side and pushed to right side of the work.

Popcorn

(Worked from the right side.) Make 5 double crochets in the specified stitch, draw up the last loop slightly, and remove the hook **(1)**. Insert the hook into the first of the 5 double crochets made, pick up the dropped loop, and draw it through. Chain 1 **(2)**.

Bullion

Chain 3. Wrap the yarn loosely around the hook 10 times, insert the hook in the next stitch, yarn over, and draw up a loop **(1)**. Wrap the yarn over the hook again and carefully draw through the coil of loops on the hook. You may find it necessary to pick the loops off the hook with your fingers, 1 at a time **(2)**. Yarn over the hook again and draw through the remaining stitch.

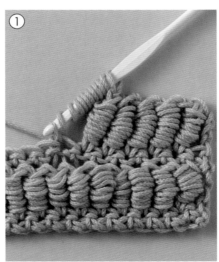 

Picot

This stitch pattern is used as an edging.

* Chain 3, work 1 single crochet in the first chain **(1)**, skip 1 stitch, and work 1 single crochet in the next stitch. Repeat from * across the row **(2)**.

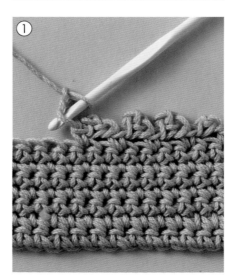 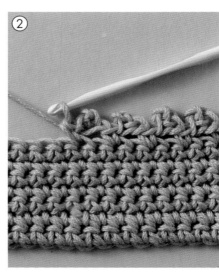

Puff Stitch

This stitch is worked the same way as the bobble stitch on page 25, but not necessarily from the wrong side. Because it is preceded and followed by double crochet stitches, this puff stitch is flatter than the bobble stitch.

Loose Puff Stitch

This stitch is worked the same as the puff stitch and bobble stitch above, but the loops are pulled up to at least ½" (1.3 cm) long.

Crochet Instructions

Crochet instructions are written in a shortened form, using standard abbreviations. This greatly reduces the space and overwhelming confusion that would result if the instructions were written out completely, word for word. Diagrams with symbols that represent the stitches are often given along with the written instructions, or sometimes the diagrams stand alone.

READING WRITTEN INSTRUCTIONS

Crochet patterns are often groups of stitches that are repeated a certain number of times in a row or round. Rather than repeat the instructions for the stitch group over and over, the group is enclosed between brackets [ ] immediately followed by the number of times to work the stitches.

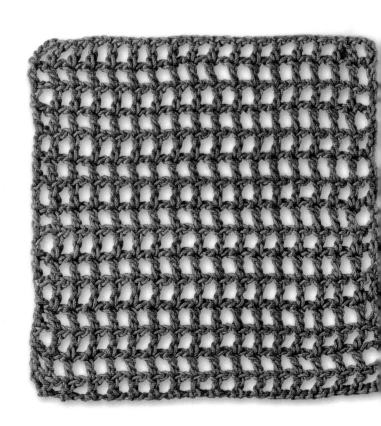

For example: [ch 1, sk 1, 1 dc in next st] 4 times.

This is a much shorter way to say "chain 1, skip 1 stitch, work 1 double crochet in the next stitch, chain 1, skip 1 stitch, work 1 double crochet in the next stitch, chain 1, skip 1 stitch, work 1 double crochet in the next stitch, chain 1, skip 1 stitch, work 1 double crochet in the next stitch."

Another way to indicate repeated stitch patterns is with asterisks. This same instruction could be written: * ch 1, sk 1, 1 dc in next st, repeat from * 3 times more.

Parentheses are used to clarify or reinforce information: Ch 3 (counts as 1 dc). They may be used at the end of a row to tell you how many total stitches you should have in that row, such as (25 sc). Sometimes this information is set off with an em dash at the row end—25 sc. Parentheses are also used to tell you which side of the work you should be on: (WS) or (RS). For multisize patterns, parentheses enclose the variations you must apply to the different sizes. For example, a pattern may include directions for size 2 (4, 6, 8). Throughout the instructions, wherever you must choose for the correct size, the choices will be written like this: ch 34 (36, 38, 40).

Abbreviations

Here is the list of standard abbreviations used for crochet. Until you can readily identify them, keep the list handy whenever you crochet.

approx	approximately
beg	begin/beginning
bet	between
BL	back loop(s)
bo	bobble
BP	back post
BPdc	back post double crochet
BPsc	back post single crochet
BPtr	back post triple crochet
CC	contrasting color
ch	chain
ch-	refers to chain or space previously made, e.g., ch-1 space
ch lp	chain loop
ch-sp	chain space
CL	cluster(s)
cm	centimeter(s)
cont	continue
dc	double crochet
dc2tog	double crochet 2 stitches together
dec	decrease/decreases/decreasing
dtr	double treble
FL	front loop(s)
foll	follow/follows/following

FP	front post
FPdc	front post double crochet
FPsc	front post single crochet
FPtr	front post triple crochet
g	gram(s)
hdc	half double crochet
inc	increase/increases/increasing
lp(s)	loop(s)
Lsc	long single crochet
m	meter(s)
MC	main color
mm	millimeter(s)
oz	ounce(s)
p	picot
patt	pattern
pc	popcorn
pm	place marker
prev	previous
qutr	quadruple triple crochet
rem	remain/remaining
rep	repeat(s)
rev sc	reverse single crochet
rnd(s)	round(s)
RS	right side(s)
sc	single crochet

sc2tog	single crochet 2 stitches together
sk	skip
Sl st	slip stitch
sp(s)	space(s)
st(s)	stitch(es)
tbl	through back loop(s)
tch	turning chain
tfl	through front loop(s)
tog	together
tr	triple crochet
trtr	triple treble crochet
tr2tog	triple crochet 2 together
TSS	Tunisian simple stitch
WS	wrong side(s)
yd	yard(s)
yo	yarn over
yoh	yarn over hook
[]	Work instructions within brackets as many times as directed
*	Repeat instructions following the single asterisk as directed
**	Repeat instructions between asterisks as many times as directed or repeat from a given set of instructions

READING SYMBOLS

Symbol diagrams are another way to convey crochet instructions. Every symbol in the diagram represents a specific stitch as it appears from the right side of the work. The rows are marked on the diagram, beginning at the bottom with the foundation row (FR). The numbers alternate side to side, even rows on the right, odd rows on the left, because you will be working in alternating directions as you move from row to row, right side to wrong side. The diagram is accompanied by a key to help you identify the symbols. Though there may be some subtle differences in the way the symbols look, designers use a standard set of symbols.

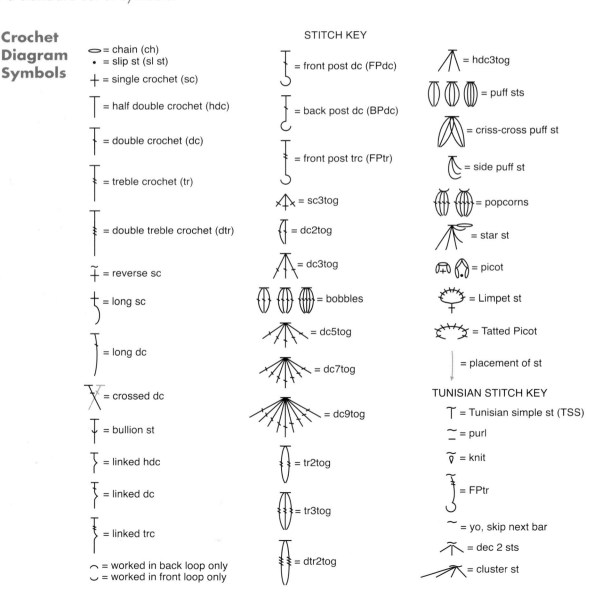

Crochet Diagram Symbols

- = chain (ch)
- = slip st (sl st)
- = single crochet (sc)
- = half double crochet (hdc)
- = double crochet (dc)
- = treble crochet (tr)
- = double treble crochet (dtr)
- = reverse sc
- = long sc
- = long dc
- = crossed dc
- = bullion st
- = linked hdc
- = linked dc
- = linked trc
- = worked in back loop only
- = worked in front loop only

STITCH KEY

- = front post dc (FPdc)
- = back post dc (BPdc)
- = front post trc (FPtr)
- = sc3tog
- = dc2tog
- = dc3tog
- = bobbles
- = dc5tog
- = dc7tog
- = dc9tog
- = tr2tog
- = tr3tog
- = dtr2tog

- = hdc3tog
- = puff sts
- = criss-cross puff st
- = side puff st
- = popcorns
- = star st
- = picot
- = Limpet st
- = Tatted Picot
- = placement of st

TUNISIAN STITCH KEY

- = Tunisian simple st (TSS)
- = purl
- = knit
- = FPtr
- = yo, skip next bar
- = dec 2 sts
- = cluster st

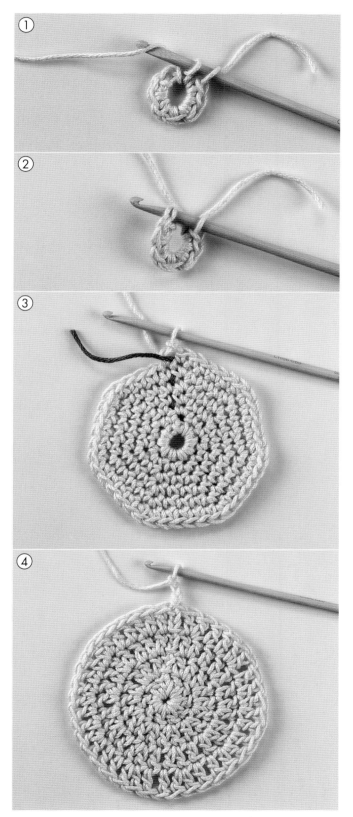

TWO WAYS TO CROCHET

Working in Rows

Many flat crochet pieces are worked back and forth in rows, beginning with a chain and foundation row. As you crochet, you alternate from right side to wrong side with each row. At the end of each row, you crochet a turning chain of 1 to 4 stitches, depending on the height of the next row of stitches. If the next row will be single crochet, the turning chain is 1 stitch; half-double crochet: 2 stitches; double crochet: 3 stitches; triple crochet: 4 stitches, etc. The directions will tell you how many chains to make. The turning chain counts as a stitch. For instance, the directions may say, "ch 3 (counts as dc)." At the end of each row, the last stitch is worked into the turning chain from the previous row.

Working in the Round

Another way to crochet is in rounds, going around in continual circles. When working in the round, the right side of the fabric is always facing you. To begin, the directions will tell you to chain a certain number of stitches and join them into a ring by slip stitching into the beginning chain. For the first round, the stitches are worked into the ring (the hook is inserted into the center of the ring), so the stitches will wrap around the beginning chain (**1**). When you reach your starting point, slip stitch into the beginning stitch. To continue on the next round, the directions will tell you to crochet a starting chain equal to the height of the stitches in the next round. Then continue, crocheting into the stitches of the previous round, and complete the round by stitching into the starting chain (**2**).

When working in rounds, it is necessary to note where the round begins and ends to keep track of rows worked. When working in single crochet, the easiest way to mark your rounds is by inserting a different colored piece of yarn in your work, then carrying it up as you work (**3**). Using a different colored yarn makes it very easy to see and pulls out easily when your work is done.

If you are working in half double crochet, double crochet, or triple crochet, the chain at the beginning of the row creates a seam stitch, so using a marker is not necessary (**4**). A typical instruction line might read, "ch 3 to begin the round, * work 1 dc in each of the next 2 sts, 2 dcs in next st (inc made), repeat from * around, join with a Sl st to the top of the beg ch 3." This would complete 1 round. The instructions will vary but they always begin with a starting chain and end with a joining at end of the round.

Invisible Join

When working in the round, connecting the end of the round to the beginning can sometimes seem awkward. Here is a way to connect the last stitch in a way that will leave the connection nearly invisible.

End the last stitch but do not join to the beginning with a slip stitch **(1)**. Cut the yarn, leaving a tail several inches long. Pull the yarn through the last stitch and set the hook aside. Thread the tail on a tapestry needle, and run the needle under the beginning stitch, pulling the tail through **(2)**. Insert the needle back through the center of the last stitch of the round and pull the tail to the back of the work (not too tightly) **(3)**. This will join the beginning to the end invisibly **(4)**. Weave the tail into the back of the work.

CHECKING YOUR GAUGE

Every pattern will tell you the exact yarn (or weight of yarn) to use, and what size hook to use to crochet an item with the same finished measurements as the project shown. It is important to choose yarn in the weight specified in order to successfully complete the project. The hook size recommended is the size an average crocheter would use to get the correct gauge. Gauge refers to the number of stitches and the number of rows in a given width and length, usually in 4" (10 cm), of crocheted fabric.

We can't all be average. Some of us crochet tighter, others looser. Before beginning to crochet a project, it is very important to take the time to check your gauge. Start by making a chain a little over 4" (10 cm) long, work the pattern stitch, using the yarn and hook called for in the instructions, until you have an approximate 4" (10 cm) square. Most crocheters do not get accurate row gauges because of the differences in how the stitch loop is picked up, so it is more accurate to check your gauge by the stitch count rather than row count. Place a pin on one side of the work and place another pin 4" (10 cm) over. Count the stitches between the pins. If you have more stitches to the inch than the instructions call for, you are working tighter than average; try a new swatch with a larger hook. If you have fewer stitches to the inch than the instructions call for, you are working looser than average; try a smaller hook. Note: It is better to change hook size to get proper gauge, rather than trying to work tighter or looser.

Usually the gauge stated means as worked. In some instances a pattern will give measurements of a garment "after blocking." This means that after an item is blocked it will stretch a little.

The same flower crocheted with three consecutive hook sizes.

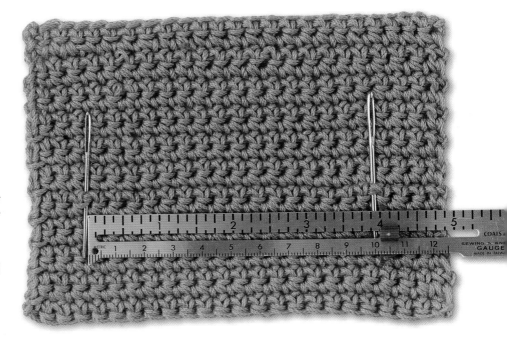

Details and Finishing Techniques

The quality of the detail work in any project is essential to the success of that project. There are various ways to sew seams, make buttonholes, insert zippers or pockets, or finish off an edge.

BUTTONHOLES

Horizontal buttonholes can be worked into the front of a crocheted garment without using a separate front band. This works best on single crochet or half double crochet. Work the front that will not have buttonholes first, and mark the edge for button placement. Using the finished front as a guide, work horizontal buttonholes in the opposite side to correspond. When you reach a placement mark, work a few stitches in from the edge—usually about ½" (1.3 cm)—chain 2, 3, or 4 sts (depending on the size of your button), skip the same number of stitches that you chained, and continue across the row. On the return row, work the number of stitches skipped into the chain space to complete the buttonhole. Continue to the next marker, and repeat.

For vertical buttonholes, from the right side, pick up stitches (page 39) along the garment edge, and work two rows of single crochet. Mark the edge for buttonhole placement. Work the buttonholes on the third and fourth rows, following the directions at left. Work the fifth row, and then add a decorative edge, if desired.

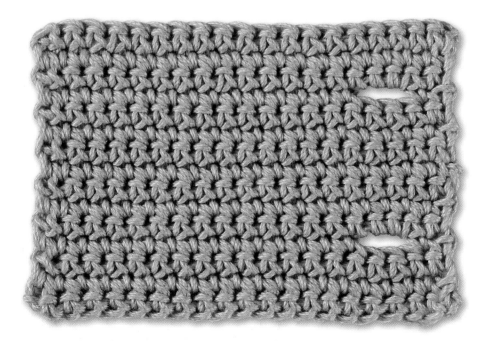

SEAMS

There are many ways to join seams in needlework. The ideal seam is flat with no bulk. You can use different kinds of seams in the same garment. Always pin your pieces together before starting to sew.

Backstitch Seam

When joining a set-in sleeve, I prefer to use the backstitch method, but use one of the more invisible methods for sewing drop shoulder, side, or underarm seams. The backstitch method does have some internal bulk, but if done properly, it is strong and does help shape the seam cap nicely. I also like to use the backstitch method when joining shaped edges. The backstitch seam is worked with right sides together.

Slip-stitch Seam

The slip-stitch join is a favorite of many because it joins pieces easily. Your stitches must be worked loosely to avoid puckering seams. Place right sides together, draw up a loop 1 stitch from the edge of seam, insert hook in next stitch, and draw up a loop; continue in this manner until seam is completed.

wrong side

right side

Whipstitch Seam

The whipstitch seam works best for sewing straight-edged seams. Holding right sides together, insert needle from front to back through inside loops, bring through and around, and repeat.

wrong side

right side

Weave Seam

I use this join when I want a really flat seam. Hold pieces to be seamed side by side and, working from the wrong side, insert needle from front to back, through 1 loop only, draw through, progress to next stitch, bring needle from back to front (not over), and proceed in this manner until seam is completed. If you draw through top loop only, a decorative ridge will be left on the right side of work. If you draw through bottom loops, the ridge will be inside work.

wrong side

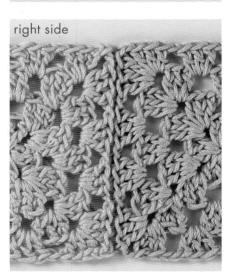

right side

Single Crochet Seam

The single crochet seam creates a decorative ridge; it is especially nice for joining motifs. Holding the pieces wrong sides together, work single crochet through the whole stitch on both motifs.

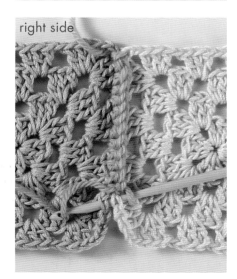

right side

wrong side

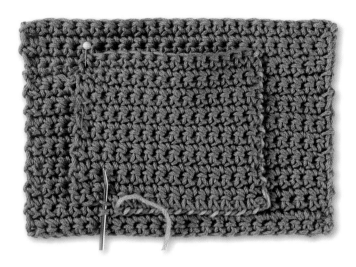

POCKETS AND ZIPPERS

Patch Pockets

Most crocheted garments use patch pockets because it is very easy to make a square of the required size, in any pattern that you happen to be using. Just pin the pocket in place and sew it to the outside of the front.

Set-in Pockets

The set-in pocket is worked a little differently. Make your pocket lining first, set aside. Begin the front of your garment and work up to the pocket opening; then insert the pocket as follows: Centering pocket on front section, pin to back of work, work across front to pocket lining, then work across the pocket lining stitches, skip the same amount of stitches on front, then work remaining front stitches, and finish front as required. When finished, sew pocket lining down to inside of garment.

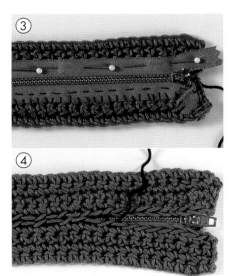

Zipper Insertion

When you insert a zipper into a garment seam, you want the garment edges to close over the zipper teeth, but still allow the zipper to operate freely. Follow these steps for properly inserting a zipper:

1. Baste the garment edges together with a contrasting thread, using the weave seam method (opposite).

2. Center the zipper face-down over the seam on the wrong side of the garment. Pin the zipper in place along both sides of the teeth.

3. Using matching thread, hand stitch the zipper to the garment using a running stitch down the center of each side, and then whipstitch the edges. By catching only the inner layer of the crocheted fabric, the zipper insertion will be nearly invisible from the right side. Turn back the tape ends at the top of the zipper and stitch them in place.

4. Remove the basting stitches from the right side.

FINISHING EDGES

Finishing a crochet cardigan with a single crochet border is a very neat way to make a button band. Here are three ways to make a plain band a little more interesting:

Reverse Single Crochet

After working 5 rows and placing your buttonholes, do not end off, do not turn. Work 1 row of reverse single crochet all around front border.

Slip-stitch Edging

This edging can be done with the same yarn, or it is also effective with a contrasting color. After the band is completed, do not end off, do not turn. Work a slip stitch from the right side, 1 stitch in from the edge; be careful not to pull too tight.

Ruffle Edging

When last row is completed, ch 3 turn, 1 sc in first st, * ch 3, 1 sc in next stitch. Repeat from * all around front edge.

Picking Up Stitches for Borders

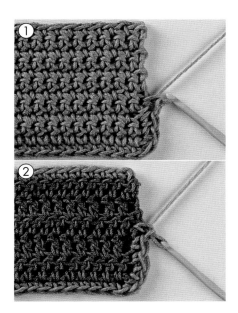

You often need to pick up stitches from the edges of a crocheted piece to add a border. Picking up stitches along the sides of a project, the row ends, is the hardest part of giving your crochet pieces a lovely finished look. It is worth the effort to practice this step until you get it right.

The general rule of thumb is to pick up 1 stitch in every other row for single crochet **(1)**. For instance, if you have worked 20 rows of single crochet, you will pick up 10 stitches along the row ends. Pick up 1 stitch for every row for double crochet **(2)**. For instance, if you have worked 20 rows of double crochet, you will pick up 20 stitches. These guidelines work for most people, but not all. Your work must lie flat, and sometimes you will have to experiment to judge how to proceed. If your edges are rippling, like a ruffle, you are picking up too many stitches; if they are pulling in, you are picking up too few stitches.

The best way to get an even edge is to divide the length to be worked into 4 parts. When the first section is done and lies flat, repeat that number of stitches for each of the following 3 sections. Work in every stitch of the top and bottom edges. Always work 3 stitches in each corner to make the project lie flat.

Setting in Drop-Shoulder Sleeves

After the shoulder seams have been sewn, place the front and back wrong side up on the work surface. Fold the sleeve in half to find the center. Place the sleeve wrong side up alongside the armhole and pin the center to the shoulder seam. Pin the remainder of the sleeve top in place, having each side reach the indent at the underarm. The body indents align to the row ends at the top of the sleeve. Holding the edges together, insert the yarn needle into the first stitch on the sleeve, then into the corresponding stitch on the body of garment, and continue in this manner going from side to side until the sleeve is sewn in place. Repeat for the opposite sleeve. Then sew the underarm seams, from the sleeve cuffs to the bottom of the body. Turn the garment right side out.

When setting a sleeve into a garment that doesn't have side seams, fold the garment in half, wrong side out. Follow the same procedure, beginning and ending at the center of the garment underarm. Then sew the sleeve underarm seam. Turn the garment right side out.

STITCH PATTERNS

Armed with the skills to make all the basic crochet stitches, you are ready to explore the wonderland of fabrics that you can create with these stitches. There are hundreds of named stitch patterns from simple to complex, smooth to highly textured, and compact and closed to lacy and open. You'll find almost 200 stitch patterns grouped by type, some with universally recognized names and others with descriptive names that seem to fit their look. Each stitch pattern is shown in a large swatch with row-by-row instructions and a symbol diagram. Refer to page 30 for a symbol key.

Basic Stitches

In this section we explore the basic stitches: slip stitch, single crochet, half double crochet, double crochet, and triple crochet, plus some common combinations and variations of these stitches.

Some basic stitches make a very dense fabric, others a lacy fabric. The size of your crochet hook and the weight of the yarn or thread play a big part in the drape of the finished project. Light and airy stitches made with a finer yarn make wonderful tops that drape well. Many stitches are suitable for blankets; heavily textured stitches are great for hats and bags.

SLIP STITCH IN THE BACK LOOP

Skill Level: Easy

The slip stitch in crochet is mostly used for joining a circle, moving from one place in your work to another, or ending off a group of stitches without adding height to your work. While there are always exceptions, making a fabric of all slip stitches worked in the whole stitch is unusual. The slip stitch, when worked in the back loop only, makes a fabric that resembles knitting; when turned vertically, it makes a very sturdy ribbed look that would be good for the bottom of crochet garments.

Ch any number of sts.

Foundation Row: Pick up a loop in second ch from hook, draw this loop through loop on hook (Sl st made), *pick up a loop in next ch, draw this loop through loop on hook (Sl st made), rep from * across row, turn.

Row 1: Ch 1, working in back loop only, Sl st in first Sl st, Sl st in each Sl st across, turn.

Rep Row 1 for pattern.

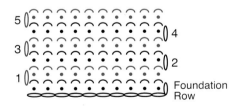

SINGLE CROCHET

Skill Level: Beginner

Ch any number of sts.

Foundation Row: Starting in 2nd ch from hook, work 1 sc in each ch across row, turn.

Row 1: Ch 1 (counts as first sc), skip first sc, 1 sc in each sc across row, turn.

Row 2: Ch 1 (counts as first sc), skip first sc, 1 sc in each sc across row, 1 sc in top of turning ch, turn.

Rep Row 2 for pattern.

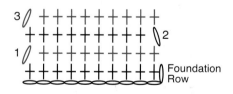

HALF DOUBLE CROCHET

Skill Level: Beginner

Ch any number of sts.

Foundation Row: Starting in 3rd ch from hook, yo hook, pick up a loop, yo hook, pull through all 3 loops on hook (hdc made), 1 hdc in each ch across row, turn.

Row 1: Ch 2 (counts as first hdc), skip first st, 1 hdc in each st across row, 1 hdc in top of turning ch, turn.

Rep Row 1 for pattern.

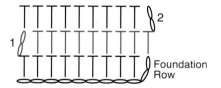

DOUBLE CROCHET

Skill Level: Beginner

Ch any number of sts.

Foundation Row: Starting in 3rd ch from hook, yo hook, pick up a loop, (yo hook, through two loops) twice (dc made), 1 dc in each ch across row, turn.

Row 1: Ch 3 (counts as a dc), skip first dc, 1 dc in each st across row, 1 dc in top of turning ch, turn.

Rep Row 1 for pattern.

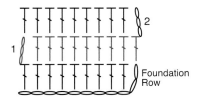

TRIPLE CROCHET

Skill Level: Beginner

Ch any number of sts.

Foundation Row: Starting in 4th ch from hook, yo hook twice, pick up a loop, (yo hook, through two loops) 3 times (tr completed), through 1 tr in each ch across row, turn.

Row 1: Ch 4 (counts as a tr), skip first tr, 1 tr in each st across row, 1 tr in top of turning ch, turn.

Rep Row 1 for pattern.

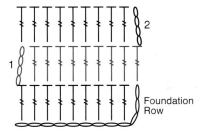

SINGLE CROCHET THROUGH THE BACK LOOP

Skill Level: Easy

Ch any number of sts.

Foundation Row: Starting in 2nd ch from hook, work 1 sc in each ch across row, turn.

Row 1: Ch 1 (counts as first sc), skip first sc, working in back loop, work 1 sc in each sc across row, turn.

Row 2: Ch 1 (counts as first sc), skip first sc, working in back loop, work 1 sc in each sc across row, work 1 sc in top of turning ch, turn.

Rep Row 2 for pattern.

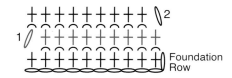

TEXTURED SINGLE CROCHET

Skill Level: Easy

Ch a multiple of 2 plus 3.

Row 1: 1 sc in 3rd ch from hook, *skip 1 ch, 2 sc into next ch, rep from * to last 2 ch, skip 1 ch, 1 sc into last ch, turn.

Row 2: Ch 1 (counts as first sc), 1 sc in first sc, *skip 1 sc, 2 sc into next sc, rep from * to last 2 sts, skip 1 sc, 1 sc in top of the turning ch, turn.

Rep Row 2 for pattern.

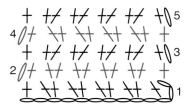

SINGLE CROCHET 3 TOGETHER

Skill Level: Easy

Sc3tog: pick up a loop in each of 3 designated sts, yo hook, draw yarn through all 4 loops on hook.

Ch a multiple of 2 plus 3.

Row 1: Starting in 3rd ch from hook, pick up a loop in next 3 chs, yo, draw through all 4 loops on hook (sc3tog made), ch 1, *pick up a loop in same ch as previous sc, pick up a loop in next 2 chs, yo, draw yarn through all 4 loops on hook (sc3tog made), ch 1, rep from * across, end 1 sc in last ch, turn.

Row 2: Ch 2, *pick up a loop in the ch-1 space, in the sc3tog, in next ch-1 space, yo, draw yarn through all 4 loops on hook, ch 1, rep from * across row, end 1 sc in tch, turn.

Rep Row 2 for pattern.

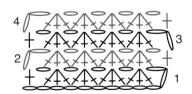

CROSSED DOUBLE CROCHET

Skill Level: Easy

Ch an even number of stitches.

Row 1: Work 1 dc in 5th ch from hook, crossing in front of dc just made, work 1 dc in last skipped ch, *skip 1 ch, work 1 dc in next ch, crossing in front of dc just made, work 1 dc in last skipped ch, rep from * across row, end 1 dc in last ch, turn.

Row 2: Ch 3 (counts as first dc), skip first 2 sts, work 1 dc in next dc, crossing in front of dc just made, work 1 dc in last skipped dc, *skip next dc, work 1 dc in next dc, crossing in front of dc just made, work 1 dc in last skipped st, rep from * across row, working 1 dc in top of tch, turn.

Rep Row 2 for pattern.

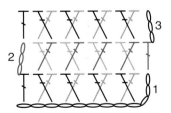

CROSS HATCH

Skill Level: Easy

Ch a multiple of 7 plus 1.

Foundation Row: Work 2 dc in 4th ch from hook, skip 3 ch, 1 sc next ch, *ch 3, 1 dc in each of the next 3 chs, skip next 3 ch, sc in next ch, rep from * across, turn.

Row 1: Ch 3, 2 dc in first st, *skip next 3 dc, [1 sc, ch 3, 3 dc] in the next ch-3 space, skip next st, rep from * across, ending skip last 2 sts, sc in the top of turning ch.

Rep Row 1 for pattern.

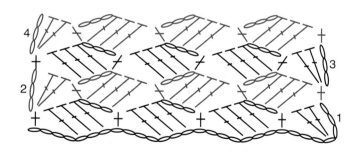

BEEHIVE STITCH

Skill Level: Intermediate

Front Post Double Crochet (FPdc): Yo hook, pick up a loop inserting hook from right to left under designated stitch, [yo, draw through 2 loops] 2 times.

Ch a multiple of 2 plus 1.

Foundation Row: Start in 4th ch from hook, work 1 dc in each ch across row, turn.

Row 1: Ch 3 (counts as a dc) skip first st, *1 FPdc in next dc, 1 dc in next dc, rep from * across, ending 1 dc in top of turning ch, turn.

Row 2: Ch 3, skip first st, *1 FPdc in the next FPdc, 1 dc in next dc, rep from * ending with 1 dc in top of turning ch, turn.

Rep row 2 for pattern.

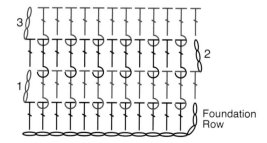

rust flick
2014

DOUBLE CROCHET LACE

Skill Level: Easy

Ch a multiple of 3.

Foundation Row: Starting in 3rd ch from hook, work 1 dc in each ch to end of row, turn.

Row 1: Ch 3 (counts as first dc), skip first 2 dc, *[1 dc, ch 1, 1 dc] in next dc, skip next 2 dc, rep from * ending with skip 1 dc, 1 dc in top of the turn ch, turn.

Row 2: Ch 3, *3 dc in next ch-1 space, rep from * across, ending with 1 dc in top of turning ch, turn.

Rep Rows 1 and 2 for pattern.

TEXTURED SC/HDC/DC COMBO

Skill Level: Easy

Ch a multiple of 3 plus 2.

Foundation Row: Starting in 2nd ch from hook, work 1 sc in each ch across row, turn.

Row 1: Ch 2, [1 sc, 1 hdc, 1 dc] in first sc, skip next 2 sc, *[1 sc, 1 hdc, 1 dc] in next sc, skip next 2 sc, rep from * across, ending with 1 sc in last sc, turn.

Row 2: Ch 2, [1 sc, 1 hdc, 1 dc] in first sc, *skip next 2 sts, [1 sc, 1 hdc, 1 dc] in next sc, rep from * ending with 1 sc in top of turning ch, turn.

Rep Row 2 for pattern.

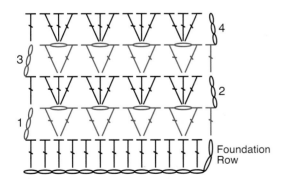

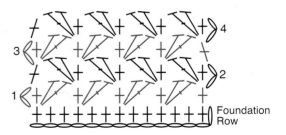

TEXTURED SC/DC #1

Skill Level: Easy

Ch an even number of sts.

Row 1: 1 sc in 4th ch from hook, *1 dc in next ch, 1 sc in next ch, rep from * across, turn.

Row 2: Ch 3 (counts as a dc), skip first st, *1 sc in next dc, 1 dc into next sc, rep from * across, ending with 1 sc in top of the turning ch, turn.

Rep Row 2 for pattern.

TEXTURED SC/DC #2

Skill Level: Easy

Ch a multiple of 3 plus 1.

Row 1: 1 sc in 4th ch from hook, 1 dc into next ch, *1 sc in next ch, 1 dc in next ch, rep from * across row (dc will be last st), turn.

Row 2: Ch 3 (counts as a dc), skip first st, *1 sc into next sc, 1 dc into next dc, rep from * ending last rep dc in top of the turn ch, turn.

Rep Row 2 only for pattern.

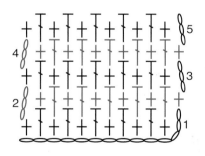

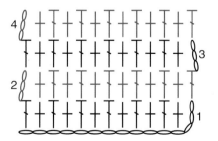

TEXTURED SC/DC #3

Skill Level: Beginner

Ch a multiple of 3.

Foundation Row: Work 2 dc in 3rd ch from hook, *skip next 2 ch [1 sc, 2 dc] in next ch, rep from * to within last 3 ch, skip next 2 ch, 1 sc in last ch, turn.

Row 1: Ch 1 (counts as a sc), work 2 dc in the first st, *skip 2 dc [1 sc, 2 dc] in the next sc, rep from * to last 3 sts, skip 2 dc, 1 sc in the top of the turning ch, turn.

Rep Row 1 for pattern.

PRIMROSE STITCH

Skill Level: Easy

Ch a multiple of 3 plus 2.

Foundation Row: Work [1 sc, ch 2, 1 sc] in 3rd ch from hook, *skip next 2 chs, [1 sc, ch 2, 1 sc] in next ch, rep from * across, ending with 1 hdc in last ch, turn.

Row 1: Ch 3, *3 dc in next ch-2 space (shell made), rep from * across, ending with 1 dc in top of turning ch, turn.

Row 2: Ch 2 (counts as first hdc), * [1 sc, ch 2, 1 sc] in 2nd dc of next shell, rep from * across, ending with 1 hdc in top of turning ch, turn.

Rep Rows 1 and 2.

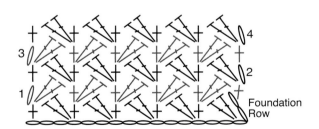

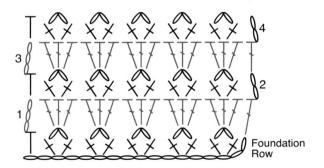

DOUBLE CROCHET SHELL

Skill Level: Easy

Ch a multiple of 6 plus 2.

Foundation Row: Starting in 2nd ch from hook, 1 sc in each ch across.

Row 1 (RS): Ch 4 (counts as dc, ch 1), 1 dc in first st (half shell made), *ch 2, skip next 2 sts, 1 sc next st, ch 2, skip next 2 sts, [1 dc, ch 1, 1 dc, ch 1, 1 dc] in next st (full shell made), rep from * across to within last 6 sts, ch 2, skip next 2 sts, 1 sc next st, ch 2, skip next 2 sts, [1 dc, ch 1, 1 dc] in last sc (half shell made), turn.

Row 2: Ch 1, 1 sc in same st, *ch 2, 1 shell in next sc, ch 2, 1 sc in 2nd dc of the next cluster, rep from * across, ending with 1 sc in the third ch of the turning ch 4, turn.

Row 3: Ch 4 (counts as a dc, ch 1), 1 dc same st (half shell made), * ch 2, 1 sc in center dc of the next cluster, ch 2, 1 shell in next sc, rep from * ending with [1 dc, ch 1, 1 dc] in the turning ch (half shell made), turn.

Rep Rows 2 and 3 for pattern.

BARS AND LOOPS

Skill Level: Easy

Ch a multiple of 2 plus 1.

Foundation Row: Starting in 2nd ch from hook, 1 sc in each ch across row, turn.

Row 1: Ch 3 (counts as first dc), skip first sc, 1 dc in each sc across row, turn.

Row 2: Ch 1, 1 sc in first dc, ch 2, 1 sc in space after next 2 dc, *ch 2, 1 sc in space after next 2 dc, rep from * ending ch 2, 1 sc in sp between the last dc and the turning ch, 1 sc in top of turn ch, turn.

Row 3: Ch 3, 2 dc in first ch-2 space, *2 dc in next ch-2 space, rep from * across, ending with 1 dc in top of turning ch, turn.

Rep Rows 2 and 3 for pattern.

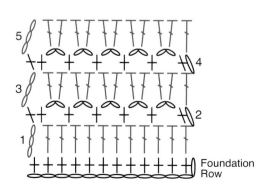

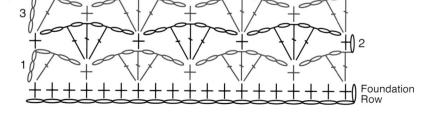

DENIM RUFFLE BAG

Here's a great handbag for everyday use, made entirely of single crochet and double crochet stitches. Single crochet stitches worked through the back loop create a ribbed effect for the bag flap. I saw a designer bag similar to this at Saks Fifth Avenue with a price tag of over $900!

YOU WILL NEED

Yarn

- Bulky-weight cotton
- Shown: Blue Jeans Cable by Schachenmayr, 100% cotton, 1.75 oz (50 g)/54 yd (50 m): Dark Denim #055, 10 balls

Hooks

- 9/I (5.5 mm) for main body of bag
- 6/G (4 mm) for strap only

Stitches

- Single crochet
- Single crochet through the back loop
- Double crochet

Gauge

- 13 sc = 4" (10 cm) using 9/I hook

Notions

- Tapestry needle
- ½ yd (0.5 m) lining fabric (optional)
- Hand-sewing needle
- Thread

Finished size

- Approximately 10" × 14" (25.4 × 35.6 cm)

(continued)

Denim Ruffle Bag (continued)

Notes

Single Crochet Decreases (sc2tog): To dec, pick up lp in next st, yo, pick up lp in next st, yo and pull through all 3 lps on hook.

Back

Foundation Row: With 9/I hook, ch 44. Starting in second ch from hook, work 1 sc in each ch across, turn—43 sc.

Row 1: Working in BL throughout, ch 1 (counts as sc), sk first st, 1 sc in next 41, 1 sc in tch, turn.

Repeat row 1 for 30 rows (15 ridges), turn.

Next row: Ch 1, sk first st, sc2tog, sc in each st until last 3 sts, sc2tog, 1 sc in tch, turn—41 sc.

Next row: Ch 1, sk first st, 1 sc in each st across, 1 sc in top of tch, turn.

Rep last 2 rows 2 times more—37 dc. Fasten off.

Front

Same as back.

Flap

Work in BL throughout.

Foundation Row: With 9/I hook, ch 32. Starting in second ch from hook, work 1 sc in each ch across, turn—31 sc.

Row 1 (RS): Ch 1, 2 sc in next st (sc inc made), 1 sc in each st to last 2 sts, 2 sc in next st (sc inc made), 1 sc in top of tch, turn.

Row 2: Ch 1 (counts as first sc), sk first st, 1 sc in each st across, 1 sc in top of tch, turn.

Rep rows 1 and 2 until 39 sts.

Rep row 2 for 14 rows more, then dec 1 st at each side every other row until 31 sts rem. Work 1 row even. Fasten off.

Ruffle

Foundation Row: With 9/I hook, ch 11. Starting in second ch from hook, 1 sc in each ch across, turn—10 sc.

Row 1: Working in BL, ch 1 (counts as sc), sk first sc, 1 sc in next 8 sc, 1 sc in top of tch, turn.

Rep row 1 for 170 rows (85 ridges). Do not fasten off, turn to work along one end of ruffle.

Beading Rnd 1: Work 1 sc in every other row end, Sl st to first sc to join. Do not turn.

Rnd 2: Ch 4, sk 1 sc, 1 dc next sc, * ch 1, sk 1 dc, 1 dc next st, rep from * around, ending ch 1, Sl st to top of beg ch to join. Fasten off.

Strap and Gusset

Make in one piece.

Foundation Row: With 6/G hook, ch 7. Starting in second ch from hook, 1 sc in each ch across, turn—6 sc.

Row 1: Ch 1 (counts as first sc), working in both loops, 1 sc in next 4 sc, 1 sc in top of tch, turn—6 sc.

Rep row 1 until strap is 60" (152.4 cm) long. Do not fasten off. Work 1 row sc around entire strap. Fasten off.

Tie

With 6/G hook, ch 200. Fasten off.

Finishing

1. If lining is desired, line back and front and part of strap that will form gusset before sewing together.

2. Sew short ends of strap together, center this seam at bottom of bag, pin back of bag to gusset, sew in place. Pin front of bag in place and sew.

3. Pin beading edge of ruffle all around flap and sew in place. Thread tie through beading row, starting and ending at center front, tie in a bow.

4. Mark row at exact center of flap, pin to back top of bag, and sew in place at back only.

5. Weave in ends using a tapestry needle.

Shell Stitches

Shell stitches are formed when three or more stitches are worked into the same chain, stitch, or space. They fan out from the base in the shape of a scallop shell. By varying the number and type of stitches in the shell, the arrangement of the shells, and how they are combined with other stitches, many different shell stitch patterns emerge. Unlike the way you work cluster stitches, which do not change the stitch count in a row, when you're working shell stitches, you must skip stitches or spaces on either side of the shell in order to keep your work flat.

Because the variety is never-ending, shell stitches lend themselves to delicate fashions, baby clothes, afghans, and a multitude of other projects. Most variations of shell stitches are easy to execute, but look very intricate, making them a favorite of beginners as well as experienced crocheters.

POSTS AND SHELLS

Skill Level: Intermediate

Front Post Double Crochet (FPdc): Yo hook, pick up a loop from front, inserting hook from right to left under designated stitch, [yo, draw through 2 loops] 2 times.

Back Post Double Crochet (BPdc): Yo hook, pick up a loop from back, inserting hook from right to left under designated stitch, [yo, draw through 2 loops] 2 times.

Ch a multiple of 6 plus 3.

Foundation Row (WS): [2 dc, ch 1, 2 dc] in 6th ch from hook (shell), *skip next 2 ch, 1 dc in next ch**, skip next 2 ch, work [2 dc, ch 1, 2 dc] in next ch (shell), rep from * across, ending last rep at **, turn.

Row 1: Ch 3 (counts as dc now and throughout), *[2 dc, ch 1, 2 dc] in next ch-1 space, skip next 2 dc of shell, FPdc in next dc, repeat from * across, ending last rep with dc in the top of the turning ch instead of last FPdc, turn.

Row 2: Ch 3, *[2 dc, ch 1, 2 dc] in next ch-1 space, skip next 2 dc of shell, BPdc in next dc, rep from * across ending last rep with dc in the top of the turning ch instead of last BPdc, turn.

Repeat Rows 1 and 2 for pattern.

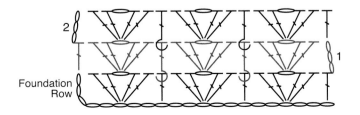

SHELLS AND ARCHES

Skill Level: Easy

Ch a multiple of 12 plus 4.

Row 1 (RS): 2 dc in third ch from hook, *skip next 2 ch, 1 sc in next ch, ch 5, skip next 5 ch, 1 sc in next ch, skip next 2 ch, 5 dc in next ch (shell), rep from * across, ending last rep with 3 dc in last ch, turn.

Row 2: Ch 1, 1 sc in first st, *ch 5, 1 sc in the next ch-5 loop, ch 5, 1 sc into 3rd dc of next shell, rep from * across, ending with last sc in top of turning ch, turn.

Row 3: Ch 5 (counts as dc, ch 2), *1 sc in next ch-5 loop, 5 dc in next sc (shell), 1 sc in next ch-5 loop**, ch 5, rep from * across, ending lat rep at **, ch 2, 1 dc in last sc, turn.

Row 4: Ch 1, 1 sc in first dc, *ch 5, 1 sc in 3rd dc of next shell, ch 5, 1 sc into next ch-5 loop, rep from * across, ending with last sc in 3rd ch of turning ch, turn.

Row 5: Ch 3 (counts as first dc), 2 dc in first st, *1 sc in next ch-5 loop, ch 5, 1 sc next ch-5 loop, 5 dc into next sc (shell), rep from * across, ending with 3 dc in last sc, turn.

Rep Rows 2–5 for pattern.

EASY SHELLS

Skill Level: Easy

Ch a multiple of 4 plus 2.

Row 1: 4 dc in 5th ch from hook, skip next 3 ch, *4 dc in next ch, skip next 3 ch, rep from * across, ending with 2 dc in last ch, turn.

Row 2: Ch 1, (counts as first sc), skip first dc, 1 sc in each dc across row, 1 sc in top of turn ch, turn.

Row 3: Ch 3 (counts as first dc now and throughout), 1 dc in first st, skip next 3 sc, *4 dc in next sc, skip next 3 sc, rep from * across to within last 2 sts, skip next sc, 1 dc in turn ch, turn.

Row 4: Rep Row 2.

Row 5: Ch 3, skip first 2sc, *4 dc in next sc, skip 3 sc, rep from * across, 1 dc in top of turning ch, turn.

Rep Rows 2–5 for pattern.

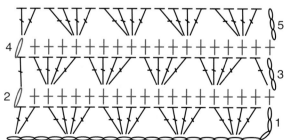

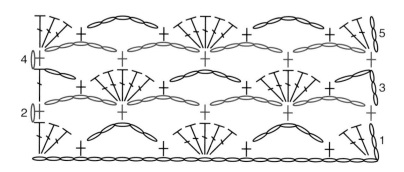

SHELLS AND PICOTS

Skill Level: Intermediate

Picot Stitch: Ch 3, work 1 sc in the base of the ch 3.

Ch a multiple of 5 plus 4.

Foundation Row: 5 dc in 6th ch from hook (shell), *ch 1, skip next 4 ch, 5 dc in next ch (shell), rep from * across to within last 3 ch, skip 2 ch, 1 dc in last ch, turn.

Row 1: Ch 5 (counts as a dc, ch 2), skip first 3 dc, 1 sc in next dc, * ch 2 [1 dc, 1 picot, 1 dc] in next ch-1 space, ch 2, 1 sc in the third dc of next shell, rep from * across to with last 3 sts, ch 2, skip next 2 dc, 1 dc in top of turning ch, turn.

Row 2: Ch 3 (counts as first dc), 5 dc in next sc, *ch 1, 5 dc in next sc, rep from * across ending with 1 dc in the 3rd ch of turning ch, turn.

Rep Rows 1 and 2 for pattern.

PETITE SHELLS

Skill Level: Beginner

Ch an even number of sts.

Foundation Row: [1 sc, ch 2, 1 sc] in 4th ch from hook (shell), *skip next ch, [1 sc, ch 2, 1 sc] in next ch, rep from * across to within last 2 ch, skip next ch, 1 hdc in last ch, turn.

Row 1: Ch 2 (counts a first hdc), *[1 sc, ch 2, 1 sc] in next ch-2 space, rep from * across, 1 hdc in top of turning ch, turn.

Rep Row 1 for pattern.

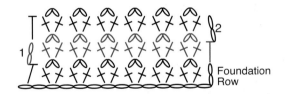

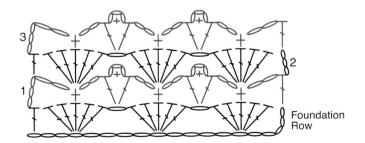

TRIPLE LOOP SHELLS

Skill Level: Experienced

Ch a multiple of 10 plus 4.

Row 1: 1 dc in 3rd ch from hook, *ch 4, skip next 4 ch, [1 sc, ch 7, 1 sc, ch 7, 1 sc, ch 7, 1 sc] in next ch, ch 4, skip next 4 ch, 1 dc in next ch, rep from * across, 1 dc in last ch, turn.

Row 2: Ch 1 (counts as first sc), skip first dc, 1 sc in next dc, *ch 1, sc in next ch-7 loop, [ch 3, 1 sc in next ch-7 loop] twice, ch 1, 1 sc in next dc, rep from * across, 1 sc in top of turning ch, turn.

Row 3: Ch 7, [1 sc, ch 7, 1 sc] in next sc, (2 petals formed), skip next sc, *ch 4, 1 dc in next sc, ch 4, skip next sc**, [1 sc, ch 7, 1 sc, ch 7, 1 sc, ch 7, 1 sc] in next sc, rep from * across, ending last rep at **, [1 sc, ch 7, 1 sc] in next sc, ch 3, 1 dc in top of turning ch turn.

Row 4: Ch 1 (counts as sc), 1 sc in next ch-3 space, ch 3, 1 sc in next ch-7 loop, *ch 1, 1 sc in next dc, ch 1, 1 sc in next ch-7 loop**, [ch 3, 1 sc in next ch-7 loop] twice, rep from * across, ending last rep at **, ch 3, 2 sc in last ch-7 loop, turn.

Row 5: Ch 3 (counts as dc), skip first sc, 1 dc in next sc, *ch 4, skip next sc, [1 sc, ch 7, 1 sc, ch 7, 1 sc, ch 7, 1 sc] in next sc, ch 4, skip next sc, 1 dc in next sc, rep from * across, 1 dc in top of turning ch, turn.

Rep Rows 2–5 for pattern.

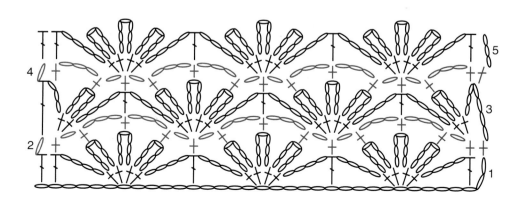

PRINCESS SHELLS

Skill Level: Intermediate

Ch a multiple of 12 plus 6.

Row 1: Work [1 tr, ch 1] 3 times in the 6th ch from hook, (half shell), skip next 5 ch, 1 sc in next ch, *ch 1, skip next 5 ch, work [1 tr, ch 1] 7 times in next ch (shell), skip next 5 ch, 1 sc next ch, rep from * across to within last 6 ch, work [ch 1, 1 tr] 3 times in last ch (half shell), turn.

Row 2: Ch 1, 1 sc in first tr, *ch 6, 1 sc in next sc, ch 6, skip next 3 tr, 1 sc in next tr, rep from * across, ending with last sc in 4th ch of beg ch-5, turn.

Row 3: Ch 1, 1 sc in first sc, *ch 6, 1 sc in next sc, rep from * across, turn.

Row 4: Ch 1, 1 sc in first sc, *ch 1, [1 tr, ch 1] 7 times in next sc, 1 sc in next sc, rep from * across, turn.

Row 5: Ch 1, 1 sc in first sc, * ch 6, skip next 3 tr, 1 sc in next tr, ch 6, 1 sc in next sc, rep from * across, turn.

Row 6: Ch 1, 1 sc in first sc, *ch 6, 1 sc in next sc, rep from * across, turn.

Row 7: Ch 5 (counts as 1 tr, ch 1), [1 tr, ch 1] 3 times in first sc, 1 sc in next sc, *ch 1, work [1 tr, ch 1] 7 times in next sc, 1 sc in next sc, rep from * across to last sc, (ch 1, 1 tr) 4 times in last sc, turn.

Rep Rows 2–7 for pattern.

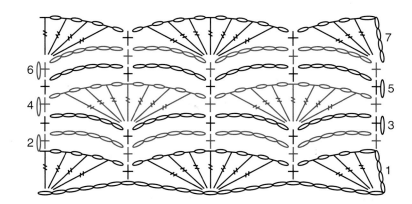

SHELL WAVES

Skill Level: Intermediate

Ch a multiple of 14 plus 2.

Row 1: 1 sc in 2nd ch from hook, 1 sc in each of next 3 ch, *skip next 3 ch, 7 dc in next ch (shell), skip next 3 ch, 1 sc in each of the next 7 ch, rep from * across, ending with 1 sc in each of last 4 ch, turn.

Row 2: Ch 1 (counts as first sc), skip first sc, 1 sc in each st across, turn.

Row 3: Ch 3 (counts as first dc), 3 dc in first sc, *skip next 3 sc, 1 sc in each of the next 7 sts, skip next 3 sc, 7 dc in next sc, rep from * across ending last rep with 4 dc in top of turn ch, turn.

Row 4: Ch 1 (counts as first sc), skip first sc, 1 sc in each st across, 1 sc in top of turning ch, turn.

Row 5: Ch 1 (counts as first sc) skip first sc, 1 sc in each of next 3 dc, *skip next 3 sc, 7 dc in next sc, skip next 3 sc, 1 sc in each of next 7 sts, rep from * across, ending last rep 1 sc in each of the next 3 dc, 1 sc in top of turning ch, turn.

Rep Rows 2–5 for pattern.

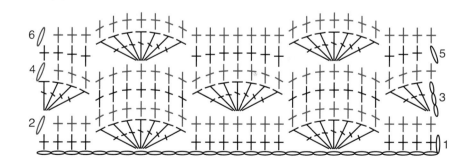

PEACOCK FAN

Skill Level: Intermediate

Ch a multiple of 10 plus 2.

Foundation Row: 1 sc in 2nd ch from hook, *skip next 4 chs, 11 tr in next ch (fan made), skip next 4 ch, 1 sc in next ch, rep from * across, turn.

Row 1: Ch 4 (counts as tr) 1 tr in first sc, *ch 5, sc in the 6th tr of next fan, ch 5**, [1 tr, ch 1, 1 tr] in next sc, rep from * across, ending last rep at **, 2 tr in last sc, turn.

Row 2: Ch 1 (counts as first sc), 1 sc in next tr, *skip next ch-5 space, 11 tr in next sc, skip next ch-5 space, 1 sc in next ch-1 space, rep from * across, ending last rep with 1 sc in last tr, 1 sc in top of turning ch, turn.

Repeat Rows 1 and 2 for pattern.

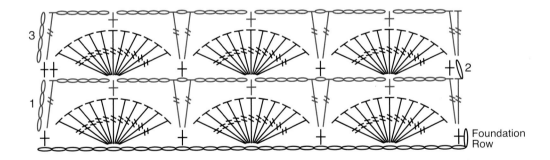

SHELLS AND V STITCH

Skill Level: Intermediate

Ch a multiple of 8 plus 2.

Foundation Row: 1 sc in 2nd ch from hook, *skip next 3 ch, 7 dc in next ch (fan made), skip next 3 ch, 1 sc in next ch, rep from * across, turn.

Row 1: Ch 4 (counts as a dc, ch 1), 1 dc in first st (counts as first V-st), *ch 5, skip next fan, [1 dc, ch 1, 1 dc] in next sc (V-st), rep from * across, turn.

Row 2: Ch 3 (counts as first dc), 3 dc in first dc (half fan made), *sc over the next ch-5 space and into the 4th dc of fan in row below, work 7 dcs in next ch 1 space, rep from * across, ending last rep with 4 dc in last ch-1 space (half fan made), turn.

Row 3: Ch 4 (counts as 1 sc, ch 3), skip next 3 dc, *[1 dc, ch 1, 1 dc] in the next sc**, ch 5, skip next fan, rep from * across, ending last rep at **, ch 3, skip next 3 dc, 1 sc in top of turning ch, turn.

Row 4: Ch 1 (counts as first sc), 1 sc over the ch-3 space and into 2nd dc of beg half fan in row below, *7 dc in next ch 1 sp, 1 sc over the ch-5 space and into the 4th dc of fan in row below, rep from * across, end last rep by working last sc over ch-3 space and into 3rd dc of last half fan, 1 sc in top of turning ch, turn.

Row 5: Ch 4 (counts as dc, ch 1), 1 dc in first sc, * ch 5, skip next fan, [1 dc, ch 1, 1 dc] in next sc, rep from * across, end last rep [1 dc, ch 1, 1 dc] in top of turning ch, turn.

Rep Rows 2–5 for pattern.

DIAGONAL SHELLS

Skill Level: Intermediate

Ch a multiple of 8 plus 5.

Foundation Row: 1 sc in 9th ch from hook, *ch 5, skip next 3 ch, 1 sc in next ch, rep from * across, turn.

Row 1: Ch 3 (counts as first dc now and throughout), 2 dc in first sc (half shell), 1 sc in next ch-5 space, *ch 5, 1 sc in next ch-5 space, 5 dc in next sc (shell), 1 sc in next ch-5 space, rep from * across, ending with ch 5, 1 sc in last ch-space, turn.

Row 2: Ch 3, 2 dc in first sc, 1 sc in next ch-5 space, *ch 5, 1 sc in center dc of next shell, 5 dc in next sc, 1 sc in next ch-5 space, rep from * across to last ch-5 space, ch 5, 1 sc in top of the turning ch, turn.

Row 3: Ch 6 (counts as 1 dc, ch 3), 1 sc in next ch-5 space, *5 dc in next sc**, 1 sc in center dc of next shell, ch 5, 1 sc in next ch-5 space, rep from * across, ending last rep at **, 1 sc in top of turning ch, turn.

Row 4: Ch 6 (counts as 1 dc, ch 3), 1 sc in center dc of next shell, *5 dc in next sc**, 1 sc in next ch-5 space, ch 5, 1 sc in center dc of next shell, rep from * across, ending last rep at **, 1 sc in 3rd ch of turning ch, turn.

Row 5: Ch 3, 2 dc in first sc, 1 sc in center dc of next shell, *ch 5, 1 sc in next ch-5 space, 5 dc in next sc, 1 sc in center dc of next shell, rep from * across, ending with ch 5, 1 sc in 3rd ch of the beg ch-6, turn.

Rep Rows 2–5 for pattern.

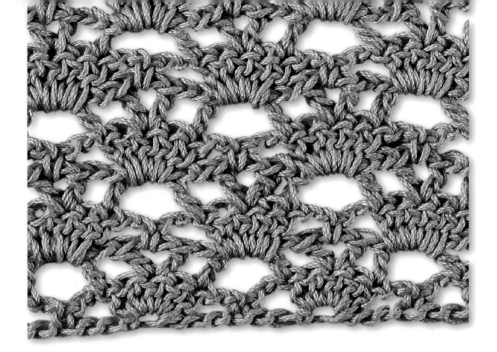

SPIDER SHELLS

Skill Level: Easy

Ch a multiple of 8 plus 2.

Foundation Row: 1 sc in 2nd ch from hook, *ch 2, skip next 3 ch, 5 dc in next ch (shell made), ch 2, skip next 3 ch, 1 sc in next ch, rep from * across, turn.

Row 1: Ch 4 (counts as dc, ch 1), skip first sc, *1 dc in next dc, ch 2, skip 1 dc, [1 dc, ch 2, 1 dc] in next dc, ch 2, skip 1 dc, 1 dc in next dc, ch 1, skip next sc, rep from * across, 1 dc in last sc, turn.

Row 2: Ch 3 (counts as dc), 2 dc in first ch-1 sp, *ch 2, skip next ch-2 space, 1 sc in next ch-2 space, ch 2, skip next ch-2 space, 5 dc in next ch-1 space, rep from * across, ending with 2 dc in last ch-1 space, 1 dc in top of turning ch, turn.

Row 3: Ch 4 (counts as dc, ch 1), 1 dc in first dc, ch 2, skip next dc, 1 dc next dc, ch 1, skip next sc, *1 dc in first dc of shell, ch 2**, skip next dc, [1 dc, ch 2, 1 dc] in next dc, ch 2, skip next dc, 1 dc in last dc of shell, ch 1, skip next sc, rep from * across, ending last rep at **, [1 dc, ch 1, 1 dc] in top of turning ch, turn.

Row 4: Ch 1 (counts as first sc), 1 sc in next ch-1 space, ch 2, skip next ch-2 space, 5 dc in next ch-1 space, *ch 2, skip next ch-2 space, 1 sc in next ch-2 space, ch 2, skip next space, 5 dc in next ch-1 space, rep from * across to within last 2 spaces, ch 2, skip next ch-2 space, 1 sc in last ch-1 space, 1 sc in top of turning ch, turn.

Rep Rows 1–4 for pattern.

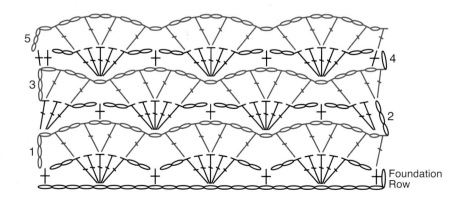

Black flick yarn
3/2014   172 Chain

TIPSY CLUSTERS

Skill level: Easy

Ch a multiple of 12 plus 4.

Foundation Row: 1 sc in 2nd ch from hook, 1 sc in each ch across row, turn.

Row 1: Ch 3 (counts as first dc), skip first sc, 1 dc in each of the next 3 sts, *skip next 2 sts, 5 dc in next st, ch 2, skip next 4 sts, 1 dc in each of next 5 sts, rep from * across ending last rep with 1 dc in each of last 4 sts, turn.

Row 2: Ch 3 (counts as first dc), skip first dc, 1 dc in each of the next 3 dc, *skip next ch-2 space, 5 dc in first dc of next shell, ch 2, skip next 4 dc of shell, 1 dc in each of the next 5 dc, rep from * across, ending last rep with 1 dc in each of the next 3 dc, 1 dc in top of turning ch, turn.

Rep Row 2 for pattern.

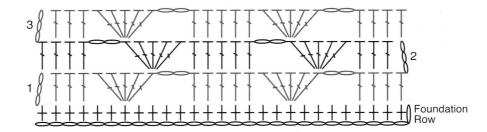

LITTLE FAN STITCH

Skill Level: Easy

Ch a multiple of 8 plus 2

Foundation Row: Sc in 2nd ch from hook, *skip next 3 ch, [1 dc, ch 1] 4 times in next st, 1 dc same st (shell made), skip next 3 ch, 1 sc in next ch, rep from * across, turn.

Row 1: Ch 6 (counts as dc, ch 3), *1 sc in center dc of next shell, ch 3, 1 dc in next sc, ch 3, rep from * across, ending with dc in last sc, turn.

Row 2: Ch 1, 1 sc in first dc, *shell in next sc, 1 sc in next dc, rep from * across, ending with last sc in 3rd ch of beg ch 5, turn.

Rep Rows 1 and 2 for pattern.

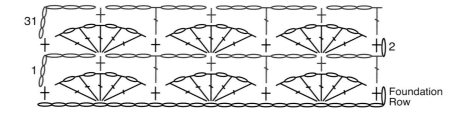

DOUBLE SHELLS AND V'S

Skill Level: Easy

Ch a multiple of 8 plus 4.

Foundation Row: 3 dc in 4th ch from hook (half shell), *skip next 3 ch [1 dc, ch 1, 1 dc) in next ch (V-st), skip next 3 ch, 7 dc in next ch (shell), rep from * across, ending with 4 dc in last ch (half shell), turn.

Row 1: Ch 3 (counts as first dc), skip first dc, 1 dc in each of the next 2 dc, *V-st in next ch-1 space, skip next 2 dc**, 1 dc in each of the next 5 dc, rep from * ending last rep at **, 1 dc in each of the next 2 dc, 1 dc in top of turning ch, turn.

Row 2: Ch 4 (counts as 1 dc, ch 1), skip first dc, 1 dc in next dc, *7 dc in ch-1 space of next V-st**, skip next 3 dc, V-st in next dc, rep from * across, ending last rep at **, dc in next dc, ch 1, dc in top of turning ch, turn.

Row 3: Ch 4, 1 dc in next ch-1 space, *skip next 2 dc, 1 dc in each of next 5 dc**, V-st in next ch-1 space of next V-st, rep from * across, ending last rep at **, 1 dc in last ch-1 space, ch 1, 1 dc in top of turning ch, turn.

Row 4: Ch 3 (counts as first dc), 3 dc in first ch-1 space, *skip next 3 dc, V-st in next dc**, 7 dc in ch-1 space of next V-st, rep from * across, ending last rep at **, 3 dc in last ch-1 space, 1 dc in top of turning ch, turn.

Rep Rows 1–4 for pattern.

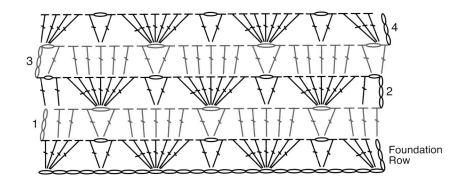

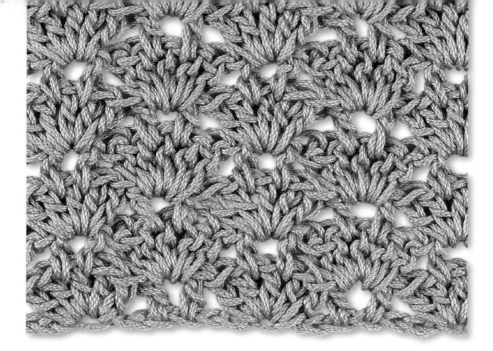

SNAPDRAGON SHELLS

Skill Level: Easy

Note: For this pattern, after the foundation row, work all stitches in the spaces between stitches.

Ch a multiple of 7 plus 6.

Foundation Row: Dc in 4th ch from hook, 1 dc next ch, *skip next 2 ch, 5 dc in next ch (shell), skip next 2 ch, 1 dc in each of next 2 ch (2-dc group), rep from * across, 1 dc in last ch, turn.

Row 1: Ch 3 (counts as first dc), skip first dc, 5 dc between next 2 dc, *1 dc in the space before and 1 dc in the space after the center dc of next shell, 5 dc between the 2 dc of the next 2-dc group, rep from * across, 1 dc top of turning ch, turn.

Row 2: Ch 3 (counts as first dc), *1 dc in the space before and 1 dc in the space after the center dc of next shell**, 5 dc between the 2 dc of next 2-dc group, rep from * across, ending last rep at **, 1 dc in top of turning ch, turn.

Rep Rows 1 and 2 for pattern.

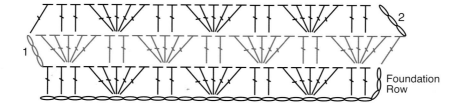

COWL NECK WARMER

A neck warmer made of silk yarn feels luxurious against your skin. This cowl collar is worked flat in a shell pattern, first in one direction and then in the other from the opposite side of the foundation chain. Worked in this way, both edges are scalloped. Then the piece is sewn together into a ring.

(continued)

Cowl Neck Warmer (continued)

YOU WILL NEED

Yarn

- Medium-weight silk yarn
- Shown: Oasis Yarn, Silk Icelandic Seduction, 100% silk, 3.5 oz (100 g)/310 yd (283.4 m), Sko2 Ruby: 1 skein

Hooks

- 5/F (3.75 mm) and 6/G (4 mm)

Stitches used

- Chain
- Double crochet
- V-stitch
- Triple crochet

Gauge

- 2 shells and 2 V-st = 4" (10 cm) on 5/F hook
- 2 shells and 1 V-st = 4" (10 cm) on 6/G hook

Notions

- Tapestry needle

Finished size

- One size fits all

First Half

Starting on inside edge of cowl, with 5/F hook, ch 124.

Foundation Row: 3 dc in 4th ch from hook (half shell made), *skip next 3 ch, [1 dc, ch 1, 1 dc] in next ch (V-st made), skip next 3 ch**, 7 dc in next ch (shell made), rep from * across, ending last rep at **, 4 dc in last ch (half shell made), turn.

Row 1: Ch 3, skip first dc, 1 dc in each of the next 2 dc, skip next 2 dc, *V-st in ch-1 space of next V-st, skip first dc of next shell**, 1 dc in each of the next 5 dc, rep from * across, ending last rep at **, 1 dc in each of the next 2 dc, 1 dc in top of the turning ch, turn.

Row 2: Ch 4 (counts as dc, ch 1), skip next dc, 1 dc in next dc, *shell in ch-1 space of next V-st**, V-st in center dc of next shell, rep from * across, ending last rep at **, skip next 2 dc, dc in next dc, ch 1, dc in top of turning ch, turn.

Row 3: Ch 4 (counts as dc, ch 1), 1 dc in first ch-1 space, *skip first dc of next shell, 1 dc in each of the next 5 dc**, V-st in ch-1 space of next V-st, rep from * across, ending last rep at **, 1 dc in last ch-1 space, ch 1, 1 dc in 3rd ch of turning ch, turn.

Row 4: Ch 3 (counts as first dc), 3 dc in first ch-1 space, *skip next 3 dc, V-st in next dc**, shell in ch-1 space of next V-st, rep from * across, ending last rep at **, 3 dc in next ch-1 space, 1 dc 3rd ch of turning ch, turn.

Rep Rows 1–4 for pattern until First Half measures 3" (7.5 cm) from beg, end off.

Second Half

With right side facing, using 6/G hook, join yarn in first ch on opposite side of foundation ch.

Foundation Row: Ch 3 (counts as first dc), 3 dc in same ch, *skip next 3 ch, [1 dc, ch 1, 1 dc] in next ch (V-st made), skip next 3 ch**, 7 dc in next ch (shell made), rep from * across, ending last rep at **, 4 dc in last ch (half shell made), turn.

Rep Rows 1–4 of First Half until Second Half measures 5" (12.7 cm) from beg, ending with Row 3 of pattern.

Last Row: Ch 4, 3 tr in first ch-1 space, *skip next 3 dc, 1 sc in next dc**, [4 tr, ch 3, 4 tr] in ch-1 space of next V-st, rep from * across, ending last rep at **, 3 tr in last ch-1 space, 1 tr in 3rd ch of turning ch, end off.

Finishing

Using tapestry needle, sew back seam; fold at foundation line with wider half to outside. Blocking is not recommended for this yarn.

Bobbles, Popcorns, and Puffs

Bobbles, popcorns, and puff stitches—commonly called clusters—all have one thing in common; they are all counted as one stitch because they begin and end in the space of one stitch and do not change the stitch count of the row.

Popcorns are worked like making an increase: you make a group of stitches in the same stitch, completing each stitch, remove the hook from the last loop, insert the hook in the first stitch of the group and into the dropped loop, then gather by drawing the dropped loop through the first stitch.

Bobbles are similar to popcorns, but each stitch is not completed; the last loop of each stitch is left on the hook, then stitches are gathered by yarn over and drawing the loop through all loops on hook.

Puffs are similar to bobbles but puffier. A long loop is drawn up from the base stitch, usually 5 times, all loops are left on hook, yarn over, then through all loops on hook.

BOBBLES AND SINGLE CROCHET

Skill Level: Easy

Bobble Stitch: [Yo, draw up a loop in designated st, yo, through 2 loops] 4 times in same st, yo, draw through all 5 loops on hook.

Ch a multiple of 4.

Foundation Row (WS): Starting in 2nd ch from hook, 1 sc in each ch across row, turn.

Row 1: Ch 1 (counts as first sc now and throughout), skip first sc, sc in each sc across, turn.

Row 2 (bobble row): Ch 1, skip first st, 1 sc in each of next 2 sts, *bobble in next st, sc in each of next 3 sc, rep from * across, ending with last sc in top of turning ch, turn.

Rows 3, 4, 5, 6, and 7: Rep Row 1.

Rep Rows 1–7 for pattern.

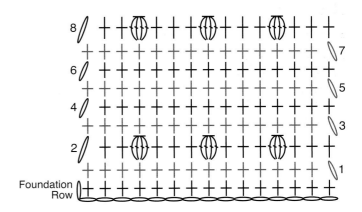

BOBBLES AND LADDERS

Skill Level: Easy

Bobble: (Yo, pick up a loop in st, yo, draw through 2 loops) 5 times, yo, draw through all 6 loops on hook.

Ch a multiple of 6 plus 3.

Foundation Row: 1 dc in 4th ch from hook, *ch 2, skip next ch, 1 sc in next ch, ch 2, skip next ch, 1 dc in each of next 3 ch, rep from * across, ending with 1 dc in each of the last 2 ch, turn.

Row 1: Ch 3 (counts as dc), skip first dc, 1 dc in next dc, *ch 3, 1 dc next dc ** (first dc of 3-dc group), bobble next dc, 1 dc next dc, rep from * across, ending last rep at **, 1 dc in top of turning ch, turn.

Row 2: Ch 3 (counts as dc), skip first dc, 1 dc next dc, *ch 2, 1 sc next ch-3 space, ch 2, 1 dc next dc**, 1 dc in top of bobble, 1 dc next dc, rep from * across, ending last rep at **, 1 dc in top of the turn ch.

Rep Rows 1 and 2 for pattern.

SIDE PUFFS

Skill Level: Intermediate

Side Puff (You will be working over the bar of dc just made): [Yo, pick up a loop around post of dc just made] 3 times, yo, draw through 6 loops on hook, yo, draw through last 2 loops.

Ch a multiple of 2 plus 1.

Row 1 (WS): Starting in 2nd ch from hook, 1 sc in each ch across row, turn.

Row 2: Ch 3 (counts as first dc), skip first sc, *1 dc in next st, side puff over the dc just made, skip 1 st, rep from * across row, end 1 dc in last st, turn.

Row 3: Ch 1 (counts as a sc), skip first st, *1 sc in the next puff st, 1 sc in next dc, rep from * across, ending with 1 sc in top of turning ch, turn.

Repeat Rows 2 and 3 for pattern.

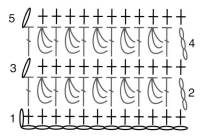

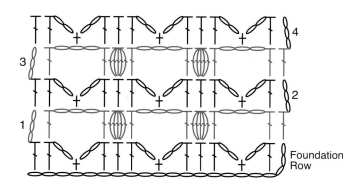

V STITCH PUFFS

Skill Level: Intermediate

Puff Stitch: [Yo hook, draw up a loop in designated stitch] 3 times, yo through all 7 loops on hook.

Ch a multiple of 3 plus 2.

Foundation Row: [Puff st, ch 2, puff st] in 6th chain from hook, *ch 1, skip 2 ch, [puff st, ch 2, puff st] in next ch, rep from * across to within last 2 ch, ch 1, skip next ch, 1 dc in last ch, turn.

Row 1: Ch 1 (counts as first sc), sc in next ch-1 space, *3 sc in the ch-2 space, 1 sc in next ch-1 space, rep from * across, sc in top of the turn ch, turn.

Row 2: Ch 4 (counts as dc, ch 1), skip first 3 sc, [puff st, ch 2, puff st] in next sc, *ch 1, skip 3 sc, [puff st, ch 2, puff st] in next sc, rep from * across to within last 3 sts, ch 1, skip 2 sc, dc in top of turning ch, turn.

Rep Rows 1 and 2 for pattern.

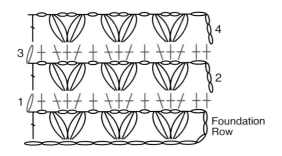

TINY MOCK POPCORNS

Skill Level: Easy

Ch a multiple of 4 plus 3.

Foundation Row: Starting in 2nd ch from hook, 1 sc in each ch across row, turn.

Row 1: Ch 1, 1 sc in first sc, *ch 4, 1 sc in each of the next 4 sc; rep from * across to within last 2 sts, ch 4, 1 sc in last sc, turn.

Row 2: Ch 1, holding ch-4 loop to back (RS), work 1 sc in first sc, 1 sc in each sc across row, turn.

Row 3: Ch 1, 1 sc in each of first 3 sc, *ch 4, 1 sc in each of next 4 sc; rep from * to within last 3 sc, ch 4, 1 sc in each of last 3 sc, turn.

Row 4: Rep Row 2.

Rep Rows 1–4 for pattern.

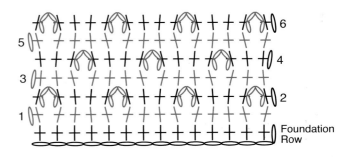

BLOCK STITCH

Skill Level: Intermediate

Ch a multiple of 2 plus 1.

Row 1: Starting in 2nd ch from hook, work 1 sc in each ch across row, turn.

Row 2: Ch 3 (counts as first dc), skip first st, 1 dc in next st, working over the bar of the dc just made [yo and pick up a loop 4 times (9 loops on hook)], pick up a loop in next sc, yo, draw through all 10 loops on hook, holding this last loop on hook, pick up a loop in next sc, ch 2, yo, draw through both loops rem on hook, *working over the ch-2 space just made [yo and pick up a loop 4 times (9 loops on hook)], pick up a loop in next sc, yo, draw through all 10 loops on hook, holding this last loop on hook, pick up a loop in next sc, ch 2, yo, draw through both loops rem on hook, rep from * across, last ch will be worked in last sc, turn.

Row 3: Ch 1 (counts as first sc), *1 sc in top of block st, 1 sc between block sts, rep from * across, skip last dc, 1 sc in top of turning ch, turn.

Row 4: Ch 1 (counts as first sc), skip first st, 1 sc in each sc across, 1 sc in top of turning ch, turn.

Rep Rows 2–4 for pattern.

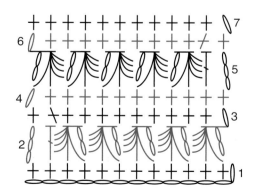

BULLIONS

Skill Level: Experienced

Bullion Stitch: Wrap yarn around widest part of the hook 10 times, pick up a loop in designated st, yo and pull through all loops on hook, ch 1.

Ch a multiple of 5.

Foundation Row: Starting in 4th ch from hook, work 1 dc in each ch across, turn.

Row 1: Ch 3 (counts as a dc now and throughout), skip first dc, 1 dc in each of the next 2 sts, * ch 2, skip 2 dc, 1 dc in each next 3 dc, rep from * across, ending with last dc in top of turning ch, turn.

Row 2: Ch 3, skip 1 dc, 1 dc in each of next 2 dc, *2 dc in the ch 2 space, 1 dc in each of the next 3 dc, rep from * ending with last dc in top of turning ch, turn.

Row 3 (bullion stitch row): Ch 3, skip first dc, 1 dc in each of the next 4 dc, *skip 1 dc, 3 bullion sts in next st, skip 1 dc, 1 dc in each of next 2 dc, rep from * across to within last 3 sts, 1 dc in each next 2 dc, 1 dc in top of turning ch, turn.

Row 4: Ch 3, skip first st, 1 dc in each of the next 4 dc, *working in the bar behind bullion sts (like a front post dc), 1 dc in next 3 bullion sts, 1 dc in each of the next 2 dc, rep from * across to within last 3 sts, 1 dc in each of the next 2 dc, 1 dc top of turning ch, turn.

Repeat Rows 1–4 for pattern.

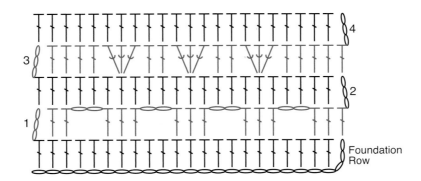

DIAMOND PUFFS

Skill Level: Intermediate

Puff Stitch: [Yo, draw up a loop] 4 times in same space, yo, draw through all 9 loops on hook.

Ch a multiple of 18 plus 8.

Row 1: 1 dc in 8th ch from hook, *ch 2, skip 2 ch, 1 dc in next ch, rep from * to end, turn.

Row 2: Ch 5 (counts as dc, ch 2 now and throughout), skip first dc, 1 dc in next dc, (ch 2, 1 dc in next dc) twice, puff st in next ch-2 space, ch 1, 1 dc in next dc, *(ch 2, 1 dc in next dc) 5 times, puff st in next ch-2 space, ch 1, 1 dc in next dc, rep from * across to within last 3 ch-2 spaces, [ch 2, 1 dc in next dc] twice, ch 2, 1 dc in 3rd ch of turning ch-5, turn.

Row 3: Ch 5, skip first dc, 1 dc in next dc, ch 2, 1 dc in next dc, * puff st in next ch-2 space, ch 1, 1 dc in next dc, ch 2, 1 dc in next dc, puff st in next ch-2 space, ch 1, 1 dc in next dc**, [ch 2, 1 dc in next dc] 3 times, rep from * across, ending last rep at **, ch 2, 1 dc in next dc, ch 2, 1 dc in 3rd ch of beg ch 5, turn.

Row 4: Ch 5, skip first dc, *1 dc in next dc, puff st in next ch-2 space, ch 1, 1 dc in next dc, ch 2, rep from * across, ending with 1 dc in 3rd ch of turning ch-5, turn.

Row 5: Rep Row 3.

Row 6: Rep Row 2.

Row 7: Ch 5, skip first dc, 1 dc in next dc, *ch 2, 1 dc in next dc, rep from * across, ending with last dc in 3rd ch of turning ch-5, turn.

Rep Rows 2–7 for pattern.

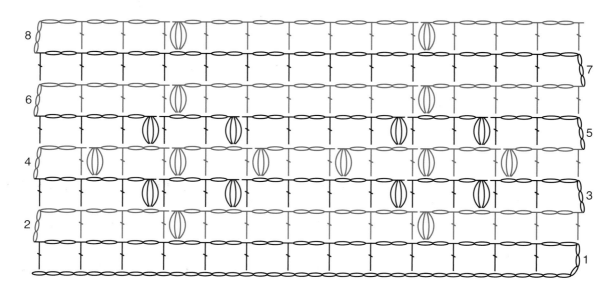

PUFFS AND BOXES

Skill Level: Easy

Puff Stitch: [Yo, draw up a loop in next dc] 5 times, yo, draw through all 11 loops on hook.

Ch a multiple of 8 plus 6.

Foundation Row: 1 dc in 6th ch from hook, *ch 1, skip 1 ch, 1 dc in next ch, rep from * across, turn.

Row 1: Ch 4 (counts as dc, ch 1 now and throughout), skip first ch-1 space, *1 dc in next dc, (1 dc in next ch-1 space, 1 dc next dc) 3 times, ch 1, rep from * across, ending with 1 dc in third ch of turning ch-4, turn.

Row 2: Ch 4, skip first ch-1 space, *1 dc in each of next 3 dc, puff st in next dc, ch 1, 1 dc in each of next 3 dc, ch 1, rep from * across, ending with 1 dc in 3rd ch of turning ch-4, turn.

Row 3: Ch 4, skip first ch-1 space, *1 dc in each of next 3 dc, 1 dc in next ch-1 space, skip next puff st, 1 dc in each of next 3 dc, ch 1, rep from * across, ending with 1 dc in 3rd ch of turning ch-4, turn.

Row 4: Ch 4, skip first ch-1 space, *1 dc in next dc, (ch 1, skip 1 dc, 1 dc in next dc) 3 times, ch 1, rep from * across, ending with 1 dc in 3rd ch of turning ch-4, turn.

Rep Rows 1–4 for pattern.

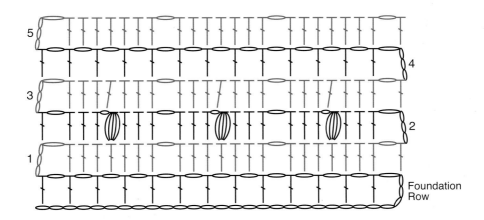

TIP

Most people use ch-3 at the beginning of the row to count as a double crochet. For a stitch pattern like this, I use ch-4 to avoid making the edges too tight.

DOUBLE POPCORNS

Skill Level: Intermediate

Popcorn Stitch: 4 dc in designated space, remove hook, place hook in top of first dc made, draw loop of last dc through, ch 1 to lock popcorn.

Front Post Double Crochet (FPdc) Stitch: Yo hook, pick up a loop from front, inserting hook from right to left under designated stitch, [yo, draw through 2 loops] 2 times.

Back Post Double Crochet (BPdc) Stitch: Yo hook, pick up a loop from back, inserting hook from right to left under designated stitch, [yo, draw through 2 loops] 2 times.

Ch a multiple of 8 plus 4.

Foundation Row: Started in 2nd ch from hook, work 1 sc in each ch across row, turn.

Row 1: Ch 3 (counts as dc now and throughout), skip first sc, 1 dc in each of the next 2 sc, *skip 2 sc, (1 dc, ch 1, 1 dc) twice in next sc, skip 2 sc, 1 dc in each of next 3 sc, rep from * across, turn.

Row 2: Ch 3, skip first dc, 1 BPdc next dc, 1 FPdc in next dc, *1 popcorn in next ch-1 space, ch 3, 1 popcorn in next ch-1 space, ch 1, 1 FPdc in next dc, 1 BPdc in next dc**, 1 FPdc in next dc, rep from * across, ending last rep at ** 1 dc in top of turning ch, turn.

Row 3: Ch 3, skip the first dc, 1 FPdc in next dc, 1 BPdc in next dc, *[1 dc, ch 1, 1 dc] twice in the next ch-3 space between popcorns, 1 BPdc in next dc, 1 FPdc in next dc**, 1 BPdc in next dc, rep from * across, ending last rep at ** 1 dc in top of turning ch, turn.

Rep Rows 2 and 3 for pattern.

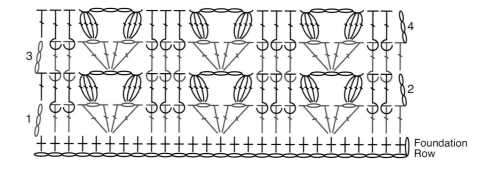

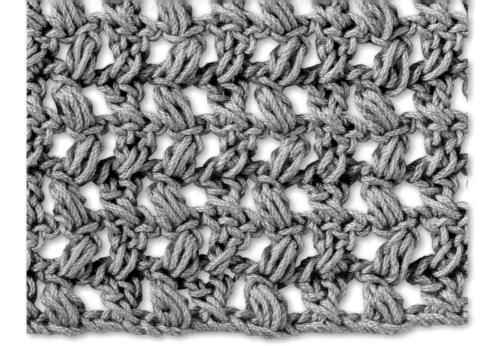

ZIGZAG PUFFS

Skill Level: Easy

Puff Stitch: [Yo hook, pick up a loop in designated st] 3 times, yo, draw through all 7 loops on hook.

Cross Stitch: 1 dc in designated st, crossing in front of dc just made, 1 dc in last skipped st.

Ch a multiple of 6 plus 2.

Foundation Row: 1 dc in 7th ch from hook, crossing in front of dc just made, 1 dc in last skipped ch (cross st made), *ch 1, skip 1 ch, puff st in next st, ch 1, skip 2 ch, 1 dc in next st, crossing in front of dc just made, 1 dc in last skipped ch (cross st made), repeat from * across to within last 2 ch, ch 1, skip 1 ch, 1 dc in last ch, turn.

Row 1: Ch 4 (counts as dc, ch 1), skip first 2 dc, work cross st, ch 1, *1 puff stitch in next puff st, ch 1, skip next dc, 1 cross st in next cross st, ch 1, rep from * across, end 1 dc in 3rd ch of turning ch, turn.

Rep Row 1 for pattern.

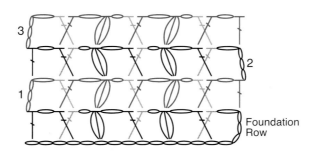

CRISSCROSS PUFFS

Skill Level: Experienced

Crisscross Puff Stitch: (Draw up a ½" (1.3 cm) long loop in specified stitch or space) 6 times, yo, draw through all 7 loops on hook, ch 1 to close puff.

Ch an even number of sts.

Foundation Row: Starting in 2nd ch from hook, work 1 sc in each ch across row, turn.

Row 1: Ch 3, draw up a loop in first sc, skip next sc, draw up a loop in next sc, (cross over the loop just picked up, draw up a loop in the first sc again, draw up a loop in same st as second loop) twice (7 loops on hook), yo, through all loops, ch 1 (1 crisscross puff made), *draw up a loop in the last sc worked, skip the next sc, pick up a loop in next sc (cross over the loop just picked up, draw up a loop in the first sc again, draw up a loop in same st as second loop) twice (7 loops on hook), yo, through all loops, ch 1, repeat from * across, 1 dc in last ch, turn.

Row 2: Ch 3, draw up a loop in the ch-1 space between the first dc and first puff st, draw up a loop in next ch-1 space between the first and second puff st, (cross over the loop just picked up, draw up a loop in the first space again, draw up a loop in second space again) twice (7 loops on hook), yo, draw through all loops, ch 1, *draw up a loop in last ch-1 space worked, pick up a loop in ch-1 sp between next 2 puffs, (cross over the loop just picked up, draw up a loop in the first space again, pick up loop in second space again) twice (7 loops on hook), yo, draw through all loops, ch 1, rep from * across, ending with last puff in space between last 2 puffs and space between the last puff and the turning ch, dc in top of turning ch, turn.

Rep Row 2 for pattern.

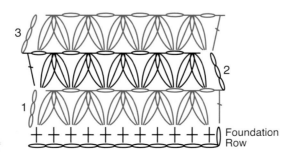

Foundation Row

CRISSCROSS PUFFS HAT

The variegated color of this silk and merino wool yarn works well in a puff stitch pattern. This hat is crocheted in rows, with the rows running vertically; then it's seamed into a cylinder and drawn together at the top. Very easy!

(continued)

YOU WILL NEED

Yarn

- Lightweight silk/merino blend
- Shown: Blue Heron Yarns Silk/Merino, 50% silk, 50% merino wool, 8 oz (227 g)/375 yd (343 m), Deep Lake: 1 skein

Hook

- 8/H (5 mm)

Stitches used

- Chain
- Single crochet
- Double crochet
- Crisscross puff stitch (page 80)

Gauge

- 8 crisscross puff sts = 4" (10 cm)

Notions

- Tapestry needle

Finished size

- Small (Medium, Large)
- 21" (22", 23") (53 [56, 58.5] cm) in circumference, 8" (8", 8½") (20.5 [20.5, 21.5] cm) deep

Hat

Ch 33 (33, 35).

Foundation Row: 1 sc in 2nd ch from hook, 1 sc in each ch across row, turn (32 [32, 34] sc).

Row 1: Ch 3, draw up a loop in first sc, skip next sc, draw up a loop in next sc, [cross over the loop just picked up, draw up a loop in the first sc again, draw up a loop in same st as second loop] twice (7 loops on hook), yo, draw through all 7 loops, ch 1 (1 criss-cross puff st made), *draw up a loop in the last sc worked, skip the next sc, pick up a loop in next sc [cross over the loop just picked up, draw up a loop in the first sc again, draw up a loop in same st as second loop] twice (7 loops on hook), yo, draw through all 7 loops, ch 1, repeat from * across, 1 dc in last ch, turn (15 [15, 16] puff sts).

Row 2: Ch 3, draw up a loop in the space between the first dc and first puff st, draw up a loop in next ch-1 space between the first and second puff st, [cross over the loop just picked up, draw up a loop in the first space again, draw up a loop in second space again] twice (7 loops on hook), yo, draw through all 7 loops, ch 1, *draw up a loop in last ch-1 space worked, pick up a loop in ch-1 sp between next 2 puffs, [cross over the loop just picked up, draw up a loop in the first space again, pick up loop in second space again] twice (7 loops on hook), yo, draw through all 7 loops, ch 1, rep from * across, ending with last puff in space between last 2 puffs and space between the last puff and the turning ch, 1 dc in top of turning ch, turn.

Rep Row 2 for pattern till piece measures 21" (22", 23") (53.5 [56, 58.5] cm) from beg, end off, leaving a tail about 1 yd (1 m) long for sewing seam and gathering top of hat.

Finishing

Thread the yarn tail onto a tapestry needle, and whipstitch (page 36) along one long end of hat. Pull on yarn to gather top of hat. Sew around a few times to secure, using same yarn. Sew back seam, end off.

Bottom Border

Rnd 1: With right side facing, join yarn on bottom edge at back seam, ch 1, sc evenly around bottom edge of hat, join with Sl st in first sc, do not turn.

Rnd 2: Ch 1, working from left to right, reverse sc in each sc around, join with Sl st in first reverse sc, end off.

Ripple Stitches

Ripple stitches all have one thing in common: a wave effect that is created by a series of increases and decreases of stitches. They are made in a variety of stitches, from single crochet to intricate shells and puffs. Ripple stitches are often used for making scarves, shawls, and afghans.

CLASSIC SINGLE CROCHET RIPPLE

Skill Level: Easy

Sc2tog: pick up a loop in each of next 2 sts, yo, draw through all 3 loops on hook.

Ch a multiple of 17 plus 15.

Foundation Row: 1 sc in 2nd ch from hook, 1 sc in each of next 5 ch, 3 sc in next ch, 1 sc in each of next 7 ch, *skip next 2 ch, 1 sc in each of next 7 ch, 3 sc in next ch, 1 sc in each of next 7 ch, rep from * across, turn.

Row 1: Ch 1, skip first st, sc2tog next 2 sts, 1 sc in each of the next 5 sc, 3 sc in next sc, *1 sc in each of the next 7 sc, skip next 2 sc, 1 sc in each of the next 7 sc, 3 sc in next sc, rep from * across to within last 7 sts, 1 sc in each of next 5 sc, sc2tog in last 2 sc, turn.

Rep Row 1 for pattern.

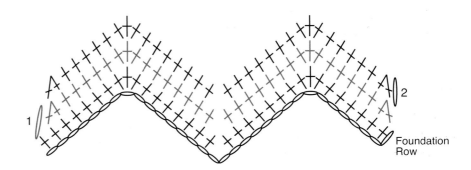

CLASSIC SINGLE CROCHET
IN BACK LOOP RIPPLE

Skill Level: Easy

Note: Work all stitches in the back loop.

Sc2tog: pick up a loop in each of next 2 sts, yo, draw through all 3 loops on hook.

Ch a multiple of 17 plus 15.

Foundation Row: 1 sc in 2nd ch from hook, 1 sc in each of next 5 ch, 3 sc in next ch, 1 sc in each of next 7 ch, *skip next 2 ch, 1 sc in each of next 7 ch, 3 sc in next ch, 1 sc in each of next 7 ch, rep from * across, turn.

Row 1: Working in back loops only, ch 1, skip first st, sc2tog next 2 sts, 1 sc in each of the next 5 sc, 3 sc in next sc, *1 sc in each of the next 7 sc, skip next 2 sc, 1 sc in each of the next 7 sc, 3 sc in next sc, rep from * across to within last 7 sts, 1 sc in each of next 5 sc, sc2tog in last 2 sc, turn.

Rep Row 1 for pattern.

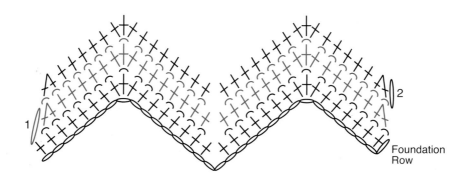

Foundation Row

CLASSIC DOUBLE CROCHET IN BACK LOOP RIPPLE

Skill Level: Easy

Dc2tog: Yo, pick up a loop in next st, yo, draw through 2 loops, yo hook, pick up a loop in next st, yo, draw through 2 loops, yo hook, draw through 3 loops on hook.

Ch a multiple of 17.

Foundation Row: 1 dc in 3rd ch from hook, 1 dc in each of next 5 ch, [1 dc, ch 2, 1 dc] in next ch, 1 dc in each of next 7 ch, skip next 2 ch, *1 dc in each of next 7 ch, [1 dc, ch 2, 1 dc] in next ch, 1 dc in each of next 7 ch, skip 2 ch, rep from * across, turn.

Row 1: Working in back loops only, ch 3 (counts as first dc), skip first st, dc2tog next 2 sts, 1 dc in each of the next 5 sts, [1 dc, ch 2, 1 dc] in next ch-2 space, *1 dc in each of the next 7 dc, skip next 2 dc, 1 dc in each of the next 7 dc, [1 dc, ch 2, 1 dc] in next dc, rep from * across to within last 8 sts, 1 dc in each of the next 5 dc, dc2tog in next 2 sts, 1 dc top of turning ch, turn.

Rep Row 1 for pattern.

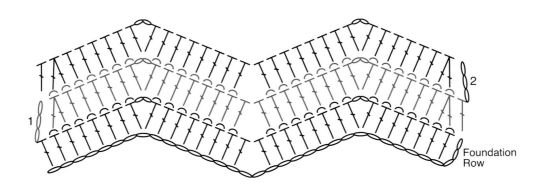

CLASSIC DOUBLE CROCHET RIPPLE

Skill Level: Easy

Dc2tog: Yo, pick up a loop in next st, yo, draw through 2 loops, yo, pick up a loop in next st, yo, draw through 2 loops, yo, draw through 3 loops on hook.

Ch a multiple of 17.

Foundation Row: 1 dc in 4th ch from hook, 1 dc in each of next 5 ch, [1 dc, ch 2, 1 dc] in next ch, 1 dc in each of next 7 ch, *skip next 2 ch, 1 dc in each of next 7 ch, [1 dc, ch 2, 1 dc] in next ch, 1 dc in each of next 7 ch, rep from * across, turn.

Row 1: Ch 3 (counts as first dc), skip first st, dc2tog next 2 sts, 1 dc in each of the next 5 sts, [1 dc, ch 2, 1 dc] in next ch-2 space, *1 dc in each of the next 7 dc, skip next 2 dc, 1 dc in each of the next 7 dc, [1 dc, ch 2, 1 dc] in next dc, rep from * across to within last 8 sts, 1 dc in each of the next 5 dc, dc2tog in next 2 sts, 1 dc top of turning ch, turn.

Rep Row 1 for pattern.

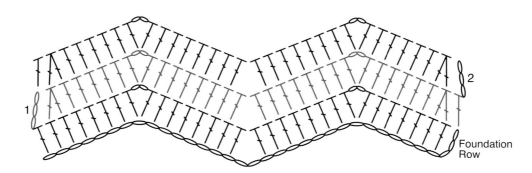

Foundation Row

KEYHOLE RIPPLE

Skill Level: Intermediate

Ch a multiple of 10 plus 3.

Foundation Row: 1 dc in 4th ch from hook, 1 dc in each of next 3 ch, *skip next 2 ch, 1 dc in each of next 4 ch, ch 2, 1 dc in each of next 4 ch, rep from * across to within last 6 ch, skip next 2 ch, 1 dc in each of next 2 ch, 2 dc in next ch, 1 dc in last ch, turn.

Row 1: Ch 3 (counts as first dc), skip first dc, 2 dc in next dc, 1 dc in each of next 2 dc, *skip next 2 dc, 1 dc in each of next 3 dc, [1 dc, ch 2, 1 dc] in next ch-2 space, 1 dc in each of next 3 dc, rep from * across to within last 6 dc, skip 2 dc, 1 dc in each of next 2 dc, 2 dc in next dc, 1 dc in top of turning ch, turn.

Rep Row 1 for pattern.

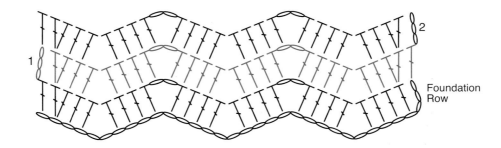

Foundation Row

BOBBLE RIPPLE

Skill Level: Intermediate

Bobble: [Yo, pick up a loop in designated space] 4 times, yo, draw through all 9 loops on hook, ch 1 to lock bobble.

Ch a multiple of 10 plus 3.

Foundation Row: 1 dc in 4th ch from hook, 1 dc in each of next 3 ch, *skip next 2 ch, 1 dc in each of next 4 ch, ch 2, 1 dc in of next 4 ch, rep from * across to within last 6 ch, skip next 2 ch, 1 dc in each of next 2 ch, 2 dc in next ch, 1 dc in last ch, turn.

Row 1: Ch 3 (counts as first dc), skip first dc, 2 dc in next dc, 1 dc in each of next 2 dc, *skip next 2 dc, 1 dc in each of next 3 dc, [bobble, ch 2, bobble] in next ch-2 space, 1 dc in each of next 3 dc, rep from * across to within last 6 dc, skip 2 dc, 1 dc in each of next 2 dc, 2 dc in next dc, 1 dc in top of turning ch, turn.

Rep Row 1 for pattern.

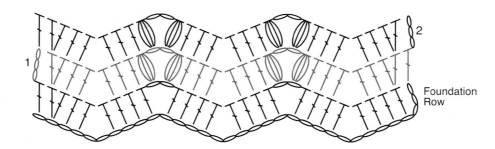

Foundation Row

Blue, brown + Multi 2014

RIPPLE GRANNY

Skill Level: Easy

Note: Work with 3 colors A, B, C; following pattern, alternate colors every 2 rows.

With A, ch a multiple of 18.

Foundation Row: 3 dc in 5th ch from hook, skip next 2 ch, 3 dc in next ch, skip next 2 ch, *[3 dc, ch 3, 3 dc] in next ch (top point), [skip next 2 ch, 3 dc in next ch] twice**, skip next 5 ch, (bottom point), [3 dc in next ch, skip next 2 ch] twice, rep from * across, ending last rep at **, 1 dc in last ch, turn.

Row 1: Ch 4, [3 dc between next two 3-dc groups] twice, *[3 dc, ch 3, 3 dc] in next ch-3 space (top point), [3 dc between the next two 3-dc groups] twice**, skip space between the next two 3-dc groups (bottom point), [3 dc between next two groups] twice, rep from * across, ending last rep at **, skip next 3 dc, 1 dc in top of turning ch, turn, draw B through last loop, drop A.

Rep Row 1, working in the following color sequence: *2 rows B, 2 rows C, 2 rows A, rep from * throughout.

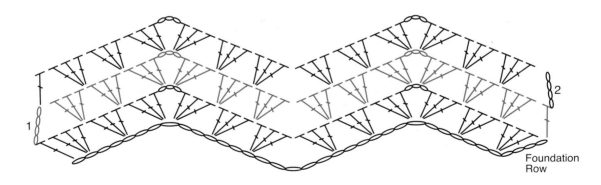

Foundation Row

FEATHER AND FAN RIPPLE

Skill Level: Easy

Dc3tog: [Yo, pick up a loop in next st, yo, draw through 2 loops] 3 times, yo, draw through 4 loops on hook.

Ch a multiple of 14 plus 3.

Foundation Row: 2 dc in 4th ch from hook, *1 dc in each of next 3 ch, [dc3tog in next 3 sts] twice, 1 dc in each of next 3 ch**, 3 dc in each of next 2 sts, rep from * across, ending last rep at **, 3 dc in the last ch, turn.

Row 1: Ch 3 (counts as first dc), 2 dc in first dc, *1 dc in each of next 3 dc, [dc3tog in next 3 sts] twice, 1 dc in each of the next 3 dc**, 3 dc in each of next 2 sts, repeat from * across, ending last rep at **, 3 dc in top of the turning ch, turn.

Rep Row 1 for pattern.

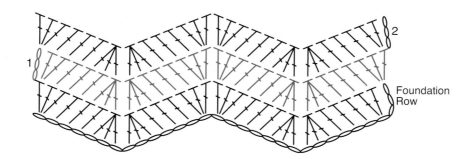

THREE-COLOR RIPPLE

Skill Level: Intermediate

Sc2tog: pick up a loop in each of next 2 sts, yo hook, draw through all 3 loops on hook.

Dc2tog: Yo, pick up a loop in next st, yo, draw through 2 loops, yo hook, pick up a loop in next st, yo, draw through 2 loops, yo, draw through 3 loops on hook.

Notes:

1. Work through the back loop throughout.

2. Work with 3 colors A, B, C.

3. Pay attention to color changes and do not end off colors at end of rows.

With A, ch a multiple of 24 plus 23.

Foundation Row: 1 dc in 4th ch from hook, 1 dc in each of next 8 ch, *[1 dc, ch 3, 1 dc] in next ch, 1 dc in each of next 10 ch**, skip next 3 ch, 1 dc in each next 10 ch, rep from * across, ending last rep at **, turn, draw B through last loop, drop A.

Row 1: Working in back loops only, with B, ch 1, skip first st, sc2tog in next 2 sts, 1 sc in each of next 8 sts, *[1 sc, ch 3, 1 sc] in next ch-3 space**, 1 sc in each next 10 sts, skip 2 sts, 1 sc in each of next 10 sts, rep from * across, ending last rep at **, 1 sc in each next 8 sts, sc2tog in next 2 sts, 1 sc in top of turning ch, turn, draw C through last loop, drop B.

Row 2: With C, rep Row 1, pick up loop with A, drop C.

Row 3: Working in back loops only, with A, ch 3 (counts as first dc), skip first st, dc2tog in next 2 sts, 1 dc in each of next 8 sts, *[1 dc, ch 3, 1 dc] in next ch-3 space**, 1 dc in each next 10 sts, skip next 2 sts, 1 dc in each of next 10 sts, rep from * across, ending last rep at **, 1 dc in each of next 8 sts, dc2tog in next 2 sts, 1 dc in top of turning ch, turn.

Repeat Rows 1–3 for pattern.

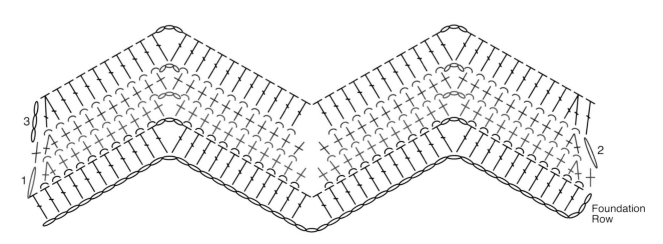

Foundation Row

LUXURY SCARF

Take a well loved stitch, add a gorgeous yarn, with standout colors, and wrap yourself in this luxuriously long, extra wide scarf. The crochet pattern is a one-row repeat. The yarn is dyed to change colors, which creates the beautiful striping pattern of the scarf.

YOU WILL NEED

Yarn

- Super fine yarn
- Shown: Kureyon Sock Yarn by Noro , 70% wool, 30% nylon, 3.5 oz (100 g)/459 yds (420 m), color S188: 3 skeins

Hook

- G-6 (4 mm) or size to obtain correct gauge

Stitches

- Chain stitch (ch)
- Slip stitch (Sl st)
- Double crochet (dc)
- Dc3tog

Gauge

- 14 sts (one patt repeat) = 3" (7.5 cm) in chevron pattern

Notions

- Tapestry needle

Size

- 17½" × 60" (44.5 × 152.5 cm)

Scarf

Dc3tog: (yo, insert hook in next st, yo, draw yarn through st, yo, draw yarn through 2 loops on hook) 3 times, yo, draw yarn through 4 loops on hook.

Ch 87.

Foundation Row: 2 dc in 3rd ch from hook, *1 dc in each of the next 3 ch, (dc3tog in next 3 ch) 2 times, 1 dc in each of the next 3 ch 3 dc in each of next 2 ch; rep from * 4 times more, 1 dc in each of the next 3 ch, (dc3tog in next 3 ch) 2 times, 1 dc in each of next 3 ch, 3 dc in last ch, turn.

Row 1: Ch 3, (counts as first dc) 2 dc in the first dc, *1 dc in each of the next 3 dc, (dc3tog in next 3 dc) 2 times, 1 dc in each of the next 3 dc, 3 dc in each of next 2 dc; rep from * 4 times more, 1 dc in each of the next 3 dc, (dc3tog in next 3 sts) 2 times, 1 dc in each of the next 3 ch, 3 dc in top of tch, turn.

Rep Row 1 until scarf measures 60" (152.5 cm) from beg. End off.

Finishing

Weave in loose ends.

Lay scarf on a towel, folded in half. Spritz with water, pat into shape, allow to dry.

Lace Stitches

The stitches included in this category are very open and lacy. They are particularly lovely when used in sweaters, tops, shawls, scarves, and baby blankets. The lace stitches, because of their open weave, are particularly great for use in warmer climates.

DUTCHESS LACE

Skill Level: Easy

Note: In this pattern 1 row will be worked in space created by a ch 3, the next row will be worked in each chain rather than the space.

Ch a multiple of 3 plus 1.

Foundation Row: [2 dc, ch 3, 1 Sl st] in 4th ch from hook, *skip next 2 ch, [2 dc, ch 3, 1 Sl st] in next ch, rep from * across, turn.

Row 1: Ch 3, *[2 dc, ch 3, 1 Sl st] in next ch-3 space, rep from * across, 1 dc in top of turning ch, turn.

Row 2: Ch 3, *working in each ch of the ch-3 of previous row, 1 dc in first ch, 1 dc in 2nd ch, ch 3, 1 Sl st in 3rd ch, rep from * across, end 1 dc in top of the turn ch, turn.

Rep Rows 1 and 2 for pattern.

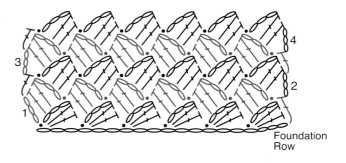

Foundation Row

LACE DIAMONDS

Skill Level: Experienced

Chain a multiple of 8 plus 4.

Row 1: 1 sc in 2nd ch from hook, 1 sc in each of the next 3 ch, *ch 5, skip next 3 ch, 1 sc in each of the next 5 ch, rep from * across, ending with 1 sc in each of the last 4 ch, turn.

Row 2: Ch 1 (counts as first sc now and throughout), skip first sc, 1 sc in each of the next 2 sc, *ch 3, 1 sc in next ch-5 loop, ch 3, skip 1 sc, 1 sc in each of the next 3 sc, rep from * across, turn.

Row 3: Ch 1, skip first sc, 1 sc in next sc, *ch 3, 1 sc in the next loop, 1 sc in next sc, 1 sc in the next loop, ch 3, skip 1 sc, 1 sc in the next sc, repeat from * across, 1 sc in top of turning ch, turn.

Row 4: Ch 3 (counts as first dc), skip first sc, 1 dc in next sc, ch 2, *1 sc in next loop, 1 sc in each of next 3 sc, 1 sc in next loop**, ch 5, rep from * across, ending last rep at ** ch 2, 1 dc in next sc, 1 dc in top of turning ch, turn.

Row 5: Ch 1, skip first dc, 1 sc next dc, *ch 3, skip next sc, 1 sc in each of next 3 sc, ch 3**, 1 sc in next loop, rep from * across, ending last rep at **, 1 sc in next dc, 1 sc in top of turning ch, turn.

Row 6: Ch 1, skip first sc, 1 sc in next sc, *1 sc in next loop, ch 3, skip next sc, 1 sc in next sc, ch 3, 1 sc in next loop, 1 sc in next sc, repeat from * across, 1 sc in top of turning ch, turn.

Row 7: Ch 1, skip first sc, 1 sc in each of the next 2 sc, 1 sc in next loop, *ch 5, 1 sc in next loop**, 1 sc in each of next 3 sc, 1 sc in next loop, rep from * across, ending last rep at **, 1 sc in each of next 2 sc, 1 sc in top of turning ch, turn.

Rep Rows 2–7 for pattern.

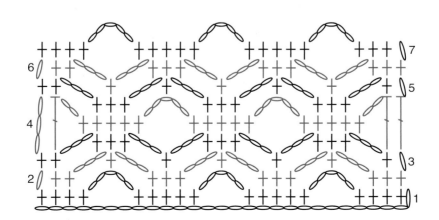

SIDE BARS

Skill Level: Easy

Ch a multiple of 2 plus 1.

Foundation Row: 1 sc in 2nd ch from hook, 1 sc in each ch across row, turn.

Row 1: Ch 1 (counts as first sc), skip first st, 1 sc in each sc across, turn.

Row 2: Ch 3 (counts as first dc), skip first st, *1 dc next st, 1 dc around the post of the dc just made, skip 1 st, rep from *, 1 dc in top of turning ch, turn.

Rep Rows 1 and 2 for pattern.

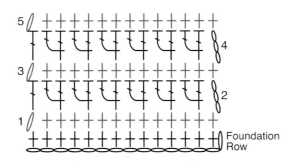

BRAIDED LACE

Skill Level: Easy

Ch an even number of sts.

Foundation Row: 1 sc in 2nd ch from hook, 1 sc in each ch across row, turn.

Row 1: Ch 1, sc in first st, *ch 5, skip next st, 1 sc in next st, rep from * across, turn.

Row 2: Ch 3, 1 sc in center ch of next ch-5 loop, *ch 1, sc in center ch of next ch-5 loop, rep from * across, 1 dc in last sc, turn.

Row 3: Ch 1, 1 sc in first sc, 1 sc in next sc, *1 sc in next ch-1 space, 1 sc in next sc, rep from * across, 1 sc in top of turning ch, turn.

Rep Rows 1–3 for pattern.

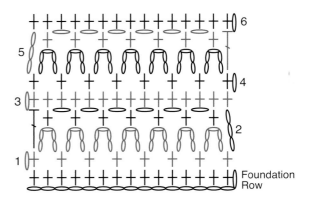

THE COMPLETE PHOTO GUIDE TO CROCHET

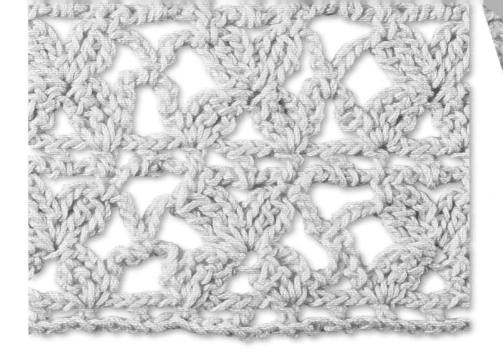

POSIES IN A ROW

Skill Level: Intermediate

Tr2tog: (Yo twice, pick up a loop in next st, [yo draw yarn through 2 loops] twice, yo twice, pick up a loop in same st, [yo draw yarn through 2 loops] twice, yo draw through all 3 loops on hook.

Triple treble crochet (trtr): Yo 4 times, [yo draw yarn through 2 loops] 5 times.

Ch a multiple of 12 plus 11.

Foundation Row: 1 dc in 8th ch from hook, *ch 2, skip next 2 ch, dc in next ch, rep from *across, turn.

Row 1 (RS): Ch 1, 1 sc in first dc, *ch 9, skip 1 dc, [1 sc, ch 4, tr2tog] in next dc, skip 1 dc, [tr2tog, ch 4, 1 sc], in next dc, rep from * across to within last 2 ch-2 spaces, ch 9, skip 1 dc, 1 sc in 3rd ch of turning ch, turn.

Row 2: Ch 10 (counts as trtr, ch 4), 1 sc in next ch-9 loop, *ch 4, [tr2tog, ch 4, Sl st, ch 4, tr2tog] in next tr2tog, ch 4, 1 sc in next ch-9 loop, rep from * across to last ch-9 loop, ch 4, 1 trtr in last sc, turn.

Row 3: Ch 1, 1 sc in first trtr, *ch 5, 1 sc in top of next tr2tog, rep from * across, ending with last 1 sc in 6th ch of turning ch, turn.

Row 4: Ch 5 (counts as 1 dc, ch 2), 1 dc in next ch-5 space, ch 2, 1 dc in next sc, *ch 2, 1 dc in next ch-5 space, ch 2, 1 dc in next sc, rep from * across, turn.

Rep Rows 1–4 for pattern.

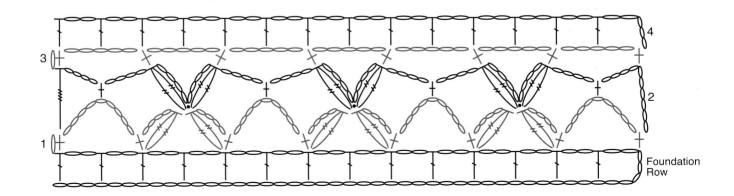

TRIANGLES

Skill Level: Intermediate

Ch a multiple of 3 plus 1.

Foundation Row: 1 sc in 2nd ch from hook, 1 sc in each ch across row, turn.

Row 1: Ch 4 (counts as hdc, ch 2), skip first st, [yo, pick up a loop in next st] 3 times, yo draw through 7 loops on hook (triangle made), *ch 2, yo, pick up a loop in same st as last st of previous triangle, [yo, pick up a loop in next st] twice, yo over draw through 7 loops on hook, rep from * across, end ch 1, 1 hdc in last sc, turn.

Row 2: Ch 1, 1 sc in first st, 1 sc in next ch-1 space, 2 sc in each ch-2 space across, 1 sc in 2nd ch of turning ch, turn.

Rep Rows 1 and 2 for pattern.

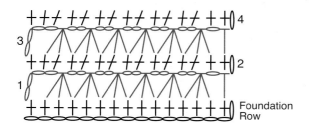

DEW DROPS

Skill Level: Easy

Dc3tog: [Yo, insert hook in next st, yo, draw yarn through st, yo, draw yarn through 2 loops on hook] 3 times, yo, draw yarn through all 4 loops on hook.

Ch a multiple of 3 plus 1.

Foundation Row: 3 dc in 5th ch from hook, *skip next 2 ch, 3 dc in next ch, rep from * across to within last 2 ch, skip next ch, 1 dc in last ch, turn.

Row 1: Ch 4 (counts as dc, ch 1), *dc3tog in next 3 dc, ch 2, rep from * across to within last 4 sts, dc3tog in next 3 dc, 1 dc in top of turning ch, turn.

Row 2: Ch 3 (counts as first dc), *3 dc in top of next cluster, rep from * across, 1 dc in 3rd ch of turning ch, turn.

Rep Rows 1 and 2 for pattern.

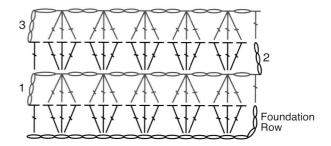

SPIDER WEBS

Skill Level: Intermediate

Ch a multiple of 9 plus 2.

Foundation Row: 1 dc in 4th ch from hook, 1 dc in each ch across row, turn.

Row 1: Ch 4 (counts as tr), skip first dc, tr in next dc, *ch 4, skip 1 dc, 1 dc in each of next 3 dc, ch 4, skip 1 dc**, 1 tr in each of next 4 dc, rep from * across, ending last rep at **, 1 tr in next dc, 1 tr in top of turning ch, turn.

Row 2: Ch 1, 1 sc in each of first 2 tr, *ch 4, 1 dc in each of next 3 dc, ch 4**, 1 sc in each of next 4 tr, rep from * across, ending last rep at **, 1 sc in next tr, 1 sc in top of turning ch, turn.

Row 3: Ch 1, 1 sc in each of first 2 sc, *ch 4, 1 dc in each of next 3 dc, ch 4**, 1 sc in each of next 4 sc, rep from * across, ending last rep at **, 1 sc in each last 2 sc, turn.

Row 4: Rep Row 3.

Row 5: Ch 4, 1 tr in next sc, *ch 1, 1 dc in each of next 3 dc, ch 1**, 1 tr in each of next 4 sc, rep from * across, ending last rep at **, 1 tr in in last 2 sc, turn.

Row 6: Ch 3, 1 dc in next tr, *1 dc in next ch-1 space, 1 dc in each of next 3 dc, 1 dc in next ch-1 space**, 1 dc in each of next 4 tr, rep from * ending last rep at **, 1 dc in next tr, 1 dc top of turning ch, turn.

Rep Rows 1–6 for pattern.

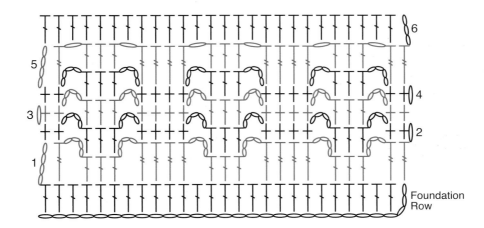

MARIELLE

Skill Level: Easy

Ch a multiple of 4.

Foundation Row: [2 tr, ch 2, dc] in 6th ch from hook, *skip next 3 ch, [2 tr, ch 2, 1 dc] in next ch, rep from * across to within last 2 ch, skip next ch, 1 tr in last ch, turn.

Row 1: Ch 3 (counts as first dc), *[2 tr, ch 2, 1 dc] in the next ch-2 space, rep from * across, 1 tr in top of turning ch, turn.

Rep Row 1 for pattern.

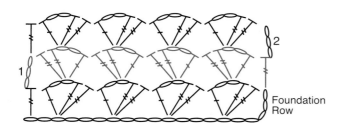

BERRY STITCH

Skill Level: Easy

Dc3tog: [Yo, insert hook in next st, yo, draw yarn through st, yo, draw yarn through 2 loops on hook] 3 times, yo, draw yarn through all 4 loops on hook.

Ch a multiple of 3 plus 1.

Foundation Row: 3 dc in 5th ch from hook, *skip 2 ch, 3 dc in next ch, rep from * across to within last 2 ch, skip next ch, 1 dc in last ch, turn.

Row 1: Ch 4 (counts as dc, ch 1), *dc3tog worked across next 3 dc (cluster made), ch 1, rep from * across, 1 dc in top of turning ch, turn.

Row 2: Ch 3 (counts as first dc), *3 dc in next dc3tog, rep from * across, 1 dc in top of turning ch, turn.

Rep Rows 1 and 2 for pattern.

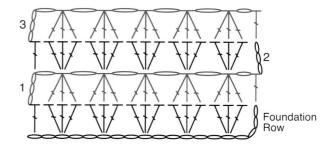

DOUBLE ARCHES

Skill Level: Easy

Ch a multiple of 8 plus 2.

Foundation Row: 1 sc in 2nd ch from hook, 1 sc in each ch across row, turn.

Row 1: Ch 1, 1 sc in first sc, ch 3, skip next 2 sc, *1 dc in each of next 3 sc, ch 3, skip 2 sc, 1 sc in next sc**, ch 3, skip 2 sc, rep from * across, ending last rep at **, turn.

Row 2: Ch 5 (counts as dc, ch 2), *1 sc in each of next 3 dc**, ch 5, skip next 2 ch-3 spaces, rep from * across, ending last rep at **, ch 2, 1 dc in last sc, turn.

Row 3: Ch 3 (counts as first dc), 1 dc in next ch-2 space, *ch 3, skip next sc, 1 sc in next sc, ch 3**, 3 dc in next ch-5 space, rep from * across, ending last rep at **, 1 dc in next ch-2 space, 1 dc in 3rd of turning ch-5, turn.

Row 4: Ch 1, 1 sc in first dc, 1 sc in next dc, *ch 5, 1 sc in each of next 3 dc, rep from * across, ending with 1 sc in last dc, 1 sc in 3rd ch of turning ch, turn.

Row 5: Ch 1, 1 sc in first sc, *ch 3, 3 dc in next ch-5 space, ch 3, skip next sc, 1 sc in next sc, rep from * across, turn.

Rep Rows 2–5 for pattern.

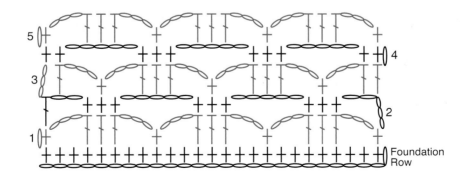

LACY LATTICE

Skill Level: Intermediate

Ch a multiple of 18 plus 17.

Foundation Row: 1 sc in second ch from hook, 1 sc in each ch across row, turn.

Row 1: Ch 4 (counts as dc, ch 2), skip first 3 sc, 1 dc in next sc, *ch 2, skip 2 sc, 1 dc in next sc, rep from * across, turn.

Row 2: Ch 1, 1 sc in first dc, 1 sc in next space, ch 3, 1 sc in next space, *[2 dc, 4 tr, 2 dc] in next sp (shell made), 1 sc in next space**, [ch 3, 1 sc in next space] 4 times, rep from * across, ending last rep at **, ch 3, 1 sc in next ch-2 space, 1 sc in second ch of turn ch, turn.

Row 3: Ch 1, 1 sc in first sc, ch 3, 1 sc in next ch-3 space, *ch 3, skip next 2 dc, 1 sc in next tr, ch 3, skip next 2 tr, 1 sc in next tr**, [ch 3, 1 sc in next space] 4 times, rep from * across, ending last rep at **, ch 3, 1 sc in next ch-3 space, ch 3, 1 sc in last sc, turn.

Row 4: Rep Row 2.

Rep Rows 3 and 4 for pattern.

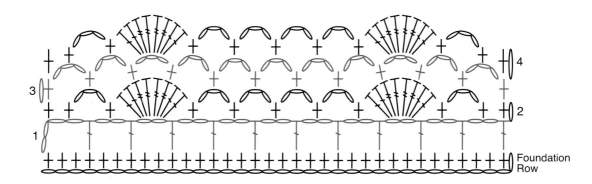

PINEAPPLES AND SHELLS

Skill Level: Experienced

Ch a multiple of 14 plus 6.

Foundation: [2 dc, ch 2, 2 dc] in fourth ch from hook, *ch 4, skip 6 ch, [1 dc, ch 4, 1 dc] in next ch, ch 4, skip 6 ch, [2 dc, ch 2, 2 dc] in next ch, rep from * across to within last 2 ch, skip next sc, 1 dc in last ch, turn.

Row 1: Ch 3 (counts as first dc), [2 dc, ch 2, 2 dc] in next ch-2 space, *ch 2, skip next ch-4 space, [(tr3tog, ch 3) 3 times, tr3tog] in next ch-4 space, ch 2, skip next ch-4 space, [2 dc, ch 2, 2 dc] in next ch-2 space, rep from * across, 1 dc in top of turning ch, turn.

Row 2: Ch 3 (counts as first dc), [2 dc, ch 2, 2 dc] in next ch-2 space, *ch 3, skip next ch-2 space, [2 sc in next ch-3 space, ch 3] 3 times, skip next ch-2 space, [2 dc, ch 2, 2 dc] in next ch 2 space, rep from * across, 1 dc in top of turning ch, turn.

Row 3: Ch 3 (counts as first dc), [2 dc, ch 2, 2 dc] in next ch-2 space, *ch 4, skip next ch-3 space, 2 sc in next ch-3 space, ch 3, 2 sc in next ch-3 space, ch 4, skip next ch-3 space, [2 dc, ch 2, 2 dc] in next ch-2 space, rep from * across, 1 dc in top of turning ch, turn.

Row 4: Ch 3, skip first 3 dc, [2 dc, ch 2, 2 dc] in next ch-2 space, *ch 4, skip next ch-4 space, [1 dc, ch 4, 1 dc] in next ch-3 space, ch 4, skip next ch-4 space, [2 dc, ch 2, 2 dc] in next ch-2 space, rep from * across, 1 dc in top of turning ch, turn.

Rep Rows 1–4 for pattern.

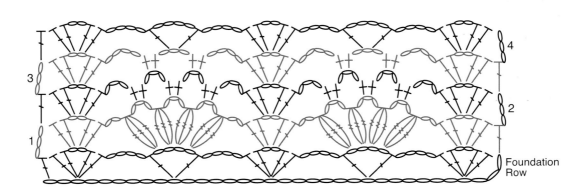

BUTTERFLY LACE

Skill Level: Intermediate

Ch a multiple of 15 plus 4.

Foundation Row: 4 dc in 6th ch from hook, *ch 5, skip next 4 ch, 1 sc in next ch, ch 5, skip next 4 ch, 4 dc in next ch**, skip next 4 ch, 4 dc in next ch, rep from * across, ending last rep at **, skip next 2 ch, 1 dc in last ch, turn.

Row 1: Ch 3 (counts as dc), skip first 4 dc, 4 dc in next dc, *ch 5, 1 sc in next sc, ch 5, 4 dc in next dc**, skip 6 dc, 4 dc in next dc, rep from * across, ending last rep at **, skip 3 dc, 1 dc in top of turning ch, turn.

Row 2: Rep Row 1.

Row 3: Ch 1, 1 sc in first dc, *ch 5, 4 dc in center ch of next ch-5 loop, 4 dc in center ch of next ch-5 loop, ch 5, skip next 3 dc, 1 sc in next dc, rep from * across, ending with last sc in top of tuning ch, turn.

Row 4: Ch 1, 1 sc in first sc, ch 5, *4 dc in next dc, skip 6 dc, 4 dc in next dc, ch 5, 1 sc next sc**, ch 5, rep from * across, ending last rep at **, turn.

Row 5: Rep Row 4.

Row 6: Ch 3 (counts as first dc), skip first sc, *4 dc in center ch of next ch-5 loop, ch 5, skip 3 dc, 1 sc in next dc, ch 5, 4 dc in center ch of next ch-5 lp, rep from * across, 1 dc in last sc, turn.

Rep Rows 1–6 for pattern.

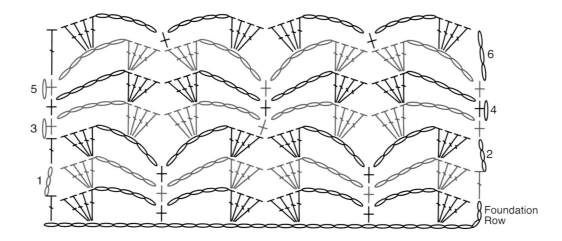

PINE TREES

Skill Level: Intermediate

Ch a multiple of 10 plus 4.

Foundation Row: 1 dc in 4th ch from hook, *ch 4, skip next 4 ch, 1 sc next ch, ch 4, skip next 4 ch, 3 dc in next ch, rep from * across, ending with 2 dc in last ch, turn.

Row 1: Ch 2 (counts as first dc), skip first dc, 2 dc in next dc, *ch 3, 1 sc in next sc, ch 3, 2 dc in next dc**, 1 dc in next dc, 2 dc in next dc, rep from * across, ending last rep at **, 1 dc top of turning ch, turn.

Row 2: Ch 2 (counts as first dc), skip first dc, 1 dc in next dc, 2 dc in next dc, *ch 2, 1 dc in next sc, ch 2, 2 dc in next dc**, 1 dc in each of next 3 dc, 2 dc in next dc, rep from * across, ending last rep at **, 1 dc in next dc, 1 dc in top of turning ch, turn.

Row 3: Ch 2 (counts as first dc), skip first dc, 1 dc in each of next 2 dc, 2 dc in next dc, *ch 1, 2 dc in next dc**, 1 dc in each of next 5 dc, 2 dc in next dc, rep from * ending last rep at **, 1 dc in each of the next 2 dc, 1 dc in top of turning ch, turn.

Row 4: Ch 1, 1 sc in first dc, *ch 4, skip next 4 dc, 3 dc in next ch-1 space, ch 4, skip next 4 dc, 1 sc in next dc, rep from * across, ending with last sc in top of turning ch, turn.

Row 5: Ch 1, 1 sc in first sc, *ch 3, 2 dc in next dc, 1 dc in next dc, 2 dc in next dc, ch 3, 1 sc in next sc, rep from * across, turn.

Row 6: Ch 5 (counts as dc, ch 2), *2 dc in next dc, 1 dc in each of next 3 dc, 2 dc in next dc, ch 2, 1 dc in next sc, ch 2, rep from * across, ending with 1 dc in last sc, turn.

Row 7: Ch 3 (counts as first dc), *2 dc in next dc, 1 dc in each of next 5 dc, 2 dc in next dc, ch 1, rep from * across, omitting last ch-1 space, 1 dc in 3rd ch of turning ch-5, turn.

Row 8: Ch 2 (counts as first dc), 1 dc in first dc, *ch 4, skip next 4 dc, 1 sc in next dc, ch 4, skip next 4 dc, 3 dc in next ch-1 space, rep from * across, ending last rep at **, 2 dc in top of turning ch, turn.

Rep Rows 1–8 for pattern.

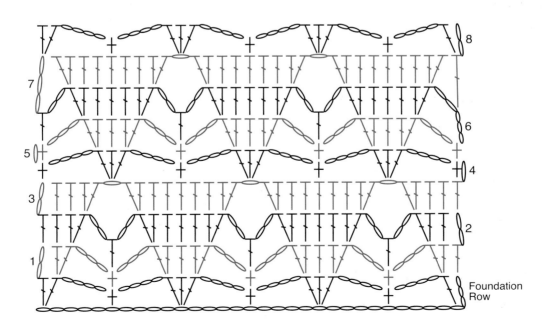

GARDEN TRELLIS SCARF

The unusual stitch in this scarf looks like a trellis of flowers. The effect is achieved by combining clusters of triple crochet with openwork.

YOU WILL NEED

Yarn

- Medium-weight cotton/rayon blend bouclé yarn
- Shown: Handpainted Yarn by Spectrum Yarns, cotton/rayon blend, 8 oz (225 g)/585 yd (538 m): Komodo Dragon, 1 skein

Hook

- Size 8/H (5 mm)

Stitches used

- Single crochet
- Double crochet
- Triple crochet
- Triple crochet 2 together
- Double triple crochet

Gauge

- 2 clusters = 4" (10 cm) on 8/H hook

Notions

- Tapestry needle

Finished size

- 6" (15 cm) wide and 64" (162 cm) long

SCARF

Foundation Row: Ch 35. Starting in eighth ch from hook, work 1 dc, * ch 2, sk 2 ch, 1 dc into next ch, rep from * (10 ch-2 sps), ch 1, turn.

Row 1: Work 1 sc in first dc, * ch 9, sk 1 dc, [1 sc, ch 4, 1 tr2tog] in next dc, sk 1 dc, [1 tr2tog, ch 4, 1 sc] in next dc, rep from * once, ch 9, sk 1 dc, 1 sc in third ch of tch (3 ch-9 loops, 2 clusters), ch 10 (counts as dtr, ch 4), turn.

Row 2: Work 1 sc in first ch-9 sp, * ch 4, [1 tr2tog, ch 4, 1 Sl st, ch 4, 1 tr2tog] in top of next tr2tog, ch 4, 1 sc in next ch-9 sp, rep from * once, ch 4, 1 dtr in last sc, (6 ch-4 lps, 2 clusters), ch 1, turn.

Row 3: Work 1 sc in first dtr, * ch 5, 1 sc in top of next tr2tog, rep from * across, ch 5, 1 sc in sixth ch of tch, (5 ch-5 sp), ch 5, (counts as 1 dc, ch 2), turn.

Row 4: Work 1 dc in next ch-5 sp, ch 2, 1 dc in next sc, *ch 2, 1 dc in next ch-5 sp, ch 2, 1 dc in next sc, rep from * across (10 ch-2 sps), ch 1, turn.

Rep Rows 1–4 for 62" (157 cm) from beg, end row 4. Work edging as foll:

EDGING

Row 1: Sk first dc, work 5 dc in next dc, 1 sc in next dc, * 5 dc in next dc, 1 sc in next dc, rep from * across (5 shells), fasten off.

Join yarn in right-hand corner at other end of scarf, ch 1, rep row 1.

FINISHING

Weave in ends using tapestry needle.

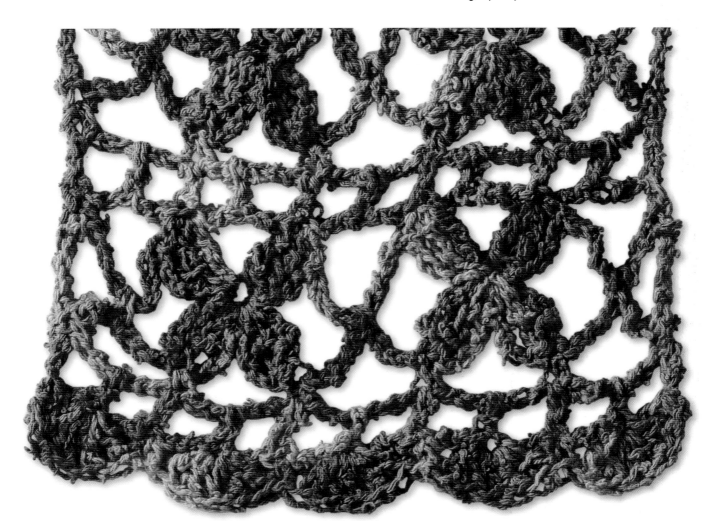

Mesh Stitches

Mesh, also called filet crochet, is usually composed of rows of open and filled squares. Traditionally, this method of crochet has been used mainly for home furnishing items, such as doilies, tablecloths, edgings, etc. More recently, crocheters have been using these open stitches for shawls, vests, and lightweight cardigans. I particularly love using the open-work stitches in my freeform work, combining them with more textured stitches for a very interesting effect. A garment made entirely in mesh stitches is also a great background for appliqués.

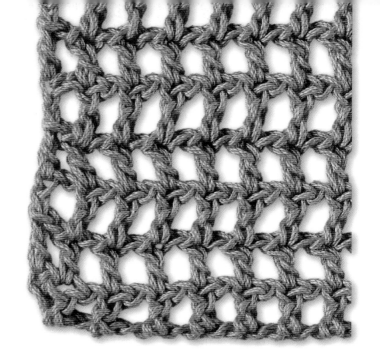

FILET MESH I

Skill Level: Easy

Ch an even number of sts.

Row 1: 1 dc in 6th ch from hook, *ch 1, skip next ch, 1 dc in next ch, rep from * across, turn.

Row 2: Ch 4 (counts as a dc, ch 1), skip first dc, *1 dc in next dc, ch 1, rep from * across row, ending 1 dc in the 3rd ch of turning ch, turn.

Rep Row 2 for pattern.

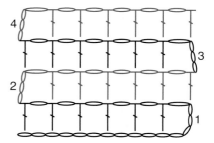

FILET MESH II

Skill Level: Easy

Ch a multiple of 3 plus 2.

Row 1: 1 dc in 8th ch from hook, *ch 2, skip next 2 ch, 1 dc in next ch, rep from * across, turn.

Row 2: Ch 5 (counts as a dc, ch 2), skip first dc, *1 dc in next dc, ch 2, rep from * across, 1 dc in the 3rd ch of turning ch, turn.

Rep Row 2 for pattern.

FILET BOXES

Skill Level: Easy

Ch a multiple of 6 plus 3.

Row 1: 1 dc in 4th ch from hook, 1 dc in next ch, *ch 3, skip next 3 ch**, 1 dc in each of the next 3 ch, rep from * across, ending last rep at **, 1 dc in last ch, turn.

Row 2: Ch 3 (counts as dc), 2 dc in first ch-3 space, *ch 3, 3 dc in next ch-3 space, rep from * across to last ch-3 space, ch 3, skip next 2 dc, 1 dc in top of turning ch, turn.

Rep Row 2 for pattern.

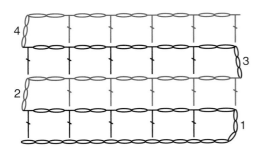

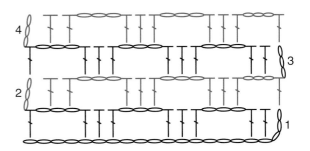

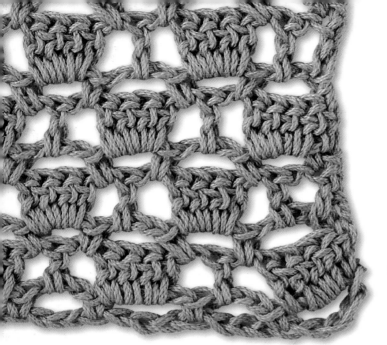

BOXES AND BARS

Skill Level: Easy

Ch a multiple of 8 plus 6.

Row 1: Sc in 2nd ch from hook, *ch 3, skip next 3 ch, 1 sc in next ch, rep from * across, turn.

Row 2: Ch 3 (counts as first dc), 4 dc in next ch-3 space, * ch 1, 1 dc in next ch-3 space, ch 1, 4 dc in next ch-3 space, rep from * across, 1 dc in last sc, turn.

Row 3: Ch 1, 1 sc in first st, ch 3, *1 sc in next ch-1 space, ch 3, rep from * across, ending with 1 sc in top of turn ch, turn.

Row 4: Ch 4 (counts as dc, ch 1), 1 dc in next ch-3 space, ch 1, *4 dc in next ch-3 space, ch 1, 1 dc in next ch-3 space, ch 1, rep from * across, 1 dc in last sc, turn.

Row 5: Ch 1, 1 sc in first dc, skip next ch-1 space, *ch 3, sc in next ch-1 space, rep from * across, ending with last sc in 3rd ch of turning ch, turn.

Rep Rows 2–5 for pattern.

PICOT MESH

Skill Level: Intermediate

Dtr: Yo 3 times, [yo, draw through 2 loops on hook] 4 times.

Note: The space in the center of the double picot is where you will be making the scs.

Ch a multiple of 5 plus 2.

Foundation Row: 1 sc in 2nd ch from hook, *[ch 4, 1 sc in 3rd ch from hook (picot made)] twice (double picot made), ch 1, skip next 4 ch, 1 sc in next ch, rep from * across, turn.

Row 1: Ch 9, (counts as 1 dtr, ch 4), 1 sc in 3rd ch from hook (picot), ch 1, 1 sc in space in the center of the next double picot, *[ch 4, 1 sc in 3rd ch from hook] twice, ch 1, 1 sc in the space in the center of the next double picot, rep from * across, ch 4, 1 sc in 3rd ch from hook, 1 dtr in last sc, turn.

Row 2: Ch 1, 1 sc in first dtr, *[ch 4, 1 sc in 3rd ch from hook] twice, ch 1, 1 sc in space in the center of the next double picot, rep from * across, ending with last sc in the 5th ch of the beg ch 9, turn.

Rep Rows 1 and 2 for pattern.

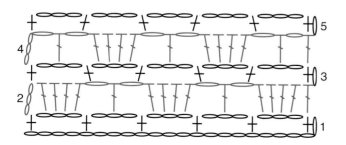
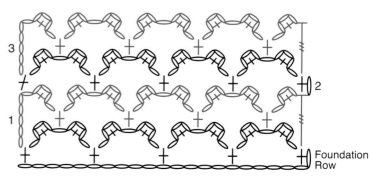

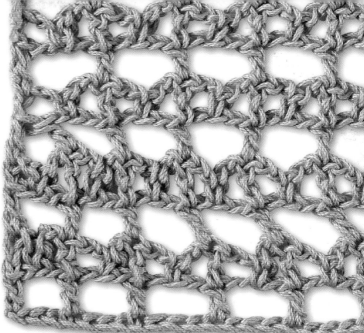

INTERTWINED LACETS

Skill Level: Easy

Ch a multiple of 8 plus 1

Foundation Row: 1 sc in 7th ch from hook, ch 2, skip the next ch, 1 dc in next ch, *ch 3, skip next 3 ch, 1 dc in next ch, ch 2, skip next ch, 1 sc in next ch, ch 2, skip next ch, 1 dc in next ch, rep from * across, turn.

Row 1: Ch 6 (counts as dc, ch 3), skip first dc, 1 dc in next dc, *ch 2, 1 sc in next ch-3 space, ch 2, 1 dc in next dc, ch 3, 1 dc in next dc, rep from * across, ending with last dc in 3rd ch of turning ch, turn.

Row 2: Ch 5 (counts as dc, ch 2), 1 sc in next ch-3 space, ch 2, *1 dc in next dc, ch 3, 1 dc in next dc, ch 2, 1 sc in next ch-3 space, ch 2, rep from * across, 1 dc in 3rd ch of turning ch, turn.

Rep Rows 1 and 2 for pattern.

LACE TRESTLES

Skill Level: Easy

Ch a multiple of 4 plus 2.

Row 1: 1 dc in 10th ch from hook, *ch 3, skip next 3 ch, 1 dc in next ch, rep from * across, turn.

Row 2: Ch 5 (counts as dc, ch 2), *1 sc in center ch of next ch-3 space, ch 2**, 1 dc in next dc, ch 2, rep from * across, ending last rep at **, 1 dc in 4th ch of turning ch, turn.

Row 3: Ch 6, (counts as dc, ch 3), *1 dc in the next dc, ch 3, rep from * across, 1 dc in the 3rd ch of turn ch, turn.

Rep Rows 2 and 3 for pattern.

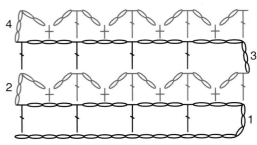

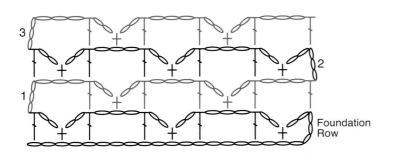

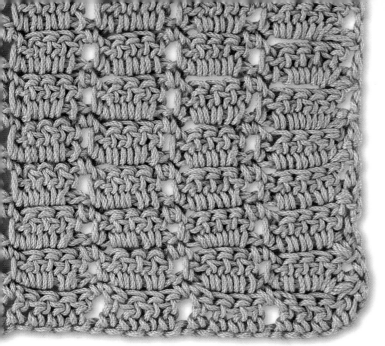

BUILDING BLOCKS

Skill Level: Easy

Ch a multiple of 5 plus 3.

Foundation Row: 1 dc in 4th ch from hook, 1 dc in each of the next 3 ch, *ch 1, skip 1 ch, 1 dc in each of next 4 ch, rep from * across to last ch, 1 dc in last ch, turn.

Row 1: Ch 1, 1 sc in first st, *ch 4, skip 4 dc, sc in the next ch-1 space, rep from * across, ending with last sc in top of turning ch, turn.

Row 2: Ch 3 (counts as first dc), 4 dc in next ch-4 loop, *ch 1, 4 dc in next ch-4 loop, rep from * across to last ch-4 loop, 1 dc in last sc, turn.

Rep Rows 1 and 2 for pattern.

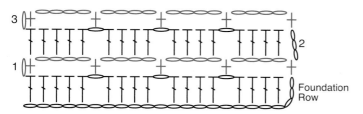

MAYA MESH

Skill Level: Easy

Ch a multiple of 8 plus 6.

Foundation Row: 1 sc in 2nd ch from hook, 1 sc in each ch across row, turn.

Row 1: Ch 1, sc in first sc, *ch 5, skip next 3 sc, 1 sc in next sc, rep from * across, turn.

Row 2: Ch 3 (counts as first dc), 3 dc in next ch-5 loop, *ch 3, 1 sc in next ch-5 loop, ch 3, 3 dc in next ch-5 loop, rep from * across to last ch-5 loop, 1 dc in last sc, turn.

Row 3: Ch 1, 1 sc in first st, *ch 5, 1 sc in next ch-3 loop, rep from * across, ending with last sc in top of turning ch, turn.

Row 4: Ch 6 (counts as dc, ch 3), 1 sc in next ch-5 loop, *ch 3, 3 dc in next ch-5 loop, ch 3, 1 sc in next ch-5 loop, rep from * across to last ch-5 loop, ch 3, 1 dc in last sc, turn.

Row 5: Ch 1, 1 sc in first st, ch 5, skip first ch-3 loop, 1 sc in next ch-3 loop, *ch 5, 1 sc next ch-3 loop, rep from * across, ending with last sc in 3rd ch of turning ch, turn.

Rep Rows 2–5 for pattern.

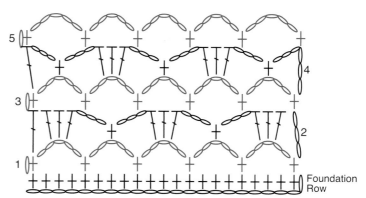

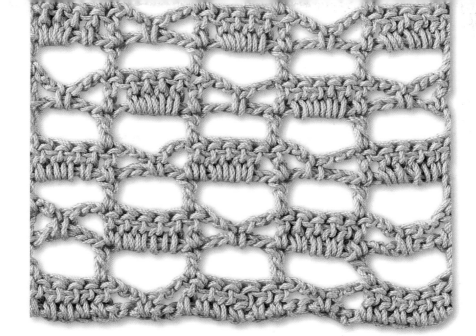

MAYA MESH II

Skill Level: Easy

Ch a multiple of 11 plus 8.

Foundation Row: 1 dc in 4th ch from hook, 1 dc in each of the next 4 ch, *ch 3, skip next 2 ch, 1 sc in next ch, ch 3, skip next 2 ch, 1 dc in each of next 6 ch, rep from * across, turn.

Row 1: Ch 8 (counts as first dc and ch 5), skip first 5 dc, 1 dc in next dc, *ch 5, 1 dc in next dc, ch 5, skip next 4 dc, 1 dc in next dc, rep from * across, ending with last dc in top of turning ch, turn.

Row 2: Ch 6, (counts as a dc, ch 3), 1 sc in next ch-5 space, ch 3, *1 dc in next dc, 4 dc in next ch-5 space, 1 dc in next dc, ch 3, 1 sc in next ch-5 space, ch 3, rep from * across, 1 dc in 3rd ch of turning ch, turn.

Row 3: Ch 8 (counts as dc, ch 5), skip next 2 ch-3 spaces, *1 dc in next dc, ch 5, skip next 4 dc, 1 dc in next dc, ch 5, rep from * across, 1 dc in 3rd ch of turning ch, turn.

Row 4: Ch 3 (counts as dc), *4 dc in next ch-5 space**, 1 dc in next dc, ch 3, 1 sc in next ch-5 space, ch 3, 1 dc in next dc, rep from * across, ending last rep at **, 1 dc in 3rd ch of turning ch, turn.

Rep Rows 1–4 for pattern.

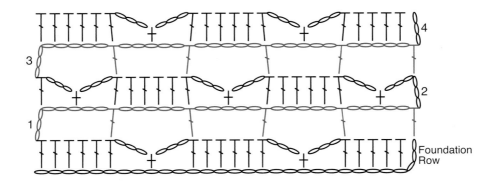

MESH JACKET

Crochet an openwork mesh jacket to ward off the chill of an over-air-conditioned office or an early spring evening. Made in baby alpaca and silk, this pale pink jacket offers just the right amount of coziness. If you prefer the jacket unembellished, make it as it is shown here. Or, if you want to try freeform crochet, add embellishments like those shown on page 257.

YOU WILL NEED

Yarn

- Fine alpaca/silk blend
- Shown: Plymouth Bristol Yarn Gallery, Buckingham, 80% baby alpaca, 20% silk, 1.75 oz (50 g)/218 yd (200 m), #9210: 6 (6, 6, 7) skeins

Hook

- 4/E (3.5 mm) for main body
- 5/F (3.75 mm) for embellishments

Stitches used

- Chain
- Double crochet
- Puff stitch

Gauge

- 8 ch-2 spaces and 9 dc = 4" (10 cm); 10 rows = 4" (10 cm) with 4/E hook

Notions

- Tapestry needle

Finished size

- Small (Medium, Large, X-large)
- Finished chest size after blocking: 39" (42", 45", 48") (99 [106.5, 114.5, 122] cm)

Notes: *Puff st: [Yo, pick up a loop] 4 times in same space, yo, pull through all 9 loops on hook.*

To decrease 1 space in mesh pattern: At beg of row, ch 3 instead of 5, 1 dc in next dc (this eliminates one ch 2 space). At end of row, eliminate last ch 2, work 1 dc in the turning ch.

Back

Ch 134 (140, 146, 152).

Row 1: 1 dc in 8th ch from hook,*ch 2, skip next 2 ch, 1 dc in next ch, rep from * across, turn (43 [45, 47, 49] ch-2 spaces).

Row 2: Ch 5 (counts as dc, ch 2 now and throughout), skip first dc, 1 dc in next dc, [ch 2, 1 dc in next dc] 2, (3, 4, 5) times, 1 puff st in next ch-2 space, ch 1, 1 dc in next dc, *[ch 2, 1 dc in next dc] 5 times, 1 puff st in next ch-2 space, ch 1, 1 dc in next dc, rep from * across, ending with [ch 2, 1 dc in next dc] 2 (3, 4, 5) times, ch 2, 1 dc in 3rd ch of turning ch-5, turn.

Row 3: Ch 5, skip first dc, 1 dc in next dc, [ch 2, 1 dc in next dc] 1 (2, 3, 4) times, *1 puff st in next ch-2 space, ch 1, 1 dc in next dc, ch 2, 1 dc in next dc, 1 puff st in next ch-2 space, ch 1, 1 dc in next dc**, [ch 2, 1 dc in next dc] 3 times, rep from * across, ending last rep at **, [ch 2, 1 dc in next dc] 1 (2, 3, 4) times, ch 2 ,1 dc in 3rd ch of turning ch-5, turn.

Row 4 for size Small only: Ch 5, skip first dc, *1 dc in next dc, 1 puff st in next ch-2 space, ch 1, 1 dc in next dc, ch 2, rep from * across, ending with last dc in 3rd ch of turning ch-5, turn.

Row 4 for size Medium only: Ch 5, skip first dc, 1 dc in next dc, ch 2, *1 dc in next dc, 1 puff st in next ch-2 space, ch 1, 1 dc in next dc, ch 2, rep from * across to within last ch-2 space, 1 dc in next dc, ch 2, 1 dc 3rd ch of turning ch-5, turn.

Row 4 for size Large only: Ch 5, skip first dc, [1 dc in next dc, ch 2] twice, 1 dc in next dc, *1 puff st in next ch-2 space, ch 1, 1 dc in next dc, ch 2, rep from * across to within last 2 ch-2 spaces, [1 dc in next dc, ch 2] twice, 1 dc 3rd ch of turning ch-5, turn.

Row 4 for size X-large only: Ch 5, skip first dc, 1 dc in next dc, ch 2, [1 dc in next dc, ch 2] twice, 1 dc in next dc, *1 puff st in next ch-2 space, ch 1, 1 dc in next dc, ch 2, rep from * across to within last 3 ch-2 spaces, [1 dc in next dc, ch 2] 3 times, 1 dc 3rd ch of turning ch-5, turn.

Row 5: Rep Row 3.

Row 6: Rep Row 2.

Row 7: Ch 5, skip first dc, 1 dc in next dc, *ch 2, 1 dc in next dc, rep from * across, ending with last dc in 3rd ch of turning ch-5, turn.

Rows 8–10: Rep Row 7.

Rows 11–28: Rep Rows 2–10 (twice).

Rows 29–33: Rep Rows 2–6 (4 complete groups of puff st pattern are completed).

Work even in mesh stitch pattern only for 1 (1, 2, 3) more rows until body measures 13½" (13½", 14", 14½") (34.5 [34.5, 35.5, 37] cm) from beg.

Armhole Shaping

Sl st over first 3 (3, 4, 4) ch-2 spaces, ch 3, work mesh pattern as established to within 3 (3, 4, 4) spaces on other side, leave these sts unworked, turn, cont in mesh pattern dec 1 space each side, every row 3 (3, 4, 4) times, then work even on rem sts until armhole measures 7½" (8", 8½", 9") (19 [20.5, 21.5, 23] cm) from beg of armhole shaping.

Neck Shaping

Work in mesh pattern across 7 (8, 9, 10) ch-2 spaces, end off yarn. Skip center 17 (17, 15, 13 ch-2 spaces), rejoin yarn in next dc, ch 5, work in mesh pattern across (7 [8, 9, 10] ch-2 spaces), end off.

Left Front

Ch 62 (68, 74, 80).

Row 1: 1 dc in 8th ch from hook,*ch 2, skip next 2 ch, 1 dc in next ch, rep from * across, turn (19 [21, 23, 25] ch-2 spaces).

Work same as Back to armhole.

Armhole Shaping

Starting at armhole edge, Sl st over first 3 (3, 4, 4) ch-2 spaces, ch 3, work in mesh pattern as established across to end of row, turn, keeping front edge even, cont in pattern as established, dec 1 space each armhole side, every row 3 (3, 4, 4) times.

V Neck Shaping

When armhole dec are completed, work armhole side even and dec 1 space at neck edge every other row until 7 (8, 9, 10) ch-2 spaces rem, work even until armhole measures 8" (8½", 9", 9½"), (20.5 [21.5, 23, 24] cm) end off.

Right Front

Work same as Left Front to armhole.

Armhole Shaping

Starting at neck edge, work across row to within last 3 (3, 4, 4) ch-2 spaces, turn, ch 3, work in mesh pattern as established to end of row, turn, keeping front edge even, cont in pattern as established, dec 1 space each armhole side, every row 3 (3, 4, 4) times.

V Neck Shaping

When armhole dec are completed, keep arm side even and dec 1 space at neck edge every other row until 7 (8, 9, 10) ch-2 spaces rem, work even till armhole measures 8" (8½", 9", 9½") (20.5 [21.5, 23, 24] cm), end off.

Sleeve (make 2)

Ch 80 (86, 92, 98).

Row 1: 1 dc in 8th ch from hook,*ch 2, skip next 2 ch, 1 dc in next ch, rep from * across, turn (25 [27, 29, 31] ch-2 spaces).

Rows 2–10: Work same as Back.

Rows 11–15: Rep Rows 2–6.

Work 1 (1, 2, 3) more rows even.

Cap Shaping

Sl st over first 3 (3, 4, 4) ch-2 spaces, ch 3, work in mesh pattern as established to within 3 (3, 4, 4) spaces on other side, leaving these sts unworked, turn. Cont in mesh pattern, dec 1 space each side, every row 3 (3, 4, 4) times. Work even on rem sts until cap measures 6" (6½", 7", 7½") (15 [16.5, 18, 19] cm) from beg of cap shaping. Dec 1 space each side of next 2 rows, end off.

Sleeve Bell Bottom

Same for all sizes, worked in the round.

Sew underarm seam of sleeve.

Rnd 1: With RS facing, join yarn at seam, ch 1, work 70 sc evenly spaced around bottom of sleeve, working the sts in the ch-2 spaces, join with a Sl st to first sc.

Rnd 2: Ch 3 (counts as half a V-st now and throughout), *skip next 2 sc, [2 dc, ch 2, 2 dc] in next sc (shell made), skip next 2 sc, [1 dc, ch 2, 1 dc] in next sc (V-st made), rep from * around end 1 dc in same sc as beg ch 3, ch 2, join to top of beg ch-3, forming last V-st (12 shells, 12 V-sts).

Rnd 3: Ch 3, *[2 dc, ch 2, 2 dc] in center ch-2 space of next shell, V-st in center ch-2 space of next V-st, rep from * around, ending with 1 dc in ch-2 space of last V-st, ch 2, join with a Sl st to top of beg ch-3.

Rnds 4–7: Rep Rnd 3.

Rnds 8–13: Ch 3, *[3 dc, ch 2, 3 dc] in center ch-2 space of next shell, V-st in center ch-2 space of next V-st, rep from * around, ending with 1 dc in ch-2 space of last V-st, ch 2, join with a Sl st to top of beg ch-3.

Rnd 14: Ch 3, 1 dc in same st as ch 3, *[3 dc, ch 3, 3 dc] in center ch-3 sp of next shell, [2 dc, ch 3, 2 dc] in center ch-3 space of next V-st, rep from * around, ending with 2 dc in ch-3 space of last V-st, ch 3, join with a Sl st to top of beg ch 3, end off.

Sweater Edging

Use a tapestry needle to sew shoulder seams.

Row 1: Starting at bottom right front, join yarn, ch 1, work 2 sc in each open space all around front and neck edges to bottom left front corner, turn.

Row 2: Ch 1, skip first sc, 1 sc in each sc across, turn.

Row 3: Ch 1, skip first sc, 1 sc in each sc to beg of V-neck shaping on Right Front, ch 61 for tie, 1 sc in 2nd ch from hook, 1 sc in each ch across, 1 sc in each sc across neck edge to bottom of V-neck shaping on Left Front, ch 61 for tie, 1 sc in 2nd ch from hook, 1 sc in each ch across, 1 sc in each sc across to bottom of Left Front, do not turn, cont in sc along bottom edge, working 2 sc in each ch-2 space, join with a Sl st in first sc at bottom of Right Front, end off.

Finishing

Pin Sleeves in place centering on shoulder seam and matching underarm seams, sew in place.

Blocking

Lay garment flat on a towel-padded surface, spritz lightly with water, and pat into shape. Do not iron or press flat; allow to thoroughly dry.

Color Combinations

Blending color combinations into your crochet work can be lots of fun. Many stitches do not lend themselves to changing colors while you work, but the stitches in this section use color changes very effectively. The possibilities for making colorful jackets, hats, scarves, afghans, and baby items are endless. Besides being colorful, the use of two or more colors in interesting stitch combinations makes a strikingly textured fabric.

WAVES

Baby blanket lt green + white 2011

Skill Level: Easy

Note: Use 2 colors A and B. Colors are carried up sides.

With A, ch a multiple of 8 plus 2.

Foundation Row: With A, sc in 2nd ch from hook, *1 sc in next ch, 1 hdc in next ch, 1 dc in each of next 3 ch, 1 hdc next ch, 1 sc in each of next 2 ch, rep from * across, turn.

Row 1: With A, ch 1 (counts as first sc), skip first st, 1 sc in each st across. Drop A, draw B through last loop, turn.

Row 2: With B, ch 3 (counts as first dc), skip first st, *1 dc in next st, 1 hdc next st, 1 sc in each of next 3 sts, 1 hdc next st, 1 dc in each of the next 2 sts, rep from * across, ending with last dc in top of turning ch, turn.

Row 3: With B, ch 1 (counts as first sc), skip first st, 1 sc in each st across, ending with 1 sc in top of turning ch. Drop B, draw A through last loop, turn.

Row 4: With A, ch 1 (counts as first sc), skip first st, 1 sc next st, *1 hdc next st, 1 dc in each of next 3 sts, 1 hdc in next st**, 1 sc in each of the next 3 sts, rep from * across, ending last rep at **, 1 sc next st, 1 sc in top of turning ch, turn.

Rep Rows 1–4 for pattern.

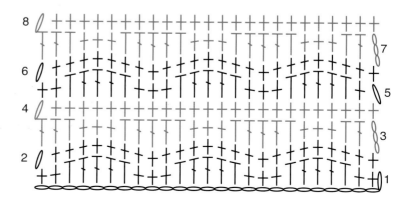

HOUNDSTOOTH

Skill Level: Experienced

Use 2 colors A and B.

Notes:

1. Colors are carried along sides, not ended off at each row.

2. In order to form the points of the houndstooth pattern, form and work on new chains at every other row.

With A, ch a multiple of 4.

Row 1: With A, *1 sc in 2nd ch from hook, 1 hdc in next ch, 1 dc in next ch (point made), skip next 3 ch, 1 sc in next ch**, ch 4, rep from * across, ending last rep at **, turn. Drop A, draw B through last loop, turn.

Row 2: With B, ch 4, *1 dc in next dc, 1 hdc in next hdc, 1 sc in next sc**, 1 tr in next sc, rep from * across, ending last rep at **, turn.

Row 3: With B, ch 4, *1 sc in 2nd ch from hook, 1 hdc in next ch, 1 dc in next ch, skip 3 sts, 1 sc in next st, ch 4, rep from * across, ending with last sc in top of turning ch, turn. Drop B, draw A through last loop, turn.

Rep Rows 2 and 3, alternating colors every 2 rows.

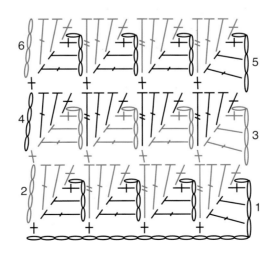

TRICOLOR SAND STITCH

Skill Level: Easy

Use 3 colors A, B, and C. Work one row each of colors A, B, and C throughout, carrying yarn loosely up sides.

Chain an even number of stitches.

Foundation Row: With A, 1 sc in 4th ch from hook (counts as sc, ch 1), *ch 1, skip next ch, 1 sc in next ch, rep from * across, turn. Drop A, draw B through last loop.

Row 1: With B, ch 2 (counts as sc, ch 1), skip first sc, *1 sc in next ch-1 space, ch 1, skip next sc, rep from * across, ending with 1 sc in last ch-1 space of turning ch, turn. Drop B; draw C through last loop.

Row 2: With C, rep Row 1.

Rep Row 1, alternating A, B, and C, for pattern.

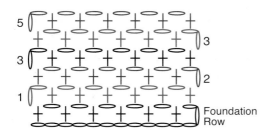

TWO-COLOR INTERLACED SHELLS

Skill Level: Intermediate

Notes:

1. Use 2 colors, A and B. Pay attention to color changes.

2. When dropping a color, always pick up a long loop so as not to lose the stitch.

3. After the Foundation Row, do not turn at the end of every row.

With A, ch a multiple of 6 plus 4.

Row 1: With A, work 2 dc in 4th ch from hook, *skip next 2 ch, 1 sc next ch, skip next 2 ch**, 5 dc in next ch, rep from * across, ending last rep at **, 3 dc in last ch, do not turn. Drop A.

Row 2: Join B in first st of last row. With B, ch 1, 1 sc in first st, *ch 2, *(yo, draw up a loop in next st, yo, draw through 2 loops) 5 times, yo, draw through 6 loops on hook (cluster made), ch 2, 1 sc in next dc**, ch 2, rep from * across, ending last rep at **. Drop B.

Row 3: Join A in first st of last row, ch 3 (counts as first dc), 2 dc in the first sc, *1 sc in next cluster**, 5 dc in next sc, rep from * across, ending last rep at **, 3 dc in last sc. Drop A.

Rep Rows 2 and 3 for pattern.

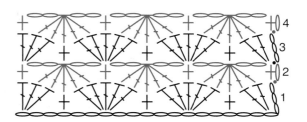

CLEVER BLOCKS

Skill Level: Experienced

Use 3 colors A, B, and C. Work one row each of colors A, B, and C throughout, carrying yarn loosely up sides.

With A, ch a multiple of 6 plus 5.

Foundation Row: 1 dc in 4th ch from hook, 1 dc in next ch, *ch 3, skip next 3 ch, 1 dc in each of the next 3 ch, rep from * across, turn. Drop A, draw B through last loop **(1)**.

Row 1: With B, ch 3, skip next 3 dc, *working over next ch-3 space, 1 dc in each of next 3 skipped ch in foundation ch, ch 3, skip next 3 dc, rep from * across, 1 sc in top of turning ch, turn. Drop B; draw C through last loop **(2)**.

Row 2: With C, ch 3 (counts as first dc), skip first st, working over ch-3 space, 1 dc in each of next 2 skipped dc 2 rows below,*ch 3, skip 3 sts, working over next ch-3 space, 1 dc in each of next 3 skipped dc 2 rows below, rep from * across, turn. Drop C, draw A through last loop.

Row 3: With A, ch 3, skip next 3 dc, *working over next ch-3 space, 1 dc in each of the next 3 skipped dc 2 rows below, rep from * across, sc in top of turning ch, turn. Drop A, draw B through last loop.

Rep Rows 2 and 3 for pattern, alternating colors A, B, and C throughout **(3)**.

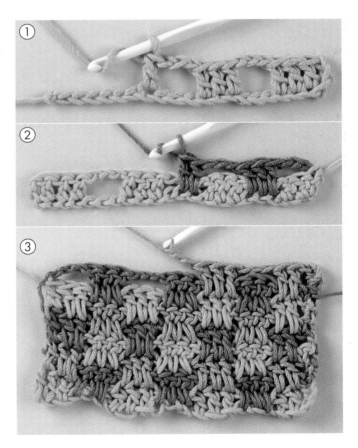

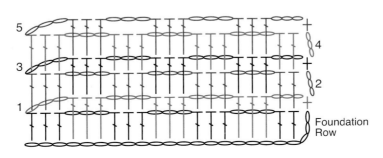

COTTON CANDY

Skill Level: Intermediate

Notes:

1. Use 2 colors, A and B. Pay attention to color changes.

2. When dropping a color, always pick up a long loop so as not to lose the stitch.

3. After the Foundation Row, do not turn at the end of every row.

With A, ch a multiple of 8 plus 6.

Foundation Row (WS): With A, 1 sc in 2nd ch from hook, 1 sc in each ch across row, turn.

Row 1: With A, ch 1, 1 sc in first sc, *ch 5, skip next 3 sc, 1 sc in next sc, rep from * across, do not turn. Drop A.

Row 2: Join B in first st of last row. With B, ch 3 (counts as first dc), 4 dc in next ch-5 loop, *ch 3, 1 sc in next ch-5 loop, ch 3**, 5 dc in next ch-5 loop, rep from * across, ending last rep at **, 4 dc in last ch-5 loop, 1 dc in last sc, do not turn. Drop B.

Row 3: Join A in first st of last row. With A, ch 1, 1 sc in first dc, *ch 5, 1 sc in next ch-3 loop, rep from * across, ending with last sc in last dc. Drop A.

Row 4: Join B in first st of last row. With B, ch 6 (counts as dc, ch 3), 1 sc in next ch-5 loop, *ch 3, 5 dc in next ch-5 loop, ch 3, 1 sc in next ch-5 loop, rep from * across to last ch-5 loop, ch 3, 1 dc in last sc, do not turn. Drop B.

Row 5: Join A in first st of last row. With A, ch 1, 1 sc in first st, skip next ch-3 loop, *ch 5, 1 sc in next ch-3 loop, rep from * across, ending with last sc in last dc. Drop A.

Rep Rows 2–5 for pattern.

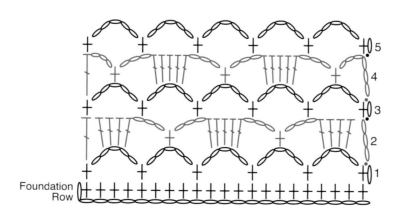

BOBBLES AND STRIPES

Skill Level: Easy

Bobble: Yo, pick up a loop in next stitch, yo and through 2 loops, [yo, pick up a loop in the same stitch, yo and through 2 loops] 2 times, yo, draw through all 4 loops on the hook.

Note: Use 3 colors A, B, and C. Colors may be carried loosely up sides of work. After first 3 rows, change colors every other row.

With A, ch a multiple of 4.

Foundation row (WS): With A, 1 sc in 2nd ch from hook, 1 sc in each ch across row, turn.

Row 1: With A, ch 1 (counts as first sc now and throughout), skip first st, sc in each sc across row, turn.

Row 2: With A, ch 1, skip first st, 1 sc in each of next 2 sts, *bobble in next st, sc in each of next 3 sc, rep from * across, ending with last sc in top of the turning ch, turn. Drop A, draw B through last loop.

Rows 3–4: With B, ch 1, skip first st, 1 sc in each st across row, 1 sc top of turning ch, turn. At end of last row, drop B; draw C through last loop.

Row 5: With C, ch 1, skip first st, working in back loops only, 1 sc in each st across, 1 sc in top of turning ch, turn.

Row 6: With C, ch 1, skip first st, 1 sc in each st across row, turn. Drop C, draw A through last loop.

Rep Rows 1–6 for pattern.

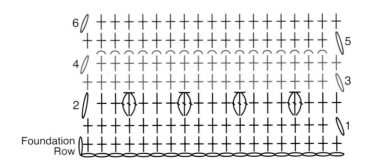

CABLE LOOPS

Skill Level: Easy

Note: Use 2 colors A and B. After first 6 rows in A, alternate A and B, every 4 rows. Do not break yarn at end of rows, but carry it loosely up sides.

With A, ch a multiple of 4 plus 1.

Foundation Row (WS): With A, 1 sc in 2nd ch from hook, 1 sc in each ch across row, turn.

Row 1: Ch 1 (counts as first sc now and throughout), skip first st, 1 sc in each st across, turn.

Row 2: Ch 1, skip first st, 1 sc in each st across, ending with 1 sc in top of turning ch, turn.

Row 3: Ch 1, skip first st, sc in next st, *ch 12, sc in each of the next 4 sts, rep from * across, ending last rep with 1 sc in the next st, 1 sc in the top of the turning ch, turn.

Rows 4–6: Keeping loops to front of work, ch 1, skip first sc, 1 sc in each sc across, 1 sc in top of turning ch, turn. Drop A, draw B through last loop.

Rows 7–10: With B, rep Rows 3–6. Drop B, draw A through last loop.

Rep Rows 3–10 for desired length.

Before completing last row, chain loops together by pulling each loop through the one below.

Last Row: With next color in sequence, ch 1, skip first st, *inserting hook in next ch-12 loop, 1 sc in next sc, 1 sc in each of next 3 sc, rep from * across, ending with 1 sc in last sc, 1 sc in top of turning ch.

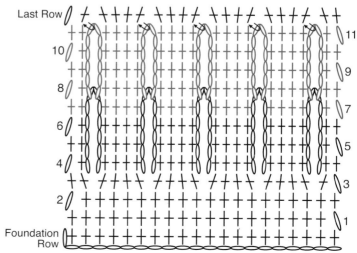

THE COMPLETE PHOTO GUIDE TO CROCHET

MOCK WEAVING

Skill Level: Experienced

Note: Use 2 colors A and B. Do not end colors after each change, but carry up sides of work.

Long Double Crochet: Yo, pick up a loop in designated space, draw loop up to height of current row, [yo, draw through 2 loops on hook] twice.

With A, ch a multiple of 4 plus 1.

Foundation: With A, 1 sc in 2nd ch from hook, 1 sc in each ch across row, turn.

Row 1: With A, ch 1, 1 sc in each sc across, turn. Drop A. Draw B through last loop.

Row 2: With B, ch 1, sc in first sc, 1 sc in each of the next 2 sc, *[working over sts in previous 2 rows, long dc in next ch of foundation ch] twice, skip 2 sc behind 2 long dc just worked, 1 sc in each of next 2 sc, rep from * across, ending with 1 sc in last sc, turn.

Row 3: With B, ch 1, 1 sc in first sc, *ch 2, skip next 2 sc, 1 sc in each of next 2 dc, rep from * across, ending with 1 sc in last sc, turn. Drop B. Draw A through last loop.

Row 4: With A, ch 1, 1 sc in first sc, *[working over sts in previous 2 rows, long dc in next sc 3 rows below] twice, skip ch-2 space behind 2 long dc just worked, ch 2, skip 2 sc, rep from * across, end 2 long dc, 1 sc in last ch, turn.

Row 5: With A, ch 1, 1 sc in first sc, *1 sc in each next 2 dc**, 2 sc in next ch-2 space, rep from * ending last rep at **, 1 sc in last sc, turn.

Row 6: With B, ch 1, 1 sc first sc, *1 sc in each next 2 sc, [working over sts in previous 2 rows, long dc in next sc 3 rows below] twice, rep from * across to within last 3 sts, 1 sc in each last 3 sc, turn.

Row 7: With B, Rep Row 3.

Rep Rows 4–7 for pattern.

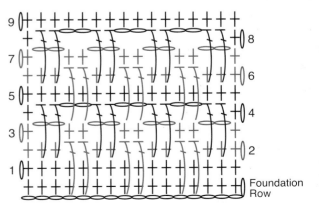

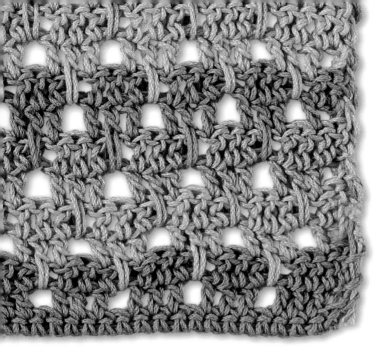

Row 4: With B, ch 3, skip first dc, 1 dc in next dc, ch 1, *1 dc in each of next 3 dc, ch 1, rep from * across, 1 dc next dc, 1 dc in top of turning ch, turn. Drop B. Draw C through last loop.

Row 5: With C, ch 3, skip first dc, 1 dc in next dc, *working over sts in previous row, 1 long dc in ch-1 space 2 rows below, 1 dc in next dc**, ch 1, skip 1 dc, 1 dc in next dc, rep from * across, ending last rep at **, 1 dc in top of turning ch, turn.

Row 6: With C, ch 3, skip first dc, *1 dc in each next 3 dc, ch 1, rep from * across to within last 4 sts, 1 dc in each of next 3 dc, 1 dc in top of turning ch, turn. Drop C. Draw A through last loop.

Rep Rows 3–5 for pattern, alternating colors A, B, and C, every 2 rows.

LARKSFOOT

Skill Level: Intermediate

Long Double Crochet: Yo, pick up a loop in designated space, draw loop up to height of current row, [yo, draw through 2 loops on hook] twice.

Notes:

1. Use 3 colors A, B, and C. After first 6 rows, pattern repeat is 4 rows, alternating colors every 2 rows.

2. Colors may be carried very loosely up side of work.

3. When working the long dc, you are working in the ch-1 space 2 rows below.

With A, ch a multiple of 4 plus 2.

Foundation Row: With A, 1 sc in 2nd ch from hook, 1 sc in each ch across row, turn.

Row 1: With A, ch 3 (counts as first dc now and throughout), skip first sc, *1 dc in each of next 3 sc, ch 1, skip 1 st, rep from * across to within last 4 sts, 1 dc in each of last 4 sts, turn.

Row 2: With A, ch 3, skip first dc, *1 dc in each of next 3 dc, ch 1, rep from * across to within last 4 sts, 1 dc in each of last 3 dc, 1 dc in top of turning ch, turn. Drop A. Draw B through last loop.

Row 3: With B, ch 3, skip first dc, 1 dc in next dc, *ch 1, skip next dc, 1 dc next dc**, working over sts in previous row, 1 long dc in ch-1 space 2 rows below, 1 dc next dc, rep from * across, ending last rep at **, 1 dc next dc, 1 dc in top of turning ch, turn.

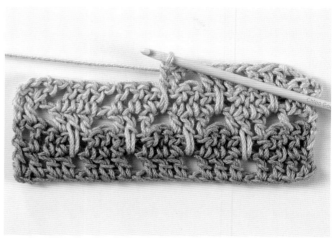

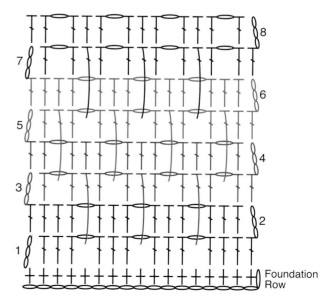

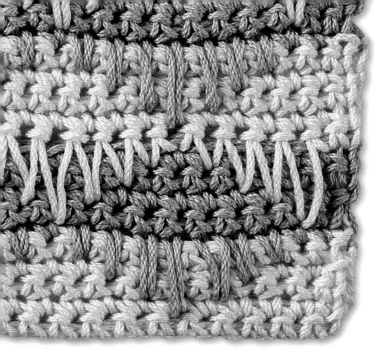

FLAME STITCH

Skill Level: Experienced

Long Single Crochet (Lsc): Draw up a loop in designated stitch, draw loop up to top of row being worked, complete as a single crochet.

Notes:

1. Colors cannot be carried up sides and must be cut and restarted on other side.

2. Use two colors A and B.

3. When instructions state to work in the next stitch in any row below, the long single crochet takes the place of the next single crochet in the current row, so skip the stitch behind the long single crochet.

With A, ch a multiple of 8 plus 4.

Foundation Row (WS): With A, 1 sc in 2nd ch from hook, 1 sc in each ch across row, turn.

Rows 1–4: With A, ch 1, 1 sc in each sc across, turn. At end of last row, drop A. With right side facing, join B in first st of last row.

Row 5 (RS): With B, ch 1, sc in first 2 sc, *1 Lsc in the next st 1 row below, 1 Lsc in next st 2 rows below, 1 Lsc in next st 3 rows below, 1 Lsc in next st 4 rows below, 1 Lsc in next st 3 rows below, 1 Lsc in next st 2 rows below, 1 Lsc in next st 1 row below, 1 sc in next sc, rep from * across, ending with 1 sc in last sc, turn.

Rows 6–9: With B, rep Rows 1–4. Drop B. With wrong side facing, join A in first st of last row.

Row 10 (WS): With A, ch 1, 1 sc in first sc, *1 Lsc in next st 4 rows below, 1 Lsc in next st 3 rows below, 1 Lsc in next st 2 rows below, 1 Lsc in next st 1 row below, 1 sc in next sc, 1 Lsc in the next st 1 row below, 1 Lsc in next st 2 rows below, 1 Lsc in next st 3 rows below, rep from * across, 1 Lsc in next st 4 rows below, 1 sc in last sc, turn.

Rows 11–14: With A, rep Rows 1–4.

Rep Rows 5–14 for pattern.

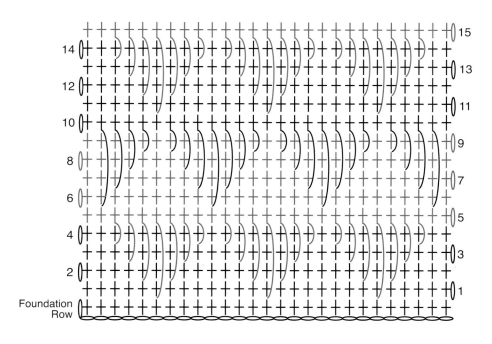

MITERED SQUARE

Skill Level: Easy

Note: Use 2 colors A and B. Alternate colors every other row.

Single Crochet 3 Together (sc3tog): Draw up a loop in each of next 3 sts, yo, through all 4 loops on hook.

With A, ch 33.

Foundation Row: With A, 1 sc in 2nd ch from hook, 1 sc in each of first 14 ch, sc3tog in next 3 ch, 1 sc in each of next 15 ch, turn.

Row 1: Ch 1 (counts as sc now and throughout), skip first sc, 1 sc in each of the next 13 sc, sc3tog in next 3 sts, 1 sc in each of the next 14 sc, turn. Drop A, pick up B.

Row 2: With B, ch 1, skip first sc, 1 sc in each of the next 12 sc, sc3tog in next 3 sts, 1 sc in each of the next 12, 1 sc in top of turning ch, turn.

Row 3: Ch 1, skip first sc, 1 sc in each of the next 11 sc, sc3tog in next 3 sts, 1 sc in each of the next 11 sc, 1 sc in top of turning ch, turn. Drop B, pick up A.

Rows 4–14: Continue in this manner, working 1 fewer st before and after the center sc3tog, until 3 sts remain, changing color every other row.

Row 15: Ch 1, sc3tog in next 3 sts.

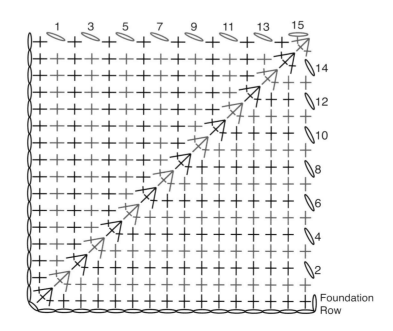

THE COMPLETE PHOTO GUIDE TO CROCHET

MITERED SQUARE THROUGH BACK LOOP

Skill Level: Easy

Work the same as Mitered Square (opposite), except work all single crochets through the back loop for a different look.

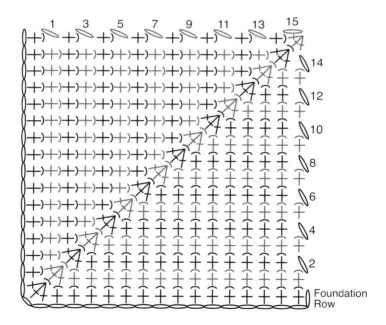

FLOWER BORDER TODDLER CARDIGAN

Pretty flowers all in a row add precious detail to this classic cardigan. Tri-color sand stitch is used for the colorful borders. The flower row stitch pattern is a little challenging but fun to do once you get the idea; the stitch is shown in detail on page 154.

Body

Body of cardigan is worked in one piece to armholes then divided for front and back sections.

Foundation Row: With 9/I hook and MC, ch 80 (84, 88). Starting in second ch from hook, work 1 sc in each ch, turn—79 (83, 87) sc.

Row 1: Ch 1 (counts as sc), sk first sc, work 1 sc in next sc, * ch 1, sk 1, rep from * across, end 1 sc in next sc, 1 sc in top of tch, turn, do not fasten off MC.

Row 2: Pick up lp with A, ch 2 (counts as sc and ch 1), sk next sc, work 1 sc in next ch-1 sp, * ch 1, sk next sc, 1 sc in next ch-1 sp, rep from * across, end ch 1, sk 1, 1 sc in top of tch, do not fasten off A, turn.

Row 3: Pick up lp with B, ch 1, work 1 sc in ch-1 sp, * ch 1, sk 1, 1 sc in next ch-1 sp, rep from * across, end 1 sc in top of tch, turn.

Rep rows 1 and 2, foll color sequence (MC, A, B) one time more, do not fasten off A and B—carry loosely up sides.

Next row, with MC, ch 1, sk first sc, work 1 sc in each sc and each ch-1 sp across, 1 sc in top of tch, turn—79 (83, 87) sc.

Beg flower patt as foll:

Row 1: With B, ch 1, sk first sc, work 1 sc in each of next 3 (5, 7) sc, * [in next sc (sc, ch 8) 3 times, sc], 1 sc in each of next 9 sc, rep from * 7 times more, end 1 sc in each of next 3 (5, 7) sc, 1 sc in top of tch, turn. Pull up lp with A, fasten off B.

Row 2: Ch 1 (counts as sc), sk first sc, work 1 sc in each of next 3 (5, 7) sc, * ch 1, sk ch lps, 1 sc in each of next 9 sc, rep from * across, end 1 sc in each of next 3 (5, 7) sc, 1 sc in top of tch, turn.

Row 3: Ch 1 (counts as sc), sk first sc, work 1 sc in each of next 0 (2, 4) sc, * 1 sc through right lp and into next sc, 1 sc in each of next 2 sc, 1 sc in ch-1 sp, 1 sc in each of next 2 sc, 1 sc through left lp and into next sc, 1 sc in each of next 3 sc, rep from * across, end 1 sc in each of next 0 (2, 4) sc, 1 sc in top of tch, turn.

Row 4: Ch 1, sk first sc, work 1 sc in each sc, 1 sc in top of tch, turn.

Row 5: Ch 1, sk first sc, work 1 sc in each of next 3 (5, 7) sc, * 6 dc through center lp and into next sc (flower bud made), 1 sc in each of next 9 sc, rep from * across, end 1 sc in each of next 3 (5, 7) sc, 1 sc in top of tch, turn.

Row 6: Ch 1 with MC (counts as sc), fasten off A, work 1 sc in each of next 3 (5, 7) sc, * ch 1, sk all dc, 1 sc in each of next 9 sc, rep from * across, end 1 sc in each of last 3 (5, 7) sc, 1 sc in top of tch, turn.

Row 7: Ch 1 (counts as sc), sk first sc, work 1 sc in each sc and in each ch-1 sp across, 1 sc in top of tch, turn.

Continuing with MC, work in sc on 79 (83, 87) sts until piece is 8" (8½", 9") [20.5 (21.8, 23) cm] from beg, ending on WS row.

Right Front

Work in sc across 18 (19, 20) sts, ch 1, turn. Working on these 18 (19, 20) sts, work even until armhole is 3" (3½", 4") [7.5 (9, 10) cm], ending at neck edge. Sl st over 6 (6, 6) sts, ch 1, cont sc on rem 12 (13, 14) sts, dec 1 st at neck edge every row two times, work even on rem 10 (11, 12) sts until armhole is 5" (5½", 6") [12.7 (14, 15) cm], fasten off.

Back

Sk 4 sts at underarm, join yarn for back, work across 35 (37, 39) sts, ch 1, turn.

Cont in sc for 4½" (5", 5½") [11.5 (12.7, 14) cm].

Shape back neck as foll: On the next row, work 10 (11, 12) sts, ch 1, turn. Work 1 more row on sts just worked, fasten off. Sk center 15 (15, 15) sts, join yarn, ch 1, work 2 rows sc on rem 10 (11, 12) sts, fasten off.

Left Front

Sk 4 sts at underarm, join yarn, work across 18, (19, 20) sts in sc until armhole is 3" (3½", 4") [7.5 (9, 10) cm], ending at arm side. Work across 12 (13, 14) sts, leave rem 6 sts not worked, turn. Complete dec as on right front, fasten off.

Sleeves

Make 2.

Note: Smaller hook used for the alternating color rows at the beginning of the sleeves makes these rows a little more snug.

With 8/H hook, ch 28 (28, 30). Work border same as back for 8 rows, fasten off A and B and cont sleeve in MC as foll:

Change to 9/I hook. On first MC row, inc 1 st each side and rep inc every 1¾" (4.5 cm) 4 (5, 5) times more—37 (39, 41) sc.

Work even until sleeve is 10" (10½", 11") [25.5 (26.7, 28) cm] from beg, fasten off.

Finishing

1. Weave in ends, using tapestry needle.

2. Sew shoulder seams.

3. Fold each sleeve in half, center and pin at shoulder seam, sew in place.

4. Sew underarm seams.

5. Work front border (see below).

6. Sew on buttons to correspond to buttonholes.

Front Border

Row 1: With 8/H hook and B, starting at bottom right front, RS facing you, work 42 (44, 46) sc along front edge to top of right front, 3 sc in last st to turn corner, 11 (12, 13) sts along top of right front, 18 (20, 22) sts along back of neck, 11 (12, 13) sts along top of left front, 3 sc in last st to turn corner, 42 (44, 46) sts to bottom, turn.

Row 2: Ch 1, sk first st, work 1 sc in each st around, making 3 sc in each corner st, fasten off B, turn.

Row 3 (start of buttonholes): Pick up lp and ch 1 with A, sk first st, work 1 sc next 1 (2, 3) st, * ch 2, sk 2 sts, 1 sc in each of next 8 sts, rep from * 3 times more, ch 5, 1 sc in same st (this lp counts as fifth buttonhole and turns corner at same time. Cont around neck edge and down left front, turn.

Row 4: Ch 1, sk first st, work 1 sc in each st around, 2 sc in each ch-sp of buttonholes, fasten off A, turn.

Row 5: Pick up lp and ch 1 with MC, work 1 sc in each st around, 3 sc in each corner st, turn.

Row 6: Ch 1, Sl st in each st around, do not work 3 Sl st in corner st, fasten off.

Three loops of chain stitches, formed in the green base row, become leaves and a stem as they are caught into stitches in the following lavender rows.

Rows of single crochet in alternating colors for the neck border and buttonband.

Heavy Textures

I love the heavy texture this group of stitches creates. Since these stitches do not drape very well, they are most suitable for crocheting heavy outerwear. But the stitches also make wonderful ski hats, bags, afghans, and pillow covers. Use these stitches with a larger hook than your yarn calls for to produce a fabric that is not too stiff.

STAR STITCH

Skill Level: Intermediate

Ch a multiple of 2 plus 1.

Row 1: Pick up a loop in 2nd ch and in each of next 4 ch (6 loops on hook), yo and through all loops on hook, ch 1 (this forms eye of star), *pick up a loop in the eye of last star, pick up a loop through the back of last loop of previous star, pick up a loop through same ch as last loop of previous star, pick up a loop in each of next 2 ch (6 loops on hook), yo and through all 6 loops, ch 1, rep from * across, ending with 1 hdc in last ch (same ch as last loop of last star st), turn.

Row 2: Ch 1, 1 sc in hdc, 1 sc in eye of next star st, 2 sc in eye of each star st across, ending with 1 sc in top of turning ch, turn.

Row 3: Ch 2, pick up a loop in front strand of 2nd ch from hook, then pick up a loop in the back strand of same ch, pick up loop in each of next 3 sc, yo and through all 6 loops, ch 1, *pick up a loop in eye of last star, pick up loop in back of last loop of star, pick up loop in same sc as last loop of star, pick up a loop in each of next 2 sc, yo and through all 6 loops, ch 1, rep from * across, ending with 1 hdc in last sc (same sc as last loop of last star st).

Repeat Rows 2 and 3 for pattern.

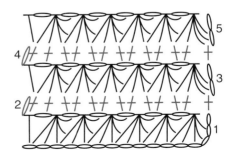

POPCORN

Skill Level: Intermediate

Popcorn: 5 dc in next st, drop loop from hook, insert hook in first dc of 5-dc group, draw dropped loop through st, ch 1 tightly to secure.

Ch an even number of stitches very loosely.

Foundation Row: 1 sc in 2nd ch from hook, 1 sc in each ch across row, turn.

Row 1: Ch 3 (count as first dc), skip first st, *popcorn in next st, 1 dc next st, rep from * across, turn.

Row 2: Ch 1, 2 sc in first dc; *skip next popcorn, 2 sc in next dc, rep from * across, ending with 1 sc top of turning ch, turn.

Rep Rows 1 and 2 for pattern.

LOOPY RIDGES

Skill Level: Easy

Ch an even number of stitches.

Foundation Row: 1 dc in 4th ch from hook, 1 dc in each ch across, turn.

Row 1 (WS): Ch 1, working in back loops of sts, 1 sc in first st, *ch 7, 1 sc in each of next 2 sc, rep from * across row, ending with ch 7, 1 sc in top of tch, turn.

Row 2: Ch 1, Sl st in first st, ch 3 (counts as a dc now and throughout), with loops pushed to front, working in back loops of sts, dc in each stitch across, turn.

Rows 3–4: Ch 3 (counts as a dc), skip first dc, working in both loops of sts, 1 dc in each st across, 1 dc in top of the turning ch, turn.

Rep Rows 1–4 for pattern.

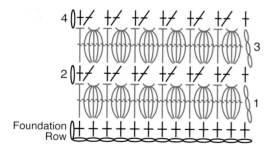

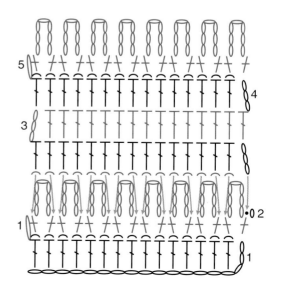

FANCIFUL FENCES

Skill Level: Intermediate

Front Post Double Crochet (FPdc): Yo hook, pick up a loop from front, inserting hook from right to left under designated stitch, [yo, draw through 2 loops] 2 times.

Ch a multiple of 8 plus 7.

Foundation Row: 1 dc in 4th ch from hook, 1 dc in each of next 3 ch, *skip next ch, [2 dc, ch 2, 2 dc] in next ch (shell made), skip next ch, 1 dc in each of next 5 ch, rep from * across, turn.

Row 1: Ch 3, skip first dc, 1 FPdc around the post of next 4 dc, *skip 2 dc of next shell, [2 dc, ch 2, 2 dc] in ch-2 space of next shell, skip next 2 dc of shell, 1 FPdc around post of each of next 5 dc, rep from * ending with 1 FPdc around the post of last 4 dc, 1 dc in top of the turning ch, turn.

Rep Row 1 for pattern.

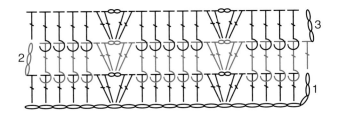

ROCKY ROAD

Skill Level: Easy

Ch a multiple of 4 plus 3.

Foundation Row: 1 sc in 2nd ch from hook, *[1 sc, ch 2, 2 dc] in next ch, skip next 2 ch, sc in next ch, rep from * across to within last ch, 1 sc in last ch, turn.

Row 1: Ch 1, 1 sc in first sc, *[sc, ch 2, 2 dc] in next sc, skip next (2 dc, ch-2), 1 sc in next sc, rep from * across, sc in last sc, turn.

Repeat Row 1 for pattern.

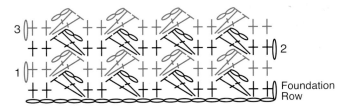

BASKETWEAVE

Skill Level: Intermediate

Front Post Double Crochet (FPdc): Yo hook, pick up a loop from front, inserting hook from right to left under designated stitch, [yo, draw through 2 loops] 2 times.

Back Post Double Crochet (BPdc): Yo hook, pick up a loop from back, inserting hook from right to left under designated stitch, [yo, draw through 2 loops] 2 times.

Ch a multiple of 8.

Foundation Row: 1 dc in 4th ch from hook, 1 dc in each ch across, turn.

Rows 1, 3, 6, 8: Ch 3 (counts as 1 dc), skip first st, *FPdc around the post of each of next 4 sts**, BPdc around the post of each of next 4 sts, rep from * across, ending last rep at **, 1 dc in top of turning ch, turn.

Rows 2, 4, 5, 7: Ch 3 (counts as 1 dc), skip first st, *BPdc around the post of next 4 sts**, FPdc around the post of each of next 4 sts, rep from *, ending last rep at **, 1 dc in top of turning ch, turn.

Repeat Rows 1–8 for pattern.

= Raised to right side of work

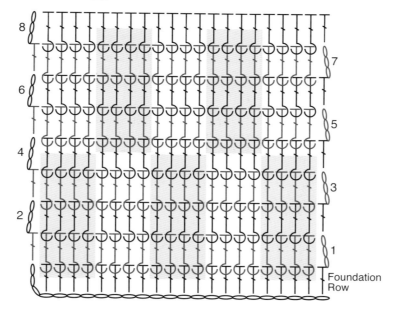

RAISED RIBS

Skill Level: Intermediate

Front Post Double Crochet (FPdc): Yo hook, pick up a loop from front, inserting hook from right to left under designated stitch, [yo, draw through 2 loops] 2 times.

Note: Always skip the sc behind the dc made in the row below.

Ch a multiple of 3 plus 2.

Row 1 (RS): 1 sc in 2nd ch from hook, 1 sc in each ch across row, turn.

Row 2: Ch 1 (counts as first sc now and throughout), skip first sc, 1 sc in each sc across, turn.

Row 3: Ch 1, skip first sc, 1 sc in next sc, *1 FPdc around the post of next sc 2 rows below, 1 sc in each of next 2 sc, rep from * across, ending with last sc in top of turning ch, turn.

Row 4: Ch 1, skip first sc, 1 sc in each st across, 1 sc in top of turning ch, turn.

Row 5: Ch 1, skip first sc, 1 sc next sc, *1 FPdc around the post of next dc 2 rows below, 1 sc in each of the next 2 sc, rep from * across, ending with last sc in top of turning ch, turn.

Rep Rows 4 and 5 for pattern.

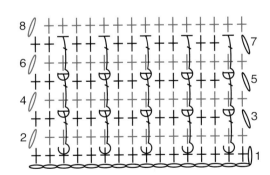

RAISED DIAGONALS

Skill Level: Intermediate

Front Post Double Crochet (FPdc): Yo hook, pick up a loop from front, inserting hook from right to left under designated stitch, [yo, draw through 2 loops] 2 times.

Note: Always skip the sc behind the dc made in the row below.

Ch a multiple of 4.

Foundation Row (RS): 1 sc in 2nd ch from hook, 1 sc in each ch across row, turn.

Row 1: Ch 1, 1 sc in each sc across, turn.

Row 2: Ch 1, 1 sc in each of first 3 sc, *1 FPdc around the base of next sc 2 rows below, 1 st to the right, 1 sc in each of next 3 sc, rep from * across, turn.

Rows 3, 5, 7: Ch 1, 1 sc in each sc across, turn.

Row 4: Ch 1, 1 sc in each of first 4 sc, *1 FPdc around the post of dc 2 rows below, 1 st to the right, 1 sc in each of next 3 sc, rep from * across, ending with 1 sc in each of last 2 sc, turn.

Row 6: Ch 1, 1 sc in first sc, 1 FPdc around the post of next sc 2 row below, 1 st to the right, *1 sc in each of next 3 sc, 1 FPdc around post of dc row below, rep from * across, ending with 1 sc in last sc, turn.

Row 8: Ch 1, 1 sc in each of first 2 sc, *1 FPdc around the post of next dc 2 rows below, 1 st to the right, 1 sc in each of next 3 sc, rep from * across to within last st, 1 sc in last sc, turn.

Rep Rows 1–8 for pattern.

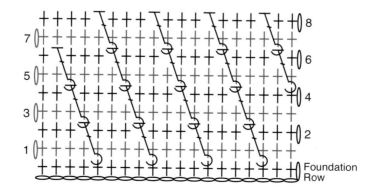

CATHERINE'S WHEEL

Skill Level: Experienced

Ch a multiple of 6 plus 2.

Foundation Row (WS): 1 sc in 2nd ch from hook, *skip 2 ch, 7 dc in next ch (shell made), skip next 2 ch, 1 sc in next ch, rep from * across, turn.

Row 1: Ch 3, skip first sc, *[yo, pick up a loop in next dc, yo through 2 loops] 3 times, yo draw through 4 loops on hook, ch 1 to form eye of cluster, ch 2, 1 sc in next dc, ch 3, *[yo, pick up a loop in next dc, yo through 2 loops] 7 times, yo, draw through 8 loops on hook, ch 1 (eye of cluster), ch 2, 1 sc next dc, ch 3, rep from * across, end [yo pick up a loop in next dc, yo through 2 loops] 4 times, yo through all 5 loops on hook, turn.

Row 2: Ch 3, 3 dc in eye of first cluster, *1 sc in next sc, 7 dc in eye of next cluster, rep from * across, ending with 4 dc in eye of last cluster, turn.

Row 3: Ch 1, 1 sc in first dc, ch 3, *[yo, pick up a loop in next dc, yo through 2 loops] 7 times, yo, draw through 8 loops on hook, ch 1 (eye of cluster), ch 2, 1 sc next dc**, ch 3, rep from * across, ending last rep at ** with last sc in turning ch, turn.

Row 4: Ch 1, 1 sc in first sc, *7 dc in the eye of next cluster, 1 sc in next sc, rep from * across, ending with last sc in top of turning ch, turn.

Rep rows 1–4 for pattern.

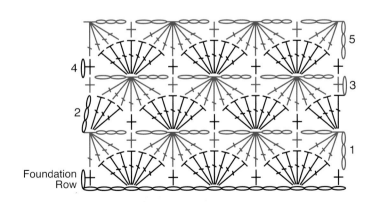

TUNISIAN AND SHELLS

Skill Level: Experienced

Ch a multiple of 8 plus 4.

Row 1 (WS): 4 dc in 4th ch from hook, *skip next 3 ch, 1 sc in next ch, skip next 3 ch, 9 dc in next ch, rep from * across, ending last rep with 5 dc in last ch, turn **(1)**.

Row 2 (RS) (Tunisian stitch): Ch 1 *(draw up a loop in next st and retain loop on hook) 5 times (6 loops on hook), draw up a loop in next st and draw this loop through first loop on hook forming a vertical bar, (yo and through 2 loops) 5 times * (there are 6 vertical bars and 1 loop on hook), **the loop on hook counts as the first st, so skip the first bar, retaining loops on hook, draw up a loop in each of the next 5 bars (6 loops on hook), draw up a loop in next st and through first loop on hook, (yo and through 2 loops) 5 times, rep from ** twice **(2)**, insert hook in 2nd bar, yo and through bar and loop on hook (1 st bound off), bind off 4 more sts, 1 sc in next st, rep from * across, ending bind off 5 sts, sc in top of turning ch, turn **(3)**.

Row 3: Ch 1, skip first st (ch 1 counts as first st), 1 sc in each st across, 1 sc in turning ch, turn **(4)**.

Row 4: Ch 3, yo, draw up a loop in 2nd sc, yo, draw through 2 loops on hook, (yo, draw up a loop in next sc, yo and draw through 2 loops) 2 times, yo, draw through 4 loops on hook, ch 1 tightly for eye of cluster **(5)**, *ch 3, sc in next sc, ch 3, (yo and draw up a loop in next sc, yo and through 2 loops) 9 times, yo, draw through 10 loops on hook, ch 1 tightly to form eye of cluster, rep from * across, end ch 3, sc in next st, ch 3 (yo and draw up a loop in next sc, yo and through 2 loops) 5 times, yo and through 5 loops, ch 1 tightly to form eye of cluster, turn **(6)**.

Row 5: Ch 3, 4 dc in eye of first cluster, skip next ch-3 space, 1 sc in next sc, skip next ch-3 space, *9 dc in eye of next cluster, skip next ch-3 space, 1 sc in next sc, skip next ch-3 space, rep from * across, ending with 5 dc in eye of last cluster, turn **(7)**.

Rep Rows 2–5 for pattern.

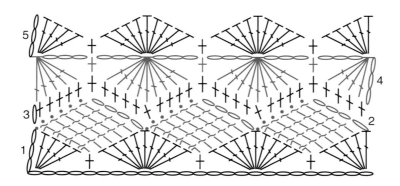

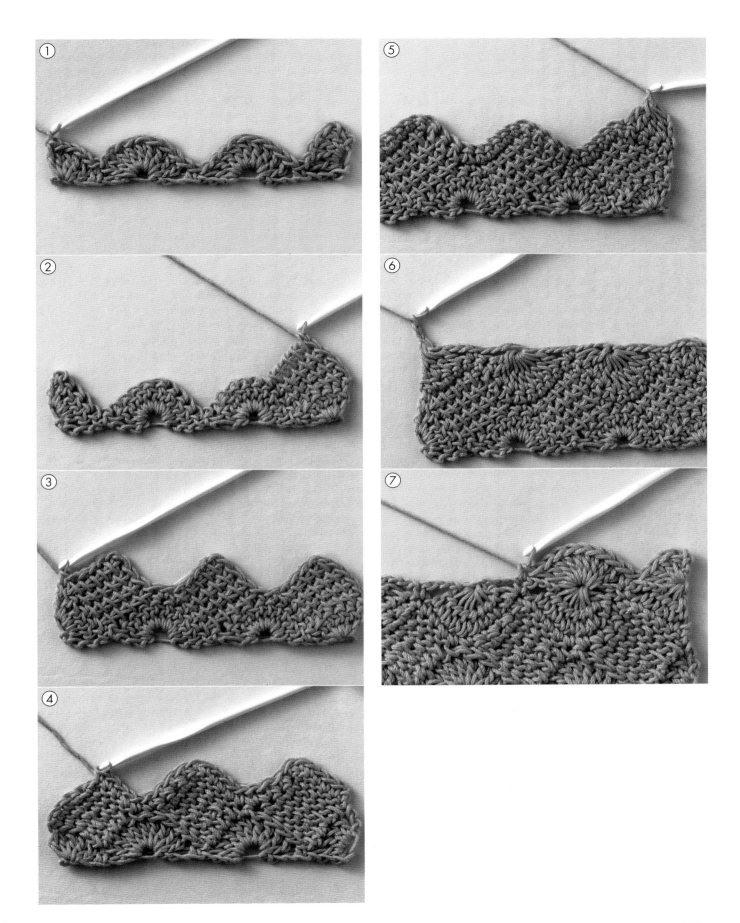

ALPACA BASKET-WEAVE THROW

The stitch called basket weave creates a deep, sophisticated texture. It may look complicated, but it is actually easy to make with front post and back post double crochet stitches. This pumpkin-colored yarn is wonderfully soft.

Alternating groups of back post and front post double crochet stitches form basket-weave effect.

YOU WILL NEED

Yarn

- Bulky-weight bouclé yarn
- Shown: Alpaca Bouclé by Plymouth, 90% alpaca, 10% nylon, 1.75 oz (50 g)/70 yd (64 m): color #2037, 20 balls

Hooks

- 11/L (8 mm)
- 10½/K (6.5 mm)

Stitches used

- Single crochet
- Double crochet
- Front post double crochet
- Back post double crochet
- Block stitch

Gauge

- 8 dc = 4" (10 cm) on 11/L (8 mm) hook

Notions

- Tapestry needle

Finished size

- 40" × 46" (102 × 117 cm)

Throw

Throw is worked in 1 piece.

Foundation Row: Using 11/L (8 mm) hook, ch 80. Beg in fourth ch from hook, work 1 dc in each ch (78 dc, counting st formed by starting in fourth ch) turn.

Rows 1, 3, 6, 8: Ch 3 (counts as a dc), sk first st, * FPdc around post of each of next 4 sts, BPdc around post of each of next 4 sts, rep from * across, end FPdc around post of each of next 4 sts, 1 dc in top of tch, turn.

Rows 2, 4, 5, 7: Ch 3 (counts as a dc), sk first st, * BPdc around post of each of next 4 sts, FPdc around post of each of next 4 sts, rep from * across, end BPdc around post of each of next 4 sts, 1 dc in top of tch, turn.

Rep Rows 1–8 until throw measures 42" (107 cm) from beg, do not fasten off.

Border

See page 72 for directions on Block Stitch.

Row 1: With RS facing you, beg in top right corner, using 10½/K (6.5 mm) hook, pick up and work 108 sc along side to first corner, [1 sc, ch 2, 1 sc] in corner, 76 sc along bottom to next corner, [1 sc, ch 2, 1 sc] in second corner, 108 sc along other side, [1 sc, ch 2, 1 sc] in third corner, 76 sc along top edge, ending with [1 sc, ch 2, 1 sc] to form fourth corner, join with Sl st to first sc.

Row 2: Ch 3, [work 1 dc in each of next 2 sts, block st, * 1 dc in each of next 3 sts, block st, rep from *] to first corner (27 block sts, 2 dc bet each block), 5 dc in corner ch-2 sp, rep bet [ ] to next corner (19 block sts, 2 dc bet each block), 5 dc in corner ch-2 sp, rep patt for rem 2 sides, join with Sl st to beg ch 3.

Rows 3 and 4: Ch 1, * work 1 sc in each st, 3 sc in center corner st, rep from * around, join with Sl st to beg ch 1, fasten off.

Finishing

Weave in ends using tapestry needle. Do not block.

Geometric border of block stitches and double crochet stitches

Unusual Stitches

I call this group "Unusual Stitches" because they do not fit into any of the other categories. Some of them are heavily textured; others are not. Most of them employ an unusual placement of hook or yarn. Some take practice to master. Once you learn these stitches, you will love the fabrics you've created and will be able to turn out some great projects.

LINKED HALF DOUBLE CROCHET

Skill Level: Intermediate

Ch any number of stitches.

Row 1: 1 sc in 2nd ch from hook, 1 sc in each ch across row, turn.

Row 2: Ch 2 (counts as first hdc), pick up a loop in 2nd ch from hook, leave on hook, pick up a loop in next sc (3 loops on hook), yo, draw through all 3 loops, *pick up a loop in second bar on side of hdc just completed, pick up a loop in next sc (3 loops on hook), yo, draw through all 3 loops, rep from * across, ending with last linked hdc in top of turning ch, turn.

Rep Row 2 for pattern.

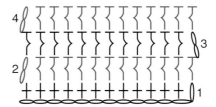

LINKED DOUBLE CROCHET

Skill Level: Intermediate

Ch any number of stitches.

Row 1: 1 sc in 2nd ch from hook, 1 sc in each ch across row, turn.

Row 2: Ch 2 (counts as first dc), pick up a loop in 2nd ch from hook, leave on hook, pick up a loop in next sc (3 loops on hook), [yo, draw through 2 loops] twice, *pick up a loop in 2nd bar on side of dc just completed, pick up a loop in next sc (3 loops on hook), [yo, draw through 2 loops] twice, rep from * across, ending with last linked dc in top of turning ch, turn.

Rep Row 2 for pattern.

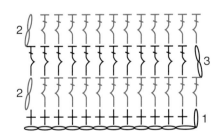

LINKED TRIPLE CROCHET

Skill Level: Intermediate

Ch any number of stitches.

Row 1: 1 sc in 2nd ch from hook, 1 sc in each ch across row, turn.

Row 2: Ch 3 (counts as first tr), pick up a loop in second ch from hook, leave on hook, pick up a loop in next ch, leave on hook, pick up a loop in next sc (4 loops on hook), [yo, draw through 2 loops] 3 times, *pick up a loop in 2nd bar on side of tr just completed, pick up a loop in 3rd bar, pick up a loop in next sc (4 loops on hook), [yo, draw through 2 loops] 3 times, rep from * across, ending with last linked tr in top of turning ch, turn.

Rep Row 2 for pattern

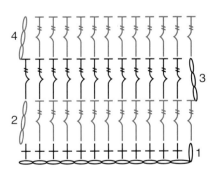

SINGLE CROCHET THERMAL STITCH

Skill Level: Experienced

Ch an even number of sts.

Row 1: Working in back loops only, 1 sc in 2nd ch from hook, 1 sc in each ch across row, turn.

Row 2: Ch 1 (counts as sc), skip first st, *insert hook into skipped loop of beginning ch and through front loop of next sc, pick up a long loop, yo, draw through both loops to complete a sc, rep from * across, turn.

Row 3: Ch 1 (counts as sc), skip first st, *insert hook into skipped loop of previous row and through front loop of next sc, pick up a long loop, yo, and through both loops to complete a sc, rep from * across, 1 sc in top of turning ch, turn.

Rep Row 3 for pattern.

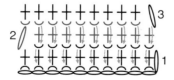

DOUBLE CROCHET THERMAL STITCH

Skill Level: Experienced

Ch an even number of sts.

Row 1: Working in back loops only, 1 dc in 4th ch from hook, 1 dc in each ch across row, turn.

Row 2: Ch 3, *yo, insert hook into skipped loop of beginning ch, and through front loop of next dc, pick up a long loop, [yo, draw through 2 loops] twice to complete a dc, rep from * across, 1 dc in top of turning ch, turn.

Row 3: Ch 3 (counts as dc), skip first st, *yo, insert hook into skipped loop of previous row, and through front loop of next dc, pick up a long loop, [yo, draw through 2 loops] twice to complete a dc, rep from * across, 1 dc in top of turning ch, turn.

Rep Row 3 for pattern.

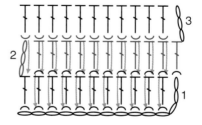

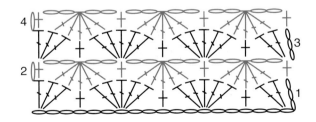

PADDED CLUSTERS

Skill Level: Intermediate

Front Post Double Crochet (FPdc): Yo hook, pick up a loop from front, inserting hook from right to left under designated stitch, [yo, draw through 2 loops] twice. Always skip the sc behind the FPdc just made.

Ch a multiple of 4 plus 1.

Foundation Row: 1 dc in 4th ch from hook, 1 dc in each ch across row, turn.

Row 1: Ch 3 (counts as first dc now and throughout), skip first st, 1 dc in next st, *skip next st, 1 sc in next st, skip next st**, 3 dc in next st, rep from * across, ending last rep at **, 1 dc in next st, 1 dc in top of turning ch, turn.

Row 2: Ch 3, skip first st, 1 dc in next st, *3 FPdc around the post of next sc**, skip next st, 1 sc in next dc, skip next st, rep from * across, ending last rep at **, 1 dc in next st, 1 dc in top of turning ch, turn.

Row 3: Ch 3, skip first st, 1 dc in next st, *skip next st, 1 sc in next dc, skip next st**, 3 FPdc around the post of next sc, rep from * across, ending last rep at **, 1 dc in next st, 1 dc in top of turning ch, turn.

Rep Rows 2 and 3 for pattern.

INTERLACED SHELLS

Skill Level: Intermediate

Ch a multiple of 6 plus 4.

Row 1: 2 dc in 4th ch from hook, *skip 2 ch, 1 sc next ch, skip 2 ch, 5 dc in next ch, rep from * across, ending with 3 dc in last ch, turn.

Row 2: Ch 1, sc in first dc, *ch 2, [yo, pick up loop in next st, yo through 2 loops hook] 5 times, yo, draw through 6 loops on hook, ch 2, 1 sc in next dc, rep from * across, ending with last sc in top of turning ch, turn.

Row 3: Ch 3 (counts as first dc), 2 dc in the first sc, *1 sc in next cluster, 5 dc in next sc, rep from * across, ending with 3 dc in top of turning ch, turn.

Rep Rows 2 and 3 for pattern.

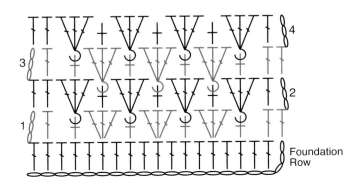

CROSSED PUFFS

Skill Level: Experienced

Long Triple Crochet (Long tr): Yo twice, pick up a half-inch (1.3 cm) long loop in designated stitch, (yo, draw through 2 loops on hook) 3 times.

Ch a multiple of 6 plus 3.

Foundation Row: 1 sc in second ch from hook, 1 sc in each ch across row, turn.

Row 1: Ch 4 (counts as first tr now and throughout), skip first sc, *skip next 3 sc, 1 tr in each of next 3 sc, working over last 2 tr made, 1 Long tr in each of last 3 skipped sc (crossed puff made), rep from * across, 1 tr in last sc, turn.

Row 2: Ch 4, skip first st, *skip next 3 tr of next crossed puff, 1 tr in each of next 3 tr, working over last 3 tr, 1 long tr in each of last 3 skipped tr, rep from * across, 1 tr in top of turning ch, turn.

Rep Row 2 for pattern.

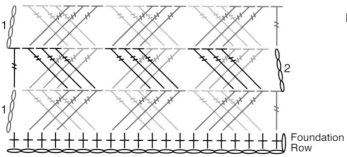

REVERSIBLE V STITCH

Skill Level: Intermediate

V-stitch (V-st): [1 dc, ch 1, 1 dc] in same st.

Front Post Double Crochet (FPdc): Yo hook, pick up a loop from front, inserting hook from right to left under designated stitch, [yo, draw through 2 loops] twice.

Note: Always skip the sc behind the FPdc just made.

Ch a multiple of 4 plus 3.

Foundation Row: V-st in 5th ch from hook, *skip next ch, 1 sc in next ch**, skip next ch, V-st in next ch, rep, from * across, ending last rep at **, turn.

Row 1: Ch 2 (counts as first hdc now and throughout), *1 sc in ch-1 space of next V-st**, [FPdc, ch 1, FPdc] around the post of next sc, rep from * across, ending last rep at **, 1 hdc in top of turning ch, turn.

Row 2: Ch 2, *[FPdc, ch 1, FPdc] around the post of next sc**, 1 sc in ch-1 space of next V-st, rep from * across, ending last rep at **, 1 hdc in top of turning ch, turn.

Rep Rows 1 and 2 for pattern.

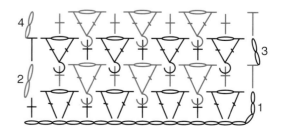

BOW TIES

Skill Level: Easy

Bow Ties are made by creating chains of 7 stitches on 3 rows, then gathering the center of the chains with 1 single crochet over all 3 chains on the 4th row.

Ch a multiple of 13 plus 1.

Foundation Row: 1 sc in 2nd ch from hook, 1 sc in each ch, turn.

Row 1: Ch 1 (counts as first sc now and throughout), skip first st, 1 sc in each of the next 2 sts, *ch 7, skip next 7 sc, 1 sc in each of the next 6 sc, rep from * across, ending last rep with 1 sc in each of last 3 sc, turn.

Row 2: Ch 1, skip first sc, 1 sc in each of next 2 sc, *ch 7, skip next ch-7 loop, 1 sc in each of the next 6 sc, rep from * across, ending last rep with 1 sc in each of last 2 sc, 1 sc in top of turning ch, turn.

Row 3: Rep Row 2.

Row 4: Ch 1, skip first sc, 1 sc in each of next 2 sc, *ch 3, 1 sc over all 3 ch-7 loops in previous 3 rows, ch 3 (bow tie made), 1 sc in each of the next 6 sc, rep from * across, end last rep 1 sc in each of the last 2 sc, 1 sc in top of turning ch, turn.

Row 5: Ch 1, skip first st, 1 sc in each of the next 2 sc *ch 7, skip next bow tie, 1 sc in each of the next 6 sc, rep from * across, ending last rep with 1 sc in each of last 2 sc, 1 sc in top of turning ch, turn.

Rep Rows 2–5 for pattern.

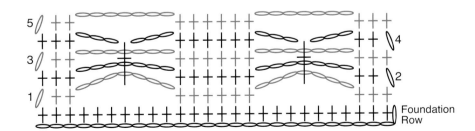

FALLING LEAVES

Skill Level: Experienced

Note: When working stitches in row below, skip the comparable stitch on current row.

Ch a multiple of 4 plus 2.

Foundation Row (RS): 1 sc in 2nd ch from hook, 1 sc in each ch across row, turn.

Row 1: Ch 1 (counts as first sc now and throughout), skip first st, 1 sc in each st across row, turn.

Row 2: Ch 3 (counts as first dc now and throughout), skip first sc, 1 dc in each of next 3 sts, *[yo, insert hook from right to left under next sc 2 rows below, yo, draw up a long loop to the height of current row] twice, yo, draw through 4 loops on hook, yo, draw through last 2 loops (leaf made), skip sc behind st just made, 1 dc in each next 3 sc, rep from * across, 1 dc in top of turning ch, turn.

Row 3: Ch 1, skip first st, 1 sc in each st across, 1 sc in top of turning ch, turn.

Row 4: Ch 3, skip first sc, 1 dc next st, *[yo, insert hook from right to left under next dc 2 rows below, yo, draw up a long loop to the height of current row] twice, yo, draw through 4 loops on hook, yo, draw through last 2 loops (leaf made), skip sc behind st just made**, 1 dc in each next 3 sc, rep from * across, ending last rep at **, 1 dc in next dc, 1 dc in top of turning ch, turn.

Row 5: Rep Row 3.

Row 6: Ch 3, skip first sc, 1 dc in each of next 3 sc, *[yo, insert hook from right to left under next dc 2 rows below, yo, draw up a long loop to the height of current row] twice, yo, draw through 4 loops on hook, yo, draw through last 2 loops (leaf made), skip sc behind st just made, 1 dc in each next 3 sc, rep from * across, 1 dc in top of turning ch, turn.

Rep Rows 3–6 for pattern.

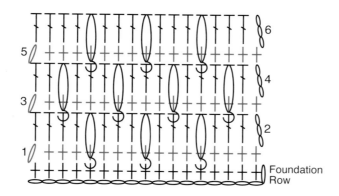

LIMPET STITCH

Skill Level: Experienced

Limpet Stitch: [Wrap yarn clockwise around left index finger, pick up a loop from right to left under back strand] 8 times **(1)**, *yo, and holding the last stitch on hook, gently draw yarn through all 9 loops on hook, sc in next st to complete the limpet* **(2)**.

Notes:

1. The Limpet Stitch is worked from the wrong side to present on right side.

2. When adding new loops on hook, work over the thumb rest to keep stitches from becoming too tight.

Ch a multiple of 4.

Foundation Row: 1 sc in 2nd ch from hook, 1 sc in each ch across row, turn.

Row 1 (WS): Ch 1, (counts as a sc now and throughout), skip first sc, 1 sc in each of next 2 sc, *limpet st in next sc, 1 sc in each of next 3 sc, rep from * across, turn.

Row 2: Ch 1 (counts as first sc now and throughout), skip first sc, 1 sc in each sc and limpet stitch across, 1 sc in top of turning ch, turn.

Row 3: Ch 1, skip first sc, 1 sc in each of next 4 sc, *limpet st in next sc, 1 sc in each of next 3 sc, rep from * across to within last 2 sts, 1 sc in next sc, 1 sc in top of turning ch, turn.

Row 4: Rep Row 2.

Rep Rows 1–4 for pattern.

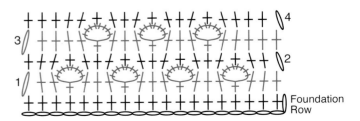

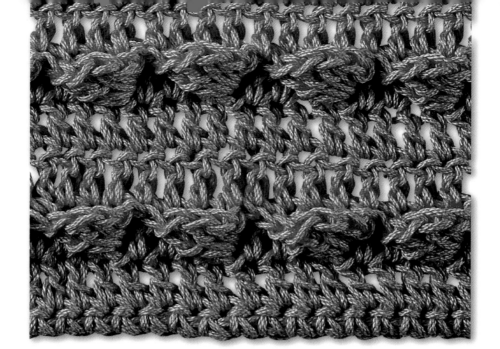

POCKET STITCH

Skill Level: Experienced

Ch a multiple of 4 plus 2.

Foundation Row (WS): 1 sc in 2nd ch from hook, 1 sc in each ch across row, turn.

Row 1: Ch 3 (counts as first dc now and throughout), skip first sc, 1 dc in each sc across row, turn.

Row 2: Ch 3, skip first dc, 1 dc in each dc across row, 1 dc in top of turning ch, turn.

Row 3: Ch 1, skip first dc, Sl st in next dc, [1 sc, 1 hdc, 3 dc] over the post of the dc under last Sl st (pocket st made), skip next 2 dc, 1 Sl st in each of the next 2 dc, *[sc, hdc, 3 dc] around the post of the dc under last Sl st, skip next 2 dc, 1 Sl st in each next 2 dc, rep from * across, ending with 1 Sl st in top of turning ch, turn **(1)**.

Row 4: Ch 3, skip first st, *1 dc in each of next 2 skipped sts below pocket st, 1 dc in each of next 2 Sl sts, rep from * across, ending with 1 dc in last Sl st, 1 dc in top of turning ch, turn.

Row 5: Ch 3 (counts as first dc), skip first dc, 1 dc in each dc across, 1 dc in top of turning ch, turn.

Rep Rows 2–5 for pattern.

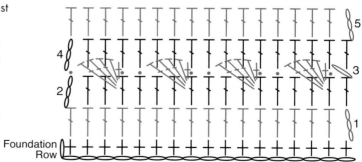

TATTED PICOT STITCH

Skill Level: Experienced

Tatted Picot: [Wrap yarn counterclockwise around left index finger, pick up a loop from left to right under front strand, then wrap yarn clockwise around left index finger, pick up a loop from right to left under back strand] 4 times, yo, gently draw yarn through all 9 loops on hook **(1)**.

Ch a multiple of 4 plus 1.

Foundation Row (RS): 1 dc in 4th ch from hook, 1 dc in each ch across row, turn.

Row 1: Ch 3 (counts as first dc now and throughout), skip first st, 1 dc in each st across row, 1 dc in top of turning ch, turn.

Row 2: Ch 1, 1 sc in first dc, *work 1 Tatted Picot, skip 2 dc**, 1 sc in each of next 3 dc, rep from * across, ending last rep at **, 1 sc in top of turning ch, turn.

Row 3: Ch 3, skip first sc, *1 dc in each of next 2 skipped dc 2 rows below**, 1 dc in each of next 3 sc, rep from * across, ending last rep at **, 1 dc in top of turning ch, turn.

Row 4: Ch 1, 1 sc in first dc, 1 sc in each of next 3 dc, *work 1 Tatted Picot, skip 2 dc, 1 sc in each next 3 dc, rep from * across, ending with last sc in top of turning ch, turn.

Row 5: Ch 3, skip first sc, 1 dc in each of the next 2 sc, *1 dc in each of the next 2 skipped dc 2 rows below, 1 dc in each of next 3 sc, rep from * across to within last st, 1 dc in top of turning ch, turn.

Rep Rows 2–5 for pattern.

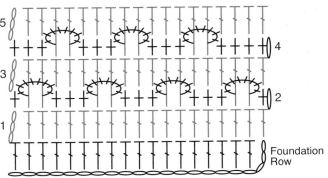

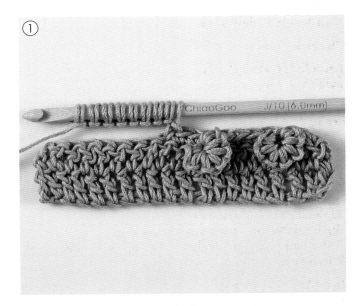

CABLES

Skill Level: Intermediate

Front Post Double Crochet (FPdc): Yo hook, pick up a loop from front, inserting hook from right to left under designated stitch, [yo, draw through 2 loops] twice.

Note: Always skip the sc behind the FPdc just made.

Ch a multiple of 6 plus 3.

Foundation Row (WS): 1 sc in 2nd ch from hook, 1 sc in each ch across row, 1 sc in turning ch, turn.

Row 1: Ch 1 (counts as first sc now and throughout), skip first sc, 1 sc in each st across, 1 sc in top of turning ch, turn.

Rows 2, 4, 6, 8: Ch 1, skip first sc, 1 sc in each sc across, 1 sc in top of turning ch, turn.

Row 3: Ch 1, skip first sc, sc in next 2 sc, *FPdc around the post of next sc 2 rows below, 1 sc next st, FPdc around the post of next sc 2 rows below, sc in next 3 sts, rep from * across, ending with last sc in top of turning ch, turn.

Row 5: Ch 1, skip first st, sc in next 2 sc, *FPdc around the post of next FPdc 2 rows below, sc in next st, FPdc around the post of next FPdc 2 rows below, sc in next 3 sc, rep from * across, ending with last sc in top of turning ch, turn.

Row 7 (cable cross row): Ch 1, skip first sc, sc in next 2 sc, *skip next 2 sts, work a FPdc around the post of next FPdc 2 rows below (1), sc in next sc (2), FPdc around the post of last skipped FPdc (3), sc in next 3 sc, rep from * across, ending with last sc in top of turning ch, turn.

Row 9: Ch 1, skip first sc, sc in next 2 sc, *FPdc around the post of next FPdc 2 rows below, sc next sc, FPdc around the post of next FPdc, sc in next 3 sc, rep from * across, ending with last sc in top of turning ch, turn.

Rep Rows 4–9 for pattern.

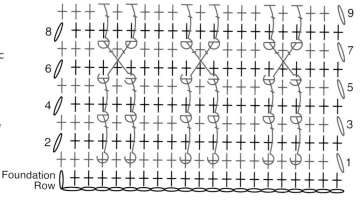

DOUBLE CABLE

Skill Level: Experienced

Front Post Double Crochet (FPdc): Yo hook, pick up a loop from front, inserting hook from right to left under designated stitch, [yo, draw through 2 loops] 2 times.

Front Post Triple Crochet (FPtr): Yo hook twice, pick up a loop from front, inserting hook from right to left under designated stitch, [yo, draw through 2 loops] 3 times.

Note: Always skip the sc behind the post st just made.

Ch a multiple of 9 plus 2.

Foundation Row (RS): 1 sc in 2nd ch from hook, 1 sc in each ch across row, turn.

Rows 1, 3, 5, 7, and 9: Ch 1 (counts as sc now and throughout), skip first sc, 1 sc in each st across row, 1 sc in turn ch, turn.

Row 2: Ch 1, skip first sc, 1 sc in each of next 2 sc, *1 FPdc around the post of each of next 2 sc 2 rows below, 1 sc in next sc, 1 FPdc around the post of each of next 2 sc 2 rows below**, 1 sc in each of the next 4 sc, rep from * across, ending last rep at **, 1 sc in each of the next 2 sc, 1 sc in top of turning ch, turn.

Rows 4 and 6: Ch 1, skip first sc, 1 sc in each of next 2 sc, *1 FPdc around the post of each of next 2 FPdc 2 rows below, 1 sc in next sc, 1 FPdc around the post of each of next 2 FPdc 2 rows below**, 1 sc in each of the next 4 sc, rep from * across, ending last rep at **, 1 sc in each of the next 2 sc, 1 sc in top of turning ch, turn.

Row 8 (cable cross row): Ch 1, skip first sc, 1 sc in each of next 2 sc, *skip next 3 sts, 1 FPtr around the post of each of next 2 FPdc 2 rows below, sc in the 3rd skipped st in current row, bring hook to front of work, and starting in the post toward outside of cable, work 1 FPtr over each of the 2 skipped FPdc**, 1 sc in each of the next 4 sc, rep from * across, ending last rep at **, 1 sc in each of the next 2 sc, 1 sc in top of turning ch, turn.

Row 10: Ch 1, skip first sc, 1 sc in each of next 2 sc, *1 FPdc around the post of each of next 2 FPtr 2 rows below, 1 sc in next sc, 1 FPdc around the post of each of next 2 FPtr 2 rows below**, 1 sc in each of the next 4 sc, rep from * across, ending last rep at **, 1 sc in each of the next 2 sc, 1 sc in top of turning ch, turn.

Row 11: Rep Row 1.

Rep Rows 4–11 for pattern.

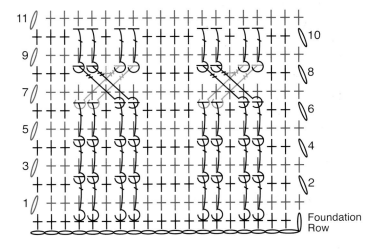

BUTTERCUPS

Skill Level: Experienced

Use 2 contrasting colors A and B.

Notes:

1. It is necessary on some rows to cut yarn and rejoin; pay attention to color changes.

2. To catch loops, you will be working from the wrong side; place hook through the designated stitch and through designated loop and work off as one stitch.

With A, ch a multiple of 10.

Foundation Row: With A, 1 sc in 2nd ch from hook, 1 sc in each ch across row, turn.

Row 1: Ch 1 (counts as first sc now and throughout), skip first sc, 1 sc in each sc across row, turn.

Row 2: Ch 1, skip first sc, 1 sc in each sc across row, 1 sc in top of turning ch, turn. End A. Pull B through last loop.

Row 3 (WS, leaf row): With B, ch 1, skip first sc, 1 sc in each of next 8 sc, *[1 sc, ch 8] 3 times in next sc, 1 sc in same sc (leaf cluster made), 1 sc in each of next 9 sc, rep from * across, ending with last sc in top of turning ch. End B. Join A through last loop.

Row 4: With A, ch 1, skip first sc, 1 sc in each of next 8 sc, *holding ch-7 loops to front, ch 1, skip 3 loops, skip next sc of leaf cluster, 1 sc in each of next 9 sc, rep from * ending with last sc in top of turning ch, turn.

Row 5: Ch 1, skip first sc, 1 sc in each of the next 5 sc, *sc in the next sc and in next ch-7 loop, catching it in place, 1 sc in each of the next 2 sc, 1 sc in next ch-1 space, 1 sc in each of the next 2 sc, sc in the next sc and in next ch-7 loop, catching it in place, 1 sc in each of the next 3 sc, rep from * across to within last 3 sts, 1 sc in each of next 2 sc, 1 sc in top of turning ch, turn.

Row 6: Ch 1, skip first sc, sc in each st across, 1 sc in top of turning ch, turn.

Row 7 (WS, flower row): Ch 1, skip first sc, 1 sc in each of the next 8 sc, *6 dc in the next st and in center ch-7 loop, catching it in place (buttercup made) **(1)**, 1 sc in each of the next 9 sc, rep from * across, ending with last sc in top of turning ch, turn.

Row 8: Ch 1, skip first sc, 1 sc in each of the next 8 sc, *ch 1, skip next 6 dc, 1 sc in each of the next 9 sc, rep from * across, ending with last sc in top of turning ch. End A. Join B through last loop.

Row 9 (WS, leaf row): With B, ch 1, skip first sc, 1 sc in each of the next 3 sc, *[1 sc, ch 8] 3 times in next sc, 1 sc in same sc (leaf cluster made), 1 sc in each of next 9, rep from * across, ending with 1 sc in each last 3 sc, 1 sc in top of turning ch. End B. Join A through last loop.

Row 10: Ch 1, skip first sc, 1 sc in each of the next 3 sc, *holding ch-7 loops to front of work, ch 1, skip 3 loops, skip next sc of leaf cluster, 1 sc in each of the next 9 sc, rep from * across, ending with 1 sc in each of the last 3 sc, 1 sc in top of turning ch, turn.

Row 11: Ch 1 (do not skip a stitch, do not count this ch 1 as first st), 1 sc in first sc, *1 sc in the next st and in next ch-7 loop, catching it in place, 1 sc in each of the next 2 sc, 1 sc in next ch-1 space, 1 sc in each of next 2 sc, 1 sc in next st and in next ch-7 loop, catching it in place, 1 sc in each of the next 3 sc, rep from * across, ending with 1 sc in top of turning ch, turn.

Row 12: Ch 1, skip first sc, 1 sc in each sc across row, turn.

Row 13: Ch 1, skip first sc, 1 sc in each of the next 3 sc, *6 dc in next sc and in center ch-7 loop, catching it in place (buttercup made), 1 sc in each of the next 9 sc, rep from * across, ending last rep with 1 sc in each of last 3 sc, 1 sc in top of turning ch, turn.

Row 14: Ch 1, skip first sc, 1 sc in each of the next 3 sc, *ch 1, skip next 6 dc, 1 sc in each of next 9 sc, rep from * across, ending last rep with 1 sc in each of next 3 sc, 1 sc in top of turning ch. End A. Join B through last loop.

Row 15 (WS, leaf row): Ch 1, skip first sc, 1 sc in each of next 3 sc, 1 sc in next ch-1 space, 1 sc in each next 4 sc, *[1 sc, ch 8] 3 times in next sc, 1 sc in same sc (leaf cluster made), 1 sc in each of next 4 sc, 1 sc in next ch-1 space, 1 sc in next 4 sc, rep from * across, ending with last sc in top of turning ch. End B. Join A through last loop.

Rep Rows 4–15 for pattern.

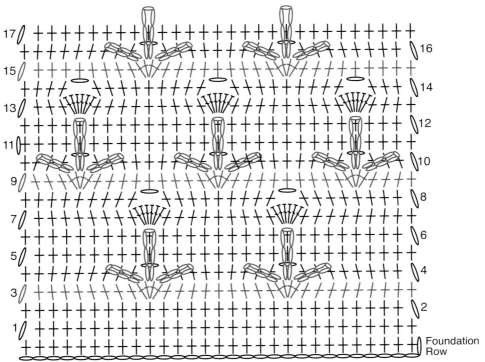

DIAMOND CROSS TRELLIS

Skill Level: Experienced

Front Post Triple Crochet (FPtr): Yo twice, working in front, place hook from right to left under designated post/posts, yo hook pull through a loop, [yo, draw through 2 loops] 3 times.

Notes:

1. When beginning the pattern, on the foundation row only, the FPtr will be made around the dc posts. On all subsequent rows, the FPtr will be made around the posts of FPtr of previous rows. At the ends of some rows you will go under only one post; in the center of the rows, you will go under 2 posts at the same time.

2. Sometimes the beginning chain will count as the first stitch and other times it will not.

Ch a multiple of 6 plus 4.

Foundation Row: 1 dc in 4th ch from hook, 1 dc in each ch across row, turn.

Row 1: Ch 1 (counts as first sc now and throughout unless otherwise stated), skip first dc, 1 sc in each dc across, 1 sc in top of turning ch, turn.

Row 2: Ch 1, skip first sc, 1 sc in each sc across, 1 sc in top of turning ch, turn.

Row 3: Rep Row 2.

Row 4 (cross row set up): Ch 1, skip first sc, 1 sc in each of the next 2 sc, 1 FPtr around the post of the second dc on the Foundation Row, *skip next 4 dc in Foundation Row, 1 FPtr around the post of next dc on the Foundation Row, skip 2 sc behind 2 FPtr just made**, 1 sc in each of the next 4 sc in current row, 1 FPtr around the post of next dc (to the left of last dc worked) in the Foundation Row, rep from * across, ending last rep at **, 1 sc in each of the next 2 sc, 1 sc in top of turning ch, turn.

Row 5: Ch 1, skip first sc, 1 sc in each of next 2 sc, *1 sc in each of next 2 skipped sts 2 rows below, 1 sc in each of next 4 sc, rep from * across, ending last rep 1 sc in each of last 2 sc, 1 sc in top of turning ch, turn.

Rows 6 and 7: Rep Row 2.

Row 8 (first cross row): Ch 1 (does not count as a st), 1 sc in first st, 1 FPtr around the posts of next 2 FPtr 4 rows below to the left of hook, skip 1 sc behind FPtr just made, 1 sc in each of next 4 sc, *1 FPtr around the posts of 2 FPtr to the right of hook already holding a FPtr**, 1 FPtr around the post of next 2 FPtr 4 rows below to the left, skip 2 sc behind 2 FPtr just made, 1 sc in each of the next 4 sc, rep from * across, ending last rep at **, skip 1 sc behind FPtr just made, 1 sc in top of turning ch, turn.

Row 9: Ch 1 (does not count as a st), 1 sc in the first sc, 1 sc in next skipped st 2 rows below, *1 sc in each of next 4 sc**, 1 sc in each of next 2 skipped sts 2 rows below, rep from * across, ending last rep at **, 1 sc in next skipped st 2 rows below, 1 sc in top of turning ch, turn.

Rows 10 and 11: Rep Row 2.

Row 12 (second cross row): Ch 1 (counts as sc), skip first sc, 1 sc in each of next 2 sc, 1 FPtr around the post of 1 FPtr 4 rows below to right, *1 FPtr around the post of next 2 FPtr 4 rows below to the left, skip 2 sc behind 2 FPtr just made, 1 sc in each of next 4 sc, 1 FPtr around the post of 2 FPtr to the right already holding a FPtr, rep from * across, 1 FPtr around the post of next FPtr to left, skip 2 sc behind 2 FPtr just made, 1 sc in each of last 2 sc, 1 sc in top of turning ch, turn.

Rep Rows 5–12 for pattern.

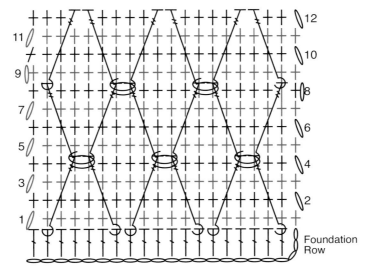

REVERSIBLE SHELLS

Skill Level: Experienced

Notes:

1. This unusual pattern uses two contrasting colors in an interesting way. Attention must be paid to beginning and end of rows and also to color changes.

2. When one color is temporarily dropped, always pick up a long loop so as not to lose the stitch.

With A, ch a multiple of 4 plus 3.

Foundation Row: With A, work 1 dc in 5th ch from hook, 3 dc in next ch, 1 dc in next ch (shell made), *skip next 2 ch, dc in next ch, 3 dc in next ch, dc in next ch, rep from * across to last ch, leave last ch unworked, drop loop from hook (pulling up a long loop so as not to lose it; loop will be picked up later). DO NOT TURN.

Row 1: Join B at right side of work (beginning of Foundation Row) with 1 sc in the 4th ch of the beg ch-4, working in front of the last row, *ch 6, skip next shell, 1 sc in next ch, rep from * across, placing last sc in last ch at end of shell stitch row. (Note: At this point you should have the same number of loops going across as you have shells.)

Row 2: Still using B, ch 2, TURN, Sl st in first dc of last shell st row, being sure to keep dropped loop and tail free from your work, ch 2, *5 dc in center st of next shell and in the ch-6 loop (shell made), rep from * across, ending with 1 sc in top of turning ch, pick up long loop, remove hook, DO NOT TURN.

Row 3: Pick up dropped A loop at end of first shell st row, *ch 6, working in front of last shell st row, skip A shell and work sc in space between 2 shells of A row, rep from * across, placing last sc in top of turning ch at end of row.

Row 4: Still using A, ch 2, TURN, Sl st in first dc of last shell stitch row, ch 2, *5 dc in center st of next shell and in ch-6 loop, rep from * across, ending with 1 sc in top of turning ch, pick up long loop, remove hook, DO NOT TURN.

Row 5: Pick up dropped B loop at end of shell st row before last row worked, working in front of last row, *ch 6, skip B shell and work sc in space between 2 shells of B row, rep from * across, placing last sc in top of turning ch at end of row.

Rep Row 2–5 for pattern ending with Row 4 of pattern (A shell row).

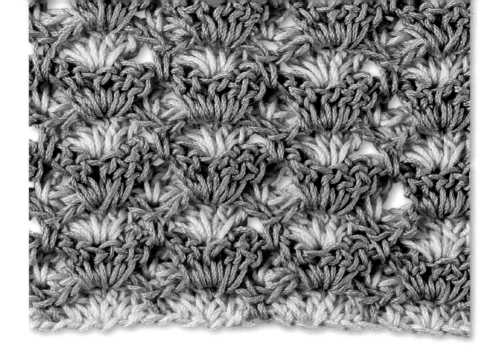

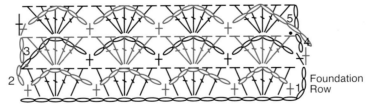

FOUR-COLOR SPIRAL

Skill Level: Experienced

Notes:

1. The Four-Color Spiral is worked in the round. Increase 12 stitches every round, always having one stitch more between increases for each round, and change colors as you work.

2. When dropping one color to pick up the next, always draw up a long loop so that you do not lose the stitch.

With A, ch 2.

Rnd 1: [1 sc, 1 hdc, 1 dc] in 2nd ch from hook, drop A, *draw up a loop with B, working into same ch, work [1 sc, 1 hdc, 1 dc], drop B*, rep from * to * with C, then rep from * to * with D, you now have a circle with 4 segments, each in a different col (3 sts each col, 12 sts in all); **(1)**. From now on you will be working entirely in dc. Place a long, different-colored thread in your work after last st to use as a marker for beginning of rnds. This marker indicates beginning of rnd. It does not denote change of color.

Rnd 2 (first inc rnd): Continuing with D, work 2 dc into each st of A, drop D, pick up the loop of A and work 2 dc into each st of next 3 B sts, drop A, pick up B, work 2 dc into each st in next 3 C sts, drop B, pick up C, work 2 dc into each of the first 3 sts of D. You have now completed one complete inc rnd; you have 4 segments, one in each color—6 dc in each color; 24 dc. You should be at the marker, but you will not be at the end of the D segment. The rnds begin and end at the marker. THE COLORS DO NOT CHANGE AT THE MARKER.

Rnd 3 (second inc rnd): Continuing with C, working into the remaining sts of D, work *[1 dc in next st, 2 dc in next st] 3 times* **(2)**, drop C, pick up D, rep from * to * on sts of A, drop D, pick up A, rep from * to * on sts of B, drop A, pick up B, rep from * to * on first 6 sts of C, you now have completed 3 rnds, you are at marker which is end of rnd, not at the end of a color—9 dc in each color; 36 dc.

Rnd 4 (third inc rnd): Following pattern as established, inc every 3rd st of each color segment—12 dc in each color; 48 dc.

Rnd 5 (fourth inc rnd): Following pattern as established, inc every 4th st of each color segment—15 dc in each color; 60 dc.

Rnd 6 (fifth inc rnd): Following pattern as established, inc every 5th st of each color segment—18 dc in each color; 72 dc.

Finishing: At end of each color segment in Rnd 6, work 1 hdc in next dc, 1 sc in next dc, 1 Sl st in next dc, end off.

①

②

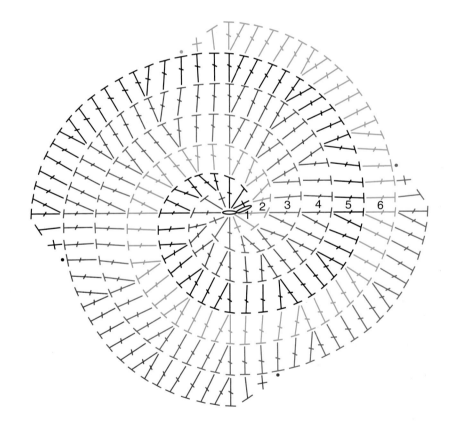

1 2 3 4 5 6

REVERSIBLE SHELLS BLANKET

The reversible shells stitch pattern makes a highly textured and warm fabric that's perfectly suited for making blankets. Choose two shades of the same color for subtle contrast, or select colors that complement each other. Either way, the result will be stunning.

YOU WILL NEED

Yarn

- Medium-weight yarn
- Shown: Patons Décor, 75 % acrylic, 25% wool, 3.5 oz (100 g)/208 yd (190 m), 87206 New Teal (A): 4 skeins; 87205 Soft New Teal (B): 3 skeins

Hook

- 8/H (5 mm)

Stitches used

- Chain
- Single crochet
- Double crochet

Gauge

- 2½ shells = 4" (10 cm)

Notions

- Tapestry needle

Finished size

- 34" x 39" (86.5 x 99 cm)

Blanket

With A, ch 98 loosely (multiple of 5 plus 3).

Foundation Row: With A, work 1 dc in 5th ch from hook, 3 dc in next ch, 1 dc in next ch (shell made), *skip next 2 ch, dc in next ch, 3 dc in next ch, dc in next ch, rep from * across to last ch, leave last ch unworked, drop loop from hook (pulling up a long loop so as not to lose it, loop will be picked up later). Do not turn.

Row 1: Join B at right side of work (beginning of Foundation Row) with 1 sc in the 4th ch of the beg ch-4, working in front of the last row, *ch 6, skip next shell, 1 sc in next ch, rep from * across, placing last sc in last ch at end of shell stitch row. (Note: At this point you should have the same number of loops going across as you have shells.)

Row 2: Still using B, ch 2, turn, Sl st in first dc of last shell st row, being sure to keep dropped loop and tail free from your work, ch 2, *5 dc in center st of next shell and in the ch-6 loop (shell made), rep from * across, ending with 1 sc in top of turning ch, pick up long loop, remove hook, do not turn.

Row 3: Pick up dropped A loop at end of first shell st row, *ch 6, working in front of last shell st row, skip A shell and work sc in space between 2 shells of A row, rep from * across, placing last sc in top of turning ch at end of row.

Row 4: Still using A, ch 2, turn, Sl st in first dc of last shell stitch row, ch 2, *5 dc in center st of next shell and in ch-6 loop, rep from * across, ending with 1 sc in top of turning ch, pick up long loop, remove hook, do not turn.

Row 5: Pick up dropped B loop at end of shell st row before last row worked, working in front of last row, *ch 6, skip B shell and work sc in space between 2 shells of B row, rep from * across, placing last sc in top of turning ch at end of row.

Rep Row 2–5 for pattern until blanket measures 35" (89 cm) from beg, ending with Row 4 of pattern (A shell row). End off.

Border

Row 1: With right side facing, join A in 2nd dc in last row of blanket, ch 4 (counts as dc, ch 1), skip next st, ** *1 dc in next st, ch 1, skip next st, rep from * across to corner, (1 dc, ch 2, 1 dc) in corner st, working across sides, [1 dc, ch 1] in each row-end st across to next corner, [1 dc, ch 2, 1 dc] in next corner st, ch 1, rep from ** around, join with Sl st in 3rd ch of beg ch-4.

Rows 2 and 3: Ch 4 (counts as dc, ch 1), *[1 dc, ch 1] in each dc to next corner, [1 dc, ch 3, 1 dc] in corner space, ch 1, rep from * around, join with Sl st to 3rd ch of beg ch-4.

Row 4 (shell row): Skip next 2 ch-1 spaces, *7 dc in next dc, skip next 2 ch-1 spaces, sc in next dc, skip next 2 ch-1 spaces, rep from * around, end off.

Motifs

The dictionary defines motif as a recurring feature or theme. For many years, crocheters have been stitching small motifs over and over again until they have enough to sew together to make afghans, bedspreads, shawls, tablecloths, etc. Thousands of stitch combinations can be used to make motifs. It is believed that the Classic American Granny motif, one of the most used and beloved motifs, was devised by early pioneers to use every yarn scrap to make warm blankets for their families. There have been hundreds of variations on this motif. In this section, I have included traditional motifs along with some freeform scrumbles (page 254) for you to try.

DOGWOOD MOTIF

Skill Level: Intermediate

4-dc cluster: [yo, pick up a loop in next st] 4 times, yo, draw through all 5 loops on hook.

5-dc cluster: [yo, pick up a loop in next st] 5 times, yo, draw through all 6 loops on hook.

Foundation: Ch 5, join with a Sl st to form a ring.

Rnd 1: Ch 3 (counts as first dc now and throughout), 4 dc in ring, ch 4, *5 dc in ring, ch 4, rep from * twice, join with Sl st to top of beg ch-3.

Rnd 2: Ch 3, 4-dc cluster over next 4 dc, *ch 7, 1 sc in the next ch-4 space, ch 7**, 5-dc cluster over next 5 dc, rep from * twice, rep from * to ** once, join with a Sl st to top of first cluster.

Rnd 3: Ch 1, *9 sc in next ch 7 space, rep from * around, join with a Sl st to beg ch-1, end off.

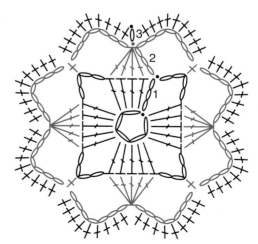

LACY WHEEL

Skill Level: Intermediate

Foundation: Ch 12, join with a Sl st to form a ring.

Rnd 1: Ch 3 (counts as first dc now and throughout), 21 dc in ring (22 dc counting the beg ch-3).

Rnd 2: Ch 3, 1 dc in same st, *ch 3, skip 1 st, 2 dc in next st, rep from * 9 times, ch 3, join with a Sl st to top of beg ch-3 (11 ch-3 loops).

Rnd 3: Ch 3, 1 dc in next dc, *ch 4, skip next ch 3 space, 1 dc in each of next 2 dc, rep from * 9 times, ch 4, join with Sl st to top of beg ch-3.

Rnd 4: Ch 3, 1 dc in next dc, *ch 5, skip the ch-4 space, 1 dc in each of next 2 dc, rep from * 9 times, ch 5, join with a Sl st to top of beg ch-3.

Rnd 5: Ch 8 (counts as sc, ch 7), 1 sc in next dc, *7 sc in next ch 5 space, 1 sc in next dc, ch 7, 1 sc in next dc, rep from * 9 times, 7 sc in next ch-5 space, join with a Sl st in the first ch of the beg ch-8, end off.

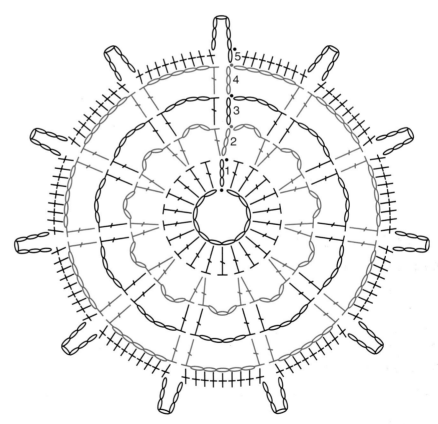

PICOTS

Skill Level: Intermediate

Note: Work stitches in chains, not in spaces.

Foundation: Ch 16, join with a Sl st to form a ring.

Rnd 1: Ch 3 (counts as first dc), 1 dc in each of the next 3 ch, ch 7, *1 dc in each of the next 4 ch, ch 7, rep from * twice, join with a Sl st to top of beg ch-3 (4 ch-7 loops).

Rnd 2: Ch 5 (counts as dc, ch 2), *skip next group of dc, working in the chains of the next ch-7 loop, work [1 dc, ch 1], in each of next 7 ch, ch 1 more, rep from * twice, end with [1 dc, ch 1] in each of the next 6 ch, join with a Sl st to the 3rd ch of beg ch-5.

Rnd 3: Ch 1, * sc in each of next 2 ch, [1 sc next dc, ch 3, 1 sc 3rd ch from hook (picot made) skip next ch-1 space] 6 times, 1 sc in next dc, rep from * 3 times more, join with a Sl st in the beg ch-1, end off.

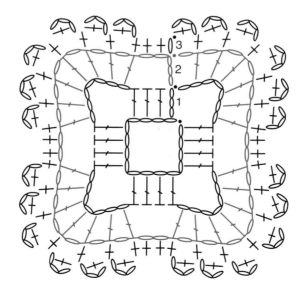

EIGHT-PETAL FLOWER

Skill Level: Intermediate

Foundation: Ch 6, join with a Sl st to form a ring.

Rnd 1: Ch 3 (counts as first dc now and throughout), 15 dc in ring, Sl st in 3rd ch of the beg ch-3 (16 dc counting the beg ch-3).

Rnd 2: Ch 5 (counts as dc, ch 2), 1 dc in first st (V-st made), *ch 1, skip next dc, [1 dc, ch 2, 1 dc] in the next dc, rep from * 6 times more, ch 1, skip next dc, join with a Sl st in 3rd ch of beg ch-5 (8 V-sts made).

Rnd 3: Sl st in first ch-2 space, ch 3, [1 dc, ch 2, 2 dc] in same ch-2 space, *ch 1, skip next ch-1 space, [2 dc, ch 2, 2 dc] in next ch-2 space, rep from * 6 times more, ch 1, skip next ch-1 space, Sl st in 3rd ch of beg ch-3.

Rnd 4: Sl st in the next dc and first ch-2 space, ch 3, work 6 dc in same space as last Sl st, 1 sc in next ch-1 space, [7 dc in next ch-2 space, 1 sc in next ch-1 space] 7 times, Sl st in 3rd ch of beg ch-3, end off.

CLOVER MOTIF

Skill Level: Intermediate

Rnd 1: Ch 10, Sl st in the first ch, [ch 9, Sl st in same ch as last Sl st] twice (3 loops formed).

Rnd 2: Ch 1, *[2 sc, 1 hdc, 11 dc, 1 hdc, 2 sc] in next ch-9 loop, Sl st in next Sl st, rep from * twice more.

Rnd 3: Sl st in first 9 sts of first loop, [ch 16, skip first 8 sts on next loop, Sl st in next dc] twice, ch 16, Sl st in same dc as last Sl st at beg of round.

Rnd 4: Ch 1, work 1 sc in same dc as last Sl st of previous round, work 19 sc in first ch-16 space [1 sc in same dc as next Sl st of previous round, 19 sc in next ch-16 space] twice, join with Sl st to first sc (60 sc).

Rnd 5: Ch 8 (counts as dc, ch 5), skip next 3 sc, [1 dc in next sc, ch 5, skip next 3 sc] 14 times, join with a Sl st in 3rd ch of beg ch-8 (15 ch-5 spaces).

Rnd 6: Sl st in first 3 ch of first space, ch 1, work 4 sc in first space, 7 sc in each of next 14 loops, 3 sc in same loop as first 4 sc, join with Sl st to first sc, end off.

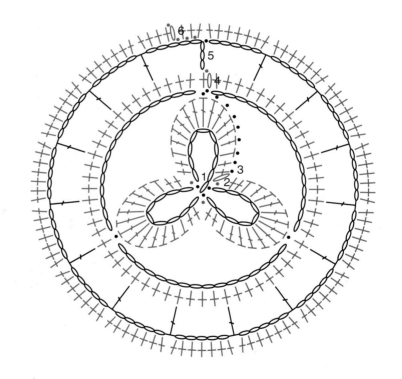

GALA GRANNY

Skill Level: Easy

Ch 6, join with a Sl st to form a ring.

Rnd 1: Ch 3 (counts as first dc), 4 dc in ring, *ch 2, 5 dc in ring, rep from * 4 times, ch 2, join with Sl st to top of beg ch-3.

Rnd 2: Ch 6 (counts as dc, ch 3), *[2 dc, ch 2, 2 dc] in next ch-2 space (shell made) ch 3, rep from * 4 times, [2 dc, ch 2, 1 dc] in last ch-2 space, join with Sl st to 3rd ch of beg ch-6 (6 shells).

Rnd 3: Ch 7 (counts as dc, ch 4), *[3 dc, ch 2, 3 dc] in next ch-2 space, ch 4, rep from * 4 times, [3 dc, ch 2, 2 dc] in last ch-2 space, join with Sl st to 3rd ch of beg ch-7.

Rnd 4: Ch 8 (counts as dc, ch 5), *[3 dc, ch 3, 3 dc] in next ch-2 space, ch 5, rep from * 4 times more, [3 dc, ch 3, 2 dc] in last space, join with Sl st to 3rd ch of beg ch-8.

Rnd 5: Ch 1, sc in same st, *7 sc in next ch-5 loop, 1 sc in each of next 3 dc, [2 sc, ch 2, 2 sc] in next ch-2 space, 1 sc in each of next 3 dc, rep from * around, omitting last sc, join with Sl st to first sc, end off.

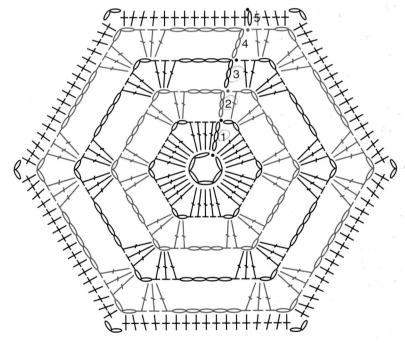

FANCY SHAMROCK

Skill Level: Intermediate

Ch 6, join with a Sl st to form a ring.

Rnd 1: Work 18 sc in ring, join with Sl st to first sc.

Rnd 2: Ch 1 (counts as first sc now and throughout), skip first sc, 1 sc in each sc around, join with Sl st to beg ch-1.

Rnd 3: Ch 1, skip first ch, 1 sc in each of next 5 sc, [ch 10, 1 sc in each of next 6] twice, ch 12, join with Sl st to beg ch-1.

Rnd 4: Ch 1, skip first ch, 1 sc in each of next 4 sc, [22 sc in next ch-10 space, 1 sc in each next 5 sc] twice, 24 sc next ch-12 space, join with Sl st to beg ch-1.

Rnd 5: Ch 1, sc in next 4 sc, *[ch 4, skip 2 sc, Sl st next sc] 7 times, sc in next sc, sc in next 5 sc] twice, rep from * once, [ch 4, skip 2 sc, Sl st next sc] 7 times, ch 4, skip next 3 sc, join with a Sl st to beg ch-1.

Rnd 6: Ch 1, skip next sc, 1 sc in next sc, [5 sc in next ch-4 space] 7 times, skip next 2 sc, Sl st in next sc, ch 18 for stem, 1 sc in 3rd ch from hook, 1 sc in each of next 15 ch, Sl st in next sc on Main Motif, [5 sc in next ch-4 space] 7 times, skip next 2 sc, 1 sc in next sc, skip next 2 sc, [5 sc next ch 4 space] 8 times, join with a Sl st in first sc, end off.

IRISH CLOVER

Skill Level: Easy

Ch 7, join with a Sl st to form a ring.

Rnd 1: Ch 1, 15 sc in ring, join with Sl st to first sc.

Rnd 2: *Ch 4, skip next sc, [1 dc, ch 2, 1 dc] in next sc, ch 4, skip next sc**, Sl st in each of next 2 sc, rep from * around, ending last rep at **, join with Sl st in last beg sc (3 petals).

Rnd 3: *[3 sc, ch 4, 3 sc] in next ch-4 loop, [2 sc, ch 4, 2 sc] in next ch-2 loop, [3 sc, ch 4, 3 sc] in next ch-4 loop, Sl st between the 2 Sl st of Rnd 2, rep from * twice, end with Sl st in base of clover.

Stem: Ch 12, working in back bump of ch sts, 1 Sl st in 2nd ch from hook, 1 Sl st in each ch across, join with a Sl st in same place where stem was started, end off.

EDWARDIAN SPIRAL

Skill Level: Experienced

Note: This motif starts with a round, then is worked in rows; this will be noted in instructions.

Ch 10, join with a Sl st to form a ring.

Rnd 1: Ch 4 (counts as dc, ch 1), [1 dc, ch 1] 11 times in ring, Sl st in 3rd ch of beg ch-4.

Begin working in rows:

Row 2: Ch 13, 1 dc in 4th ch from hook, work 12 dc over the next ch-6 portion of ch, 1 dc in next ch-1 space on Rnd 1, ch 7, turn.

*Row 3: 1 dc in 7th dc of previous row, [ch 1, skip 1 dc, 1 dc in next dc] 3 times, ch 4, turn.

Row 4: [1 dc in next ch-1 space, ch 1] 3 times, 13 dc in next ch-7 loop**, dc in next ch-1 space, ch 7.

Rep from * 9 times, rep from * to ** once, Sl st in 3rd ch of beg ch-13, turn.

Row 5: Sl st across each of first 7 dc of previous row, ch 3, Sl st in base of turning ch at outer edge of Row 1, turn, [ch 1, skip next dc, 1 dc in next dc] 3 times, ch 4, turn, [1 dc in next ch-1 space, ch 1] 3 times, Sl st in top of turning ch at outer edge of Row 1, end off.

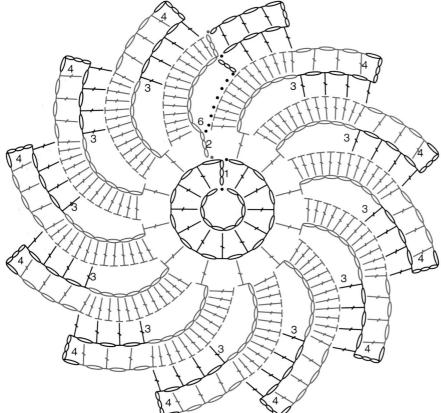

IRISH CROCHET

Skill Level: Intermediate

Picot: Ch 3, 1 sc in 3rd ch from hook.

Ch 8, join with a Sl st to form a ring.

Rnd 1: Ch 1, 18 sc in ring, join with a Sl st to first sc.

Rnd 2: Ch 8 (counts as dc, ch 5), skip next 2 sc, dc in next sc, *ch 5, skip next 2 sc, 1 dc in next sc, rep from * 4 times more, ch 5, skip 2 sc, Sl st to 3rd ch of beg ch-3 (6 loops).

Rnd 3: [1 sc, 1 hdc, 3 dc, 1 hdc, 1 sc] in each ch-5 loop around, join with Sl st to first sc (6 petals).

Rnd 4: Ch 1 (counts as first sc), *ch 5, working behind petals, 1 sc in first sc of next petal, rep from * 4 times more, ch 5, Sl st in first ch (6 loops).

Rnd 5: [1 sc, 1 hdc, 5 dc, 1 hdc, 1 sc] in each ch-5 space around, join with Sl st in first sc (6 petals).

Rnd 6: 1 sc in first sc of next petal, *ch 1, 1 picot, ch 2, 1 picot, ch 2, 1 sc in center dc of same petal, ch 1, 1 picot, ch 2, 1 picot, ch 2, 1 sc in first sc of next petal, rep from * around, omitting last sc, join with Sl st in first sc (12 loops).

Rnd 7: Sl st to center ch-2 space between first 2 picots, 1 sc in ch-2 space, *ch 8, 1 sc in ch-2 space between next 2 picots, rep from * around, omitting last sc, join with a Sl st first sc (12 ch-8 loops).

Rnd 8: 8 sc in each ch-8 loop around, join with a Sl st to first sc, end off.

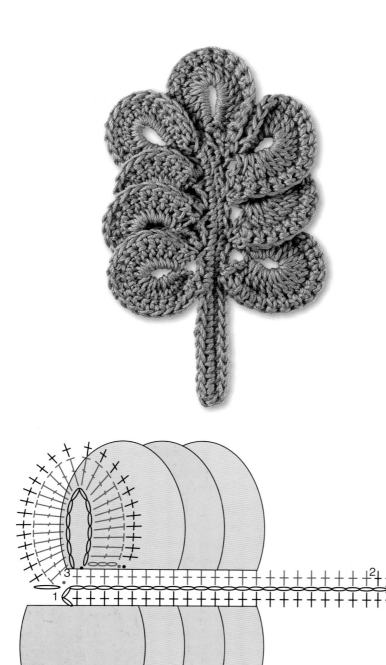

LOOPY LEAF

Skill Level: Experienced

Ch 25.

Row 1: 1 sc in 3rd ch from hook, work 1 sc in each ch across to last ch, 5 sc in the last ch, do not turn.

Row 2: Working on opposite side of beginning ch, work 1 sc in each ch to end, turn.

Row 3 (first leaf): The loops are worked individually down each side of the stem, beginning from the tip where the last sc was worked, as follows: *Ch 12, Sl st in st at base of ch just made, ch 3, skip next 2 sc, Sl st in next sc, turn, work 25 dc in the ch-12 space, Sl st in end of Row 1, turn, ch 1 (counts as first sc), skip first dc, 1 sc in each dc around loop, Sl st in same Sl st as last Sl st.

Row 4 (second leaf): Ch 12, Sl st in st at base of ch just made, ch 3, skip next 2 sc, Sl st in next sc, turn, work 25 dc in the ch-12 space, Sl st in same Sl st as last Sl st, turn, ch 1 (counts as first sc), skip first dc, 1 sc in each dc around loop, Sl st in same Sl st as last Sl st

Row 5 (third leaf): Rep Row 4.

Row 6 (fourth leaf): Rep Row 4.

To complete motif, rejoin yarn at the tip and work loops by repeating Rows 3–6 on other side of Stem, end off.

DIAMOND

Skill Level: Easy

Note: Work the center square of this motif in rows; work second part in rounds.

Ch 6.

Row 1: 1 sc in 2nd ch from hook, 1 sc in each ch across, turn.

Row 2: Ch 1, 1 sc in first sc and in each sc across, turn (5 sc).

Rows 3–6: Rep row 2.

Begin working in rounds as follows:

Rnd 1: Ch 1, 2 sc in first sc, 1 sc in each of next 3 sc, 3 sc in last sc (corner made), work 3 sc evenly spaced across side of square, 3 sc in corner, 1 sc in each of next 3 ch, 3 sc in corner, 3 sc evenly spaced across side, ending with 1 sc in first sc, join with Sl st to first sc (last corner completed).

Rnd 2: Ch 14 (counts as dc, ch 11), 1 dc in center sc of next corner, (ch 11, 1 dc in center sc of next corner) twice, ch 11, Sl st in 3rd ch of beg ch-14.

Rnd 3: Ch 1, 1 sc in first sc st, *15 sc in next loop, 1 sc in next dc, rep from * around, omitting last sc, join with Sl st to first sc.

Rnd 4: Ch 1, skip first sc, *1 sc in each of next 7 sc, 3 sc in next sc, 1 sc in each of next 7 sc, skip 1 sc, rep from * around, join with a Sl st to beg ch 1, end off.

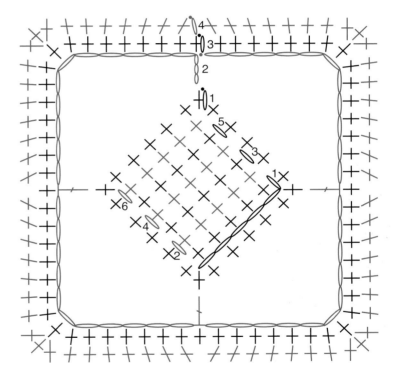

NAUTICAL WHEEL

Skill Level: Intermediate

*Beg cluster: *Yo twice, pick up a loop in designated space, [yo, draw through 2 loops on hook] twice, rep from * once, yo through all 3 loops on hook.*

*Cluster: *Yo twice, pick up a loop in designated space, [yo, draw through 2 loops on hook] twice, rep from * twice, yo through all 4 loops on hook.*

Ch 6, join with a Sl st to form a ring.

Rnd 1: Ch 5 (counts as a tr, ch 2), *[1 tr, ch 2] 11 times in ring, join with a Sl st to 3rd ch of beg ch-5 (12 tr, 12 ch-2 spaces).

Rnd 2: Sl st in next ch-2 space, ch 3, work a beg cluster in the same space, ch 3, *cluster in next ch-3 space, ch 3, rep from * 10 times, join with a Sl st to top of beg ch-3.

Rnd 3: Sl st in next ch-3 space, ch 2 (counts as first hdc), [2 hdc, ch 3, hdc in last hdc made (picot made), 2 hdc] in first ch-3 space, *[3 hdc, ch 3, 1 hdc in last hdc made (picot made), 2 hdc] in next ch-3 space, rep from * around, join with a Sl st to top of beg ch-2, end off.

SEVEN-CLUSTER MOTIF

Skill Level: Easy

Beg cluster: Ch 3, [yo, pick up loop in same st, yo, draw through 2 loops on hook] 2 times, yo, draw through 3 loops on hook.

Cluster: [Yo, pick up loop in same st, yo, draw through 2 loops on hook] 3 times, yo draw through 4 loops on hook.

Ch 6, join with a Sl st to form a ring.

Rnd 1: Work beg cluster, *ch 3, cluster in ring, rep from * 5 times, ch 3, join with Sl st to top of beg ch 3 (7 clusters).

Rnd 2: Sl st in first ch-3 space, ch 6 (counts as dc, ch 3), 1 dc in same space, *ch 5, (1 dc, ch 3, 1 dc) in next ch-3 space (V-st made), rep from * 5 times, ch 5, join with Sl st to 3rd ch of beg ch 6.

Rnd 3: Sl st in first ch-3 space, [beg cluster, ch 3, cluster] in first ch-3 space, *ch 3, sc in next ch-5 space, ch 3**, [cluster, ch 3, cluster] in next ch-3 space, rep from * 5 times, rep from * to ** once, join with Sl st to top of beg ch-3, end off.

PAISLEY

Skill Level: Easy

Notes:

1. Work with 3 colors A, B, C.

2. Work all rows from the right side.

With A, ch 16.

Row 1: With A, 1 sc in 2nd ch from hook, 1 sc in each of the next 3 ch, 1 hdc in each of the next 4 ch, 1 dc in each of the next 4 ch, 1 tr in each of the next 2 ch, 5 tr in last ch, working across opposite side of foundation ch, 1 tr in each of the next 2 ch, 1 dc in each of the next 3 ch, 1 hdc in each of the next 3 ch, 1 sc in each of the next 3 ch, leave rem sts unworked, (30 sts), do not turn, end off A.

Row 2: Working in back loops of sts, join B in first st of Row 1, 1 sc in each of the first 12 sts, 2 sc each of next 12 sts, leave rem sts unworked, (36 sc), do not turn, end off B.

Row 3: Working in back loops of sts, join C in first st of Row 2, 1 sc in each of next 8 sts, 1 hdc in each of next 12 sts, [2 dc in next st, 1 dc next st] 4 times, 1 hdc in each of the next 6 sts, 1 sc in each of the next 2 sts, 1 sc in each of the next 3 unworked sc in Row 1, (44 sts), do not turn, end off C.

Row 4: Working in back loops of sts, join A in first st of Row 3, 1 sc in each of the next 21 sts, [2 sc in next st, 1 sc in next st] 5 times, 1 sc in each of next 12 sts in Row 3, 1 sc in next 3 unworked sc in Row 2, 1 sc in next 3 unworked sc in Row 1, end off A.

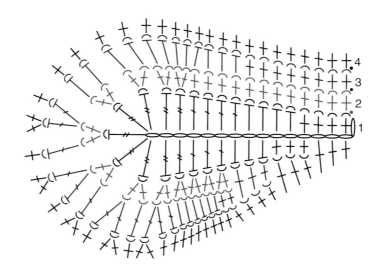

PICOT EDGE HEART

Skill Level: Intermediate

Square Center

Ch 9.

Row 1: 1 sc in 2nd ch from hook, 1 sc in each ch across row (8 sc), turn.

Row 2: Ch 1 (counts as first sc), skip first sc, 1 sc in each sc to end of row, 1 sc in top of turning ch, turn.

Rows 3–11: Rep Row 2, do not end off, turn to work across top edge of square.

Top Arches

Row 12: Skip first 3 sc, work 9 tr in next sc, skip next 3 sc, 1 Sl st in next turning ch at corner of square, work along row edges of next side of square, skip 5 rows, work 9 tr in next row edge, skip 5 rows, 1 Sl st in next corner, do not end off, do not turn.

Picot Edge

Rnd 13: Working all around outside edge of heart, ch 1, 1 sc in corner st, [ch 3, 1 sc] 6 times across bottom edge of square, [ch 3, 1 sc] 7 times across side edge of square, [ch 3, 1 sc] in each tr across top heart arches, join with Sl st to beg sc, end off.

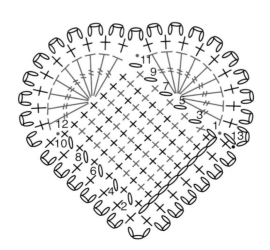

MESH HEART

Skill Level: Intermediate

Ch 12.

Row 1: 1 dc in 6th ch from hook (counts as 1 dc, ch 1, 1 dc), *ch 1, skip 1 ch, 1 dc in next ch, rep from * twice (4 ch-1 spaces), turn.

Row 2: Ch 4 (counts as 1 dc, ch 1), skip first dc, 1 dc in next dc, [ch 1, 1 dc in next dc] twice, ch 1, skip 1 ch, 1 dc in next ch, turn.

Rows 3 and 4: Rep Row 2.

Rnd 5 (worked around all 4 sides of mesh square): Ch 1, 1 sc in first dc, 1 sc in next ch-1 space, ch 3, skip next 2 ch-1 spaces 1 sc in next ch-1 space, ch 2 (center top of heart), 1 sc in next row-end st, skip next 2 rows, sc in next row-end dc, sc in next corner st, 2 sc in each ch-1 space across bottom edge, ch 3 (bottom tip of heart), 2 sc in next row-end st, 2 sc in each of next 3 row-end sts, join with Sl st in first sc.

Row 6 (top arches of heart): Work 9 dc in the next ch-3 space, 1 Sl st in the next ch-2 space at center of top of heart, 9 dc in next ch-3 space, skip next sc, Sl st to next sc, end off.

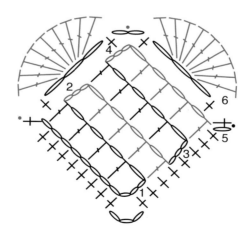

BUTTERFLY

Skill Level: Easy

Ch 15, join with a Sl st to the first ch (forming a large loop), ch 15, join with a Sl st in the same st as you joined the first loop (you now have 2 loops), ch 10, join with a Sl st in the same st as other loops are joined, ch 10, join with a Sl st in the same st as other loops are joined (2 ch-15 loops and 2 ch-10 loops).

Rnd 1: Ch 1, [5 sc, ch 4, 1 sc, ch 6, 1 sc, ch 8, 1 sc, ch 10, 1 sc, ch 8, 1 sc, ch 6, 1 sc, ch 4, 5 sc] in each of next 2 ch-15 loops, [2 sc, ch 4, 1 sc, ch 6, 1 sc ch 8, 1 sc, ch 6, 1 sc, ch 4, 2 sc], in each of next 2 ch-10 loops, join with Sl st to beg sc, end off, leaving a 12" (30.5 cm) length of yarn, wrap this around center to form body of butterfly, tie a knot underneath body.

STAR

Skill Level: Easy

Ch 2.

Rnd 1: 5 sc in 2nd ch from hook, join with Sl st to first sc.

Rnd 2: Ch 1, 3 sc in each sc, join with Sl st to first sc (15 sc).

Rnd 3: Ch 1, 1 sc in first sc, *ch 6, Sl st in 2nd ch from hook, sc in next ch, hdc in next ch, dc in next ch, tr in next ch, tr in the base of the sc at bottom of ch 6, skip next 2 sc, sc in next sc, rep from * around, omitting last sc, join with a Sl st to beg sc, end off.

PANSY

Skill Level: Easy

Ch 5, join with a Sl st to form a ring.

Rnd 1: Ch 4 (counts as dc, ch 1), 1 dc in ring, [ch 1, 1 dc in ring] twice, ch 2, 1 dc in ring, ch 2, join with a Sl st to third ch of beg ch-4.

Rnd 2: Ch 1, [1 sc, 1 hdc, 3 dc, 1 hdc, 1 sc] in each of next 3 ch-1 spaces (3 small petals), [1 Sl st, ch 2, 2 dc, 5 tr, 2 dc, ch 2, 1 Sl st] in each of next 2 ch-2 spaces (2 large petals) join with a Sl st to first sc, end off.

BULLION FLOWER

Skill Level: Experienced

Bullion Stitch: Yo 10 times, pick up a loop in designated stitch, yo and draw through 12 loops on hook, ch 1 to lock stitch. Do not pull tightly, but leave thread as long as the bullion stitch.

Ch 5, join with a Sl st to form a ring.

Rnd 1: Ch 1, 10 sc in the ring, join with a Sl st to first sc.

Rnd 2: Ch 1, 2 sc in each st around, join with a Sl st to first sc.

Rnd 3: Ch 1, sc in first st, *ch 2, (1 bullion, ch 1) 3 times in next st, ch 1 more, Sl st in next st, sc in each of next 2 sts, rep from * around (5 petals), omitting last sc, join with a Sl st to first sc, end off.

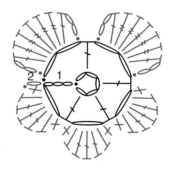

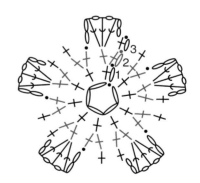

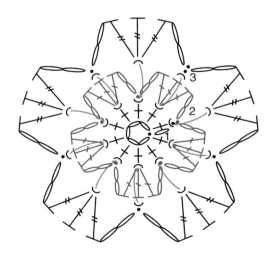

PRIMROSE

Skill Level: Easy

Work with 2 colors A and B.

With A, ch 4, join with a Sl st to form a ring.

Rnd 1: With A, ch 4 (counts as a dc, ch 1), *1 dc in ring, ch 1, rep from * 6 times, join with a Sl st in 3rd ch of beg ch-4, end off A.

Rnd 2: Join B in any ch-1 space, ch 2 (counts as first hdc), [1 dc, 1 tr, 1 dc, 1 hdc] in same space, [1 hdc, 1 dc, 1 tr, 1 dc, 1 hdc] in each ch-1 space around, join with a Sl st to beg ch-2 (8 petals).

Rnd 3: Ch 1, *[2 sc in next st] 4 times, Sl st next st, rep from * 7 times more, join with a Sl st in first sc, end off.

BRIAR ROSE

Skill Level: Easy

Ch 5, join with Sl st to form ring.

Rnd 1: Ch 1, 10 sc in ring, join with a Sl st in first sc.

Rnd 2: Working in front loops only, *ch 2, 3 dc in next st, ch 2, Sl st in next st, rep from * around (5 petals), join with Sl st in first Sl st.

Rnd 3: Working in the remaining back loops in Rnd 1, Sl st over next st, *ch 2, 3 tr in next st, ch 2, Sl st in next st, rep from * around (5 petals), join with a Sl st in first Sl st, end off.

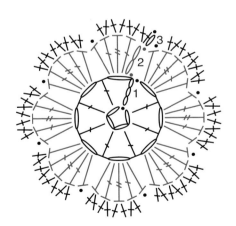

BUTTERCUP

Skill Level: Easy

Ch 4, join with a Sl st to form a ring.

Rnd 1: Ch 1, 10 sc in ring, join with a Sl st to first sc.

Rnd 2: Working in back loops only, *ch 2, [1 dc, 3 tr, 1 dc] in next st, ch 2, Sl st in next st, rep from * 4 times more , end Sl st through both loops of first sc (5 petals).

Rnd 3 (beginning cup): Bring yarn to front of work, working in remaining front loops of Rnd 1, ch 4 (counts as first tr), 2 tr in next st, *1 tr in next st, 2 tr in next st, rep from * around, join with a Sl st to top of beg ch-3 (15 tr).

Rnd 4: *Ch 3, 1 sc in third ch (picot made), skip 1 st, Sl st in next st, rep from * around, join with a Sl st in last st (7 picots made), end off.

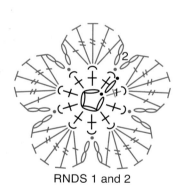

RNDS 1 and 2

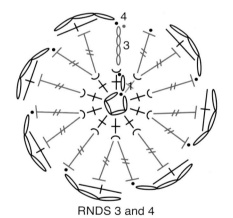

RNDS 3 and 4

DAFFODIL

Skill Level: Intermediate

Note: Make cup of flower first; then, make petals.

Cup

Ch 5, join with a Sl st to form ring.

Rnd 1: Ch 1, 10 sc in ring, join with a Sl st to first sc.

Rnd 2: Ch 3 (counts as a dc), working in the back loops for this row only, 2 dc in next sc, *1 dc in next sc, 2 dc in next sc, rep from * around (15 dc), join with a Sl st to top of beg ch-2.

Rnd 3: Ch 3 (counts as dc), 1 dc in each dc around (15 dc), join with Sl to top of beg ch-3.

Rnd 4: Rep Rnd 3.

Rnd 5: Ch 1, *skip next dc, [1 sc, 1 dc, 1 sc] in next st, rep from * around, join with Sl st to beg ch 1, end off.

Petals

Rnd 6: Join yarn in any free loop at back of Rnd 1, working in the remaining front loops, *ch 10, 4 tr in 4th ch from hook, 1 dc in each of next 2 ch, 1 hdc in each of next 2 ch, 1 sc in each of next 2 ch, skip 1 st in Rnd 1, Sl st in next st, rep from * 4 times (5 petals), join with a Sl st to first Sl st, end off.

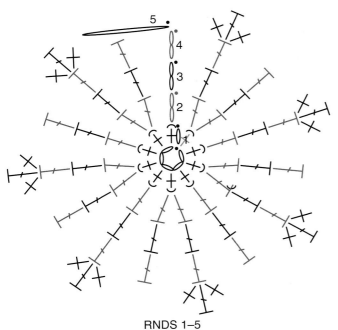

RNDS 1–5

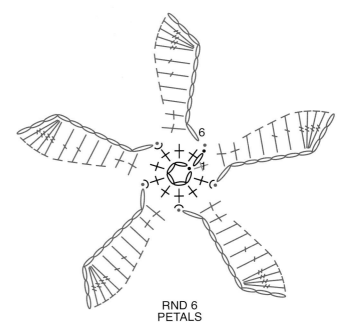

RND 6
PETALS

FIVE-PETAL FLOWER

Skill Level: Easy

Ch 5, join with a Sl st to form a ring.

Rnd 1: Ch 1, 10 sc in ring, join with a Sl st to first sc.

Rnd 2: *Ch 2, 5 tr in next sc, ch 2, Sl st in next st, rep from * 4 times more, end off.

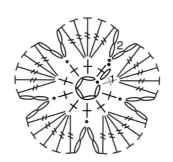

MOCK POPCORN FLOWER

Skill Level: Easy

Ch 4, join with a Sl st to form a ring

Rnd 1: Ch 1, 8 sc in ring, join with a Sl st to first sc.

Rnd 2: Ch 1, 2 sc in each sc around (16 sc), turn.

Rnd 3 (WS): Working in the back loops only, *1 tr in next st, 1 Sl st in next st, rep from * around, join with a Sl st to beg Sl st, turn.

Rnd 4 (RS): Working in the remaining back loops of Rnd 2, *ch 2, 3 tr in next st, ch 2, Sl st in next st, rep from * around, end off (8 petals).

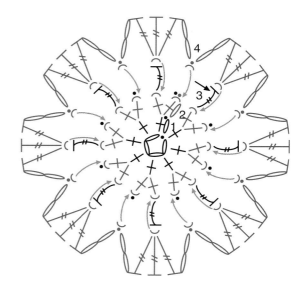

CLEMATIS

Skill Level: Easy

Note: Work with 2 colors A and B

With A, ch 4.

Rnd 1: Ch 1, 12 sc in ring, join with a Sl st to first sc, end off A.

Rnd 2: Join B in any sc, *ch 10, 1 Sl st in 2nd ch from hook, 1 sc in next ch, 1 hdc in next ch, 1 dc in each of the next 4 ch, 1 tr in each of the next 2 ch, skip 1 sc on Rnd 1, 1 Sl st in next st, rep from * around (6 petals), join with a Sl st to beg ch, end off B.

DOUBLE LOOP FLOWER

Skill Level: Easy

Ch 4, join with a Sl st to form a ring.

Rnd 1: Ch 1, 8 sc in ring, join with a Sl st to first sc.

Rnd 2: Working in front loops only, *ch 8, Sl st in next sc, rep from * 7 times (8 ch-8 loops), ending with Sl st in first Sl st.

Rnd 3: Working in remaining back loops in Rnd 1, Sl st in first sc, *ch 10, Sl st in next sc, rep from * 7 times more, (8 ch-10 loops), ending with Sl st in first Sl st, end off.

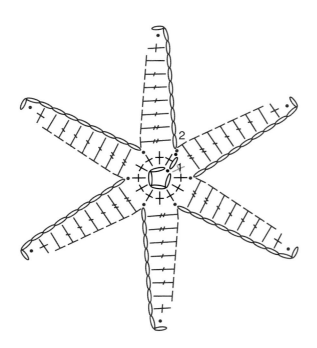

CHRYSANTHEMUM

Skill Level: Easy

Ch 5, join with a Sl st to form a ring.

Rnd 1: Ch 1, 12 sc in ring, join with Sl st to first sc.

Rnd 2: Working in front loops only, work as follows: *ch 7, 1 sc in 2nd ch from hook, 1 sc in each ch across, Sl st in next sc, rep from * 11 times more (12 petals), join with a Sl st to base of first petal.

Rnd 3: Working in the remaining back loops in Rnd 1, *ch 9, 1 sc in 2nd ch from hook, 1 sc in each ch across, Sl st in next sc, rep from * 11 times more (12 petals), join with a Sl st to base of first petal, end off.

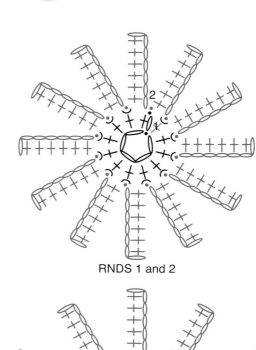

RNDS 1 and 2

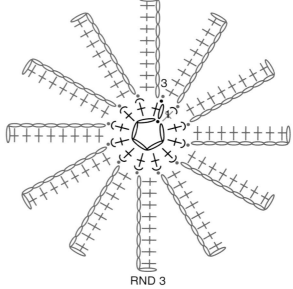

RND 3

IRISH ROSE

Skill Level: Intermediate

Ch 8, join with a Sl st to form a ring.

Rnd 1: Ch 5 (counts as a dc, ch 2), *1 dc in ring, ch 2, rep from * 6 times more, join with a Sl st to 3rd ch of beg ch (8 ch-2 spaces).

Rnd 2: [1 sc, 3 dc, 1 sc] in each ch-2 space around, join with Sl st to first sc (8 small petals).

Rnd 3: Ch 1 (counts as first sc), *ch 5, working behind petals, work 1 sc in first sc of next petal, rep from * 7 times omitting last sc, join with Sl st to beg ch (8 ch-5 loops).

Rnd 4: [1 sc, 1 hdc, 3 dc, 1 hdc, 1 sc] in each ch-5 loop around, join with a Sl st to first sc (8 medium petals).

Rnd 5: Ch 1 (counts as first sc), *ch 7, working behind petals, work 1 sc in first sc of next petal, rep from * 7 times omitting last sc, join with a Sl st to beg ch (8 ch 7 loops).

Rnd 6: [1 sc, 1 hdc, 1 dc, 3 tr, 1 dc, 1 hdc, 1 sc] in each ch-7 loop around, join with Sl st to first sc (8 large petals), end off.

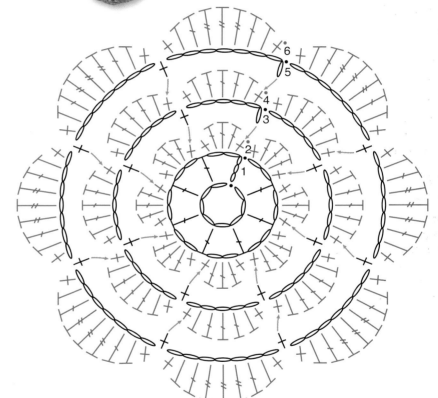

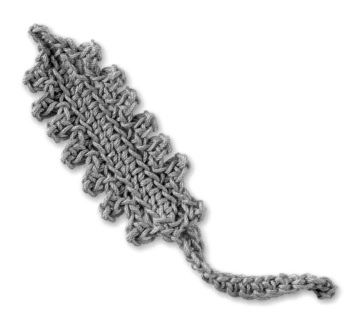

CURLY EDGE LEAF

Skill Level: Easy

Picot: Ch 3, sc in 3rd ch from hook.

Ch 16.

Row 1: 1 sc in 2nd chain from hook, 1 sc in each of the next 13 ch, 3 sc in the last chain. Working across opposite side of foundation ch, 1 sc in each ch across, 1sc in turning ch. Do not join, do not turn.

Row 2: Continue working in a spiral, working in the back loops of sts, *sc in next st [picot, Sl st in next st, sc in the next st] 7 times (7 picots)*, [sc in next st, picot, Sl st] in next st (point of leaf made). Working on other side of leaf, rep from * to * across, Sl st in next st, ch 12 for stem, 1 sc in 2nd chain from hook, 1 sc in each ch across, Sl st in next sc at base of leaf, end off.

SMALL LEAF

Skill Level: Easy

Note: Work leaf on both sides of the foundation chain.

Ch 12.

Row 1: 5 dc in the 4th ch from hook, 1 dc in each of next 4 ch, 1 hdc in each of next 2 ch, 1 sc in next ch, [sc, ch 3, sc] in last ch (point of leaf). Working across opposite side of foundation ch, 1 sc in next ch, 1 hdc in each of next 2 ch, 1 dc in each of next 4 ch, 5 dc in next ch, ch 3, Sl st in same st as last dc, end off.

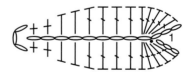

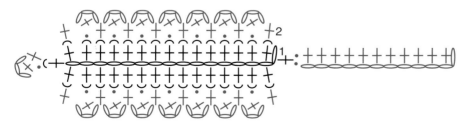

BROAD LEAF

Skill Level: Easy

Note: Work leaf on both sides of the foundation chain.

Ch 14.

First half of leaf: 5 tr in 5th ch from hook, 1 tr in each of the next 3 ch, 1 dc in each of the next 2 ch, 1 hdc in each of the next 2 ch, 1 sc in next ch, 1 Sl st in last ch, ch 3, Sl st in the same ch (point of leaf), do not turn.

Second half of leaf: Working across opposite side of foundation ch, 1 sc in next ch, 1 hdc in each of next 2 ch, 1 dc in each of next 2 ch, 1 tr in each of next 3 ch, 5 tr in last ch, ch 3, Sl st in same ch, end off.

BROAD LEAF II

Skill Level: Easy

Note: Work leaf on both sides of foundation chain.

Ch 9.

Row 1: 1 dc in 3rd ch from hook (counts as 2 dc), 1 dc in each of the next 5 ch, 3 dc in next ch (top point of leaf). Working on opposite side of foundation ch, 1 dc in each of the next 6 ch, ch 3, Sl st in the same ch as first dc, do not turn.

Row 2: Continuing around, ch 3, working in back loops only, work 1 dc in each of the next 8 dc, [1 dc, 1 tr, 1 dc] in next dc, 1 dc in each of the next 7 dc, ch 3, join with a Sl st in last dc, ch 1, Sl st in base of leaf, end off.

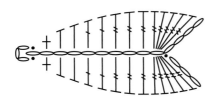

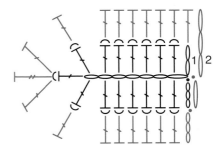

RIDGED LEAF

Skill Level: Intermediate

Notes: When working the ridged leaf, do not count the turning ch 1 as the first st;, when turning, do not skip the first st. Starting with Row 2, work sts in back loops throughout.

Ch 11.

Row 1: 1 sc in 2nd ch from hook, 1 sc in next 8 ch, 5 sc in last ch. Working across opposite side of foundation ch, 1 sc in each of next 7 ch, turn.

Row 2: Ch 1, 1 sc in each of first 9 sc, 3 sc in next sc, 1 sc in next 9 sc, turn.

Row 3: Ch 1, 1 sc in each of first 10 sc, 3 sc in next sc, 1 sc in next 8 sc, turn.

Row 4: Ch 1, 1 sc in each of next 9 sc, 3 sc next sc, 1 sc in next 9 sc, turn.

Row 5: Ch 1, 1 sc in each of next 10 sc, 3 sc in next sc, 1 sc next 8 sc, turn.

Row 6: Ch 1, 1 sc in each of next 9 sc, 3 sc in next sc, 1 sc next 9 sc, turn.

Row 7: Ch 1, 1 sc in each of next 10 sc, 3 sc in next sc, 1 sc next 8 sc, turn.

Row 8: Ch 1, 1 sc in each of next 9 sc, 3 sc in next sc, 1 sc next 9 sc, turn.

Row 9: Ch 1, 1 sc in each of next 10 sc, 3 sc in next sc, 1 sc next 10 sc, end off.

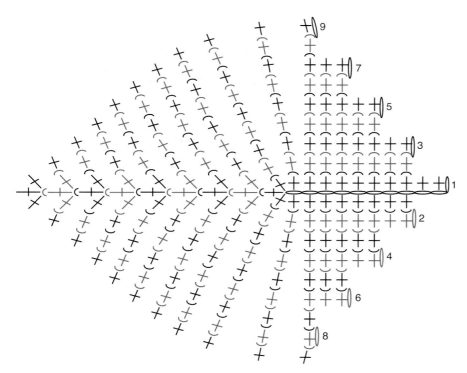

LAZY J

Skill Level: Intermediate

Reverse single crochet or rev sc (sometimes called crab or shrimp stitch): At end of row, without turning and working in front loops of sts, work 1 sc in next st to the right.

Ch 15.

First Segment

Row 1: 1 sc in 2nd ch from hook, 1 sc in next ch, 1 hdc in each of the next 3 ch, 1 dc in each of next 2 ch, 2 dc in next ch, 1 dc in each of the next 3 ch, 1 tr in each of next 3 ch, do not turn.

Row 2: Ch 1, working from left to right, working in front loops of sts, reverse sc in each st across, do not turn. (Note: This completes one segment of a Lazy J.)

Second Segment

Row 3: Ch 1, working in remaining loops of sts 2 rows below, 1 sc in first 2 sts, 1 hdc in each of next 3 sc, 1 dc in each of next 2 sts, 2 dc in next st, 1 dc in each of the next 3 sts, 1 tr in each of next 3 sts, do not turn.

Row 4: Rep Row 2.

Third and Fourth Segments

Rows 5–8: Rep Rows 3–4 twice.

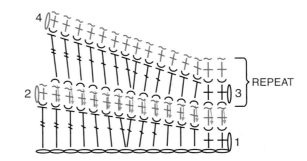

CORKSCREWS

Skill Level: Easy

Corkscrews can be made using single crochet, half double crochet, or double crochet to achieve different effects. Shown here are 3 corkscrews all worked in the same yarn on the same number of stitches, but they all look different. Corkscrews make great embellishments for hats, scarves, and freeform work.

Single Crochet Corkscrew

Ch 20, 3 sc in 2nd ch from hook, 3 sc in each ch across, end off, twist in shape.

Half Double Crochet Corkscrew

Ch 22, 3 hdc in 3rd ch from hook, 3 hdc in each ch across, end off, twist in shape.

Double Crochet Corkscrew

Ch 23, 3 dc in 4th ch from hook, 3 dc in each ch, end off, twist in shape.

REDUCED SAMPLE OF
DC CORKSCREW

REDUCED SAMPLE OF
HDC CORKSCREW

REDUCED SAMPLE OF
SC CORKSCREW

ADRIENNE SQUARE

Skill Level: Easy

Ch 8, join with a Sl st to form a ring.

Rnd 1: Ch 1, 16 sc in ring, join with Sl st to first sc.

Rnd 2: Ch 7 (counts as dc, ch 4), skip next sc, *1 dc in next sc, ch 4, skip next sc, rep from * 6 times, Sl st in 3rd ch of the beg ch-7 (8 dc, 8 ch-4 spaces).

Rnd 3: Ch 1, [1 sc, 1 hdc, 2 dc, 1 hdc, 1 sc] in each ch-4 space around (8 petals).

Rnd 4: Ch 8 (counts as dc, ch 5), *1 sc between 2 dc of next petal, ch 5, 1 sc between 2 dc of next petal, ch 5**, 1 dc between the next 2 sc, ch 5, rep from * twice, rep from * to ** once, join with Sl st to 3rd ch of beg ch-8.

Rnd 5: Ch 3 (counts as dc), 1 dc in first st (half corner made), *[4 dc in next ch-5 space] 3 times, [2 dc, ch 3, 2 dc] in next dc (full corner made), rep from * 3 times more, ending last rep, [2 dc, ch 3] in beg ch-3 of previous rnd, join with a Sl st to top of beg ch-3 (first corner complete), end off.

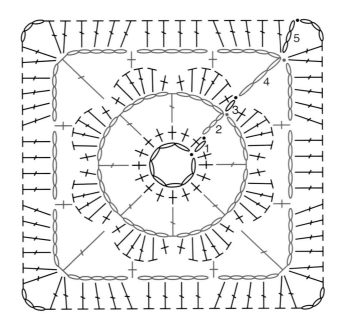

CLASSIC GRANNY

Skill Level: Easy

Note: Work in 2 colors A and B.

With A, ch 4, join with a Sl st to form a ring.

Rnd 1: With A, ch 3 (counts as a dc now and throughout), 2 dc in ring, *ch 3, 3 dc in ring, rep from * twice more, ch 3, join with a Sl st to top of beg ch-3 (four groups of 3 dc), drop A.

Rnd 2: Join B in any corner ch-3 space, ch 3 (counts as dc), 2 dc in same ch-3 space, (half corner made), *ch 2, skip 3 dc, [3 dc, ch3, 3 dc] in the next ch-3 space (corner made), rep from * twice, ch 2, 3 dc in same space as first half corner, ch 3, join with a Sl st to top of beg ch-3, drop B.

Rnd 3: Pull up a loop with A in corner ch-3 loop, ch 3, 2 dc in same ch-3 space (half corner made), *ch 2, 3 dc in next ch 2 space, ch 2, [3 dc, ch 3, 3 dc] in next corner space, rep from * twice, ch 2, 3 dc in next ch-2 space, ch 2, 3 dc in same space as first half corner, ch 3, join with a Sl st to top of beg ch-3, end off A.

Rnd 4: Pull up a loop with B in corner ch-3 loop, ch 3, 2 dc in same ch-3 space (half corner made), *[ch 2, 3 dc] in each of next 2 ch-2 spaces, ch 2**, [3 dc, ch 3, 3 dc] in corner space, rep from * twice, rep from * to ** once, 3 dc in same space as first half corner, ch 3, join with a Sl st to beg ch-3, end off B.

NICOLE'S GRANNY

Skill Level: Easy

Ch 6, join with a Sl st to form a ring.

Rnd 1: Ch 3, work 2 dc in ring, (ch 1, 3 dc in ring) 3 times, ch 1, join with a Sl st to top of ch-3.

Rnd 2: Sl st in next 2 dc, Sl st in next ch-1 space, ch 3, [2 dc, ch 1, 3 dc] in same ch-1 space (corner made), *ch 1, [3 dc, ch 1, 3 dc] in next ch-1 space, rep from * twice, ch 1, join with a Sl st to top of ch-3 (4 corners made).

Rnd 3: Sl st in next 2 dc, Sl st in next ch-1 corner space, ch 3, [2 dc, ch 1, 3 dc] in same corner ch-1 space, *ch 2, [1 dc, ch 2, 1 dc] in next ch-1 space (V-st made), ch 2**, [3 dc, ch 1, 3 dc] in next ch-1 space, rep from * twice, rep from * to ** once, join with Sl st to beg ch 3 (4 corners, 1 V-stitch between each corner).

Rnd 4: Sl st in next 2 dc, Sl st in next ch-1 corner space, ch 3, [2 dc, ch 1, 3 dc] in same corner ch-1 space, *ch 3, skip next ch-2 space, [1 dc, ch 3, 1 dc] in next ch-2 space, ch 3, skip next ch-2 space**, [3 dc, ch 1, 3 dc] in next ch-1 space, rep from * twice, rep from * to ** once, join with a Sl st to beg ch 3 (4 corners, 1 V-st between each corner), end off.

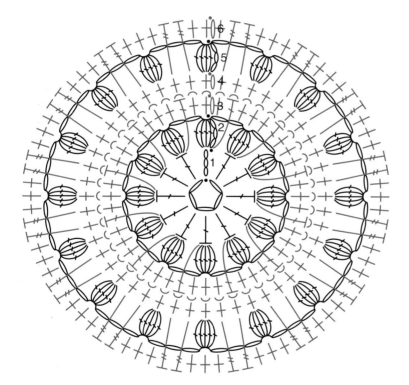

ROSE OF SHARON

Skill Level: Experienced

Popcorn: Work 5 dc in same st, drop loop from hook, insert hook in the first of the 5 dc, pick up dropped loop, tighten and draw loop through st, ch 1 to complete popcorn.

Long dc: Yo, pick up a ½ inch (1.3 cm) long loop in designated st, [yo, draw yarn through 2 loops on hook] twice.

Note: Worked with 2 colors A and B

With A, ch 5, join with a Sl st to form a ring.

Rnd 1: With A, ch 3 (counts as 1 dc), 11 dc in ring, join with a Sl st to top of beg ch-3.

Rnd 2: Ch 3, 4 dc in first st, drop loop from hook, insert hook in the top of the ch 3, pick up dropped loop, tighten, ch 1 to complete first popcorn, *ch 2, popcorn in the next dc, rep from * around (12 popcorns) ch 2, join to top of beg ch-3, drop A, draw up a loop with B.

Rnd 3: Ch 1, sc in first st, *1 sc in next ch-2 space, 1 long dc in base of next popcorn, 1 sc in same ch-2 space, 1 sc in next popcorn, rep from * around, omitting last sc, join with a Sl st to first sc.

Rnd 4: Ch 1, 1 sc in back loop of each st around, join with a Sl st in the first sc, drop B, draw up loop with A.

Rnd 5: Ch 3, 4 dc in same st as join, drop loop from hook, insert hook in the top of ch-3, pick up dropped loop, tighten, ch 1 to complete first popcorn, *ch 3, skip next 2 sc, popcorn in the next dc, rep from * around (16 popcorns in all), ch 3, join to top of beg ch-3, end off A, draw up a loop with B.

Rnd 6: Ch 1, 1 sc in first st, *1 sc in next ch-3 space, 1 long tr in each of next 2 sc 2 rows below, 1 sc in the same ch-3 space, 1 sc in next popcorn, rep from * around, join with Sl st to first sc, end off B.

JEANNINE SQUARE

Skill Level: Intermediate

Double triple crochet (dtr): Yo 3 times, pick up a loop in designated place, [yo, draw through 2 loops on hook] 4 times.

Work with 4 colors A, B, C, D.

With A, ch 6, join with a Sl st to form a ring.

Rnd 1: Ch 3 (counts as dc), 3 dc in ring, ch 3, *4 dc in ring, ch 3, rep from * twice, join with Sl st in top of beg ch-3 (4 groups of 4 dc), end off A.

Rnd 2: Join B in any ch-3 space, ch 3, *dc in same space, 1 dc in each of next 4 dc, 2 dc in next ch-3 space, 1 dtr, inserting hook from front to back, going in the beg ring and between the groups of dc, 2 dc in same corner ch-3 space, rep from * around omitting last 2 dc, join with Sl st to beg ch-3, draw C through last loop, end off B.

Rnd 3: With C, ch 3 (counts as dc), 1 dc in first st, *1 dc each next 7 dc, 2 dc in next dc, ch 3 (corner), skip next dtr**, 2 dc next dc, rep from * 2 times, rep from * to ** once, join with Sl st to top of beg ch-3, end off C.

Rnd 4: Join D in any corner ch-3 space, ch 3, dc in same ch-3 space, *1 dc in each of next 10 dc, 2 dc in ch-3 space, working over ch-3 loop, 1 dtr in next dtr in Rnd 2**, rep from * twice, rep from * to ** once, join with Sl st to top of beg ch-3, draw A through last loop, end off D.

Rnd 5: With A, ch 1, 1 sc in first st, 1 sc in each of next 15 sts, ch 2, *1 sc in each of next 16 sts, ch 2, rep from * twice, join with Sl st to first sc, end off.

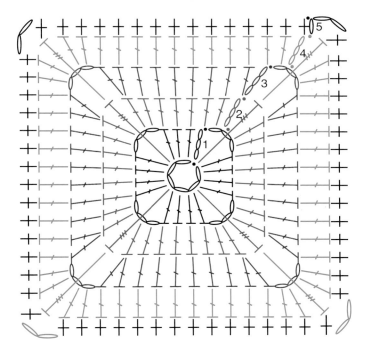

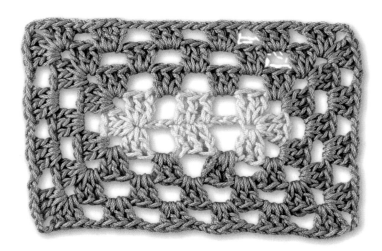

RECTANGLE GRANNY

Skill Level: Intermediate

Notes:

1. Work with 3 colors A, B, C.

2. To establish rounds, work Round 1 on both sides of the foundation chain.

3. Beginning ch-3 always counts as first double crochet of round.

With A, ch 12.

Rnd 1: [2 dc, ch 2, 3 dc, ch 2, 3 dc] in 4th ch from hook, ch 2, skip next 2 ch, 1 dc in each of the next 3 ch, ch 2, skip next 2 ch, [3 dc, ch 2, 3 dc, ch 2, 3 dc] all in last ch. Working on opposite side of foundation ch, ch 2, skip next 2 ch, 1 dc in each of the next 3 ch (these 3 dc will correspond with 3 dc already established on first side of ch), ch 2, skip next 2 ch, join with a Sl st to top of beg ch-3, end A.

Rnd 2: Join B in the last ch-2 space made, ch 3, 2 dc in same ch-2 space, *ch 2, [3 dc, ch 3, 3 dc, ch 2] in next 2 ch-2 spaces (2 corners made), [3 dc in next ch-2 sp, ch 2] twice, rep from * once, omitting last (3 dc, ch 2), join with Sl st to top of beg ch-3, end B.

Rnd 3: Join C in the first ch-2 space of last rnd, ch 3, 2 dc in same ch-2 space, ch 2, *[3 dc, ch 3, 3 dc] in next ch-2 space (corner), ch 2, 3 dc in next ch-2 space, ch 2, [3 dc, ch 3, 3 dc] in next ch-2 space (corner), [ch 2, 3 dc] in each of next 3 ch-2 spaces, ch 2, rep from * once, omitting last [3 dc, ch 2], join with Sl st to top of beg ch-3, end C.

Rnd 4: Join B in the first ch-2 space of last rnd, ch 3, 2 dc in same ch-2 space, *ch 2, [3 dc, ch 3, 3 dc] in next ch-2 space (corner), [ch 2, 3 dc in next ch-2 space] twice, ch 2, [3 dc, ch 3, 3 dc] in next ch-2 space (corner) , [ch 2, 3 dc] in each of next 4 ch-2 spaces, ch 2, rep from * once, omitting last [3 dc, ch 2], join with Sl st to top of beg ch-3, end off.

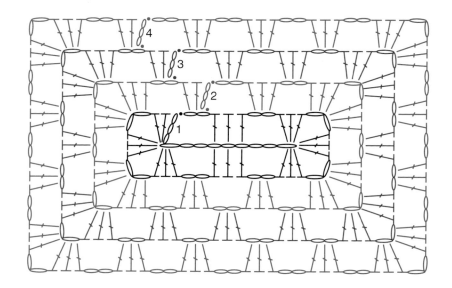

BLOOMING GRANNY

Skill Level: Easy

Popcorn: Make 5 dc in specified st, draw up the last loop slightly and remove hook, insert hook in the first of the 5 dc made, pick up the dropped loop and draw it through, ch 1.

Note: Work with 3 colors A, B, C.

With A, ch 4, join with a Sl st to form a ring.

Rnd 1: With A, ch 1, 8 sc in ring, join with a Sl st in first sc.

Rnd 2 (popcorn rnd): With A, ch 3 (counts as a dc), 4 dc in first st, insert hook in the top of the ch 3, pick up dropped loop, tighten, ch 1 to complete first popcorn, ch 1, *popcorn in next sc, ch 1, rep from * 6 times more, (8 popcorns), join with a Sl st to top of the beg ch-3, end A.

Rnd 3: Join B in any ch-1 space, ch 3 (counts as a dc now and throughout) 2 dc in same space (half corner), *ch 1, 3 dc next ch-1 sp, ch 1**, [3 dc, ch 1, 3 dc] next ch-1 space (corner), rep from * twice, rep from * to **, 3 dc in same space as beg half corner, ch 1, join with a Sl st to top of beg ch-3 (this completes first corner), end B.

Rnd 4: Join C in any corner ch-1 space, ch 3, 2 dc in same space (half corner), *[ch 1, 3 dc next ch-1 sp] twice, ch 1**, [3 dc, ch 1, 3 dc] in next ch-1 space (corner), ch 1, rep from * twice, rep from * to ** once, 3 dc in same space as beg half corner, ch 1, join with a Sl st to top of beg ch 3 (this completes first corner), end off.

BLOOMING GRANNY SQUARES BAG

The granny square has always been the most-loved crochet motif. Here it's gone floral and is hooked with brights that pop against a black background. This bag would also look great in pastels or naturals.

YOU WILL NEED

Yarn

- Lightweight cotton yarn
- Shown: Cotton Classic by Tahki/Stacy Charles, 100% cotton, 1.75 oz (50 g)/108 yd (100 m): green #3760 (C), 2 skeins; black #3002 (D), 2 skeins. Use small amounts of several other colors (A, B) for centers of squares.

Hook

- 5/F (3.75 mm)

Stitches used

- Single crochet
- Double crochet
- Popcorn

Gauge

- 1 square = 4" × 4" (10 × 10 cm)

Notions

- ½ yd (0.5 m) lining, optional
- ½ yd (0.5 m) fleece or felt, optional
- sewing needle and thread, optional
- tapestry needle
- oval ring handles, 3" × 5" (7.5 × 12.7 cm) opening

Finished size

- 12" × 14" (30.5 × 35.5 cm)

Granny Square

Make 18.

Rnds 4 and 5 will always be worked using C and D. Rnds 1, 2, 3, and foundation rnd will vary in color choices. Once center flower is completed, it is necessary to square off. This is accomplished by beg rnd with a half corner, working 3 corners around, and ending with another half corner. Rnds 3, 4, and 5 are worked in this manner.

Foundation Rnd: With A, ch 4, join with Sl st to form ring. Work 8 sc in ring, join with Sl st.

Rnd 1 (pc rnd): Ch 3 (counts as a dc), 4 dc in same st as ch 3, complete as pc, ch 1 * pc in next st, ch 1, rep from * 6 times more (8 pc sts in rnd), join with Sl st to top of beg ch 3, fasten off A.

Rnd 2: Join B in any ch-1 sp, ch 3 (counts as a dc now and throughout), 2 more dc in same sp (half corner) * 3 dc in next ch-1 sp, 3 dc, ch 1, 3 dc in next ch-1 sp (corner), rep from * 2 times more, end 3 dc in next ch-1 sp, 3 dc in same sp as beg ch 1, join with Sl st to top of beg ch 3 (this completes last corner), fasten off B.

Rnd 3: Join C in any ch-1 sp, ch 3, 2 more dc in same sp (half corner), * 3 dc in next ch-1 sp, 3 dc in next ch-1 sp, 3 dc, ch 1, 3 dc in next ch-1 sp (corner), rep from * 2 times more, end 3 dc in next ch-1 sp, 3 dc in next ch-1 sp, 3 dc in same sp as beg ch 1, join with Sl st to top of beg ch 3, fasten off C.

Rnd 4: Join D in any ch-1 sp, ch 3, 2 more dc in same sp (half corner) * [3 dc in next ch-1 sp] 3 times, 3 dc, ch 1, 3 dc in next ch-1 sp (corner), rep from * 2 times more, end [3 dc in next ch-1 sp] 3 times, 3 dc in same sp as beg ch 1, join with Sl st to top of beg ch 3, fasten off D.

Front

Sew 9 squares together in 3 rows of 3 to form the bag front.

Using C, join yarn in top right corner, RS facing you, ch 3, work 14 dc in first square, 1 dc in seam, 15 dc in second square, 1 dc in seam, 15 dc in last square, ch 3, turn (47 dc).

Row 2: Sk first st, 1 dc dec in next 2 sts, dc in each st to last 3 sts, dc dec next 2, 1 dc in last st, ch 3, turn (45 dc).

Rows 3, 4, and 5: Rep Row 2 (39 dc). Fasten off this color and join black. Cont to dec each side as established twice more (35 dc).

Work 2 rows even, fasten off, leaving a long end for sewing.

Back

Work same as front.

Gusset

Foundation Row: Using C, ch 9. Starting in second ch from hook, work 1 sc in each ch to end (8 sc), ch 1, turn.

Row 1: Sk first st, sc in second st and in each st to end, 1 sc in top of tch (8 sc), ch 1, turn.

Rep Row 1 until piece measures 36" (91.5 cm).

Finishing

1. Line the bag, if desired. Line only the rectangular area behind the granny squares, avoiding the upper section below the handles.

2. Pin the gusset between the front and back, stopping at the top of the squares. Sew the gusset in place.

3. Place a handle at the top of the front, and turn the last 2 rows of stitches to the inside over the handle. Stitch in place. Repeat for the other handle.

Edgings and Trims

Edgings are crocheted separately and then sewn onto a finished garment, accessory, or home décor item. Some are crocheted in a predetermined length, working from edge to edge in long rows. Others are started at one narrow end and worked in many short rows to the desired length. Decorative edging can turn a very simple item into an elegant fashion piece.

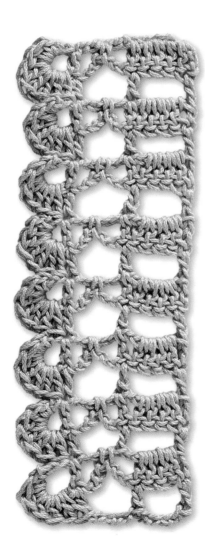

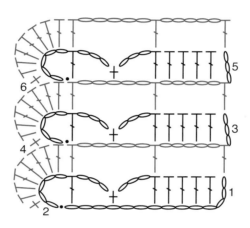

VENETIAN TRIM

Skill Level: Intermediate

Note: Work from the narrow end.

Ch 14.

Row 1: 1 dc in 4th ch from hook, 1 dc in each of the next 4 ch, ch 3, skip next 2 ch, 1 sc in next ch, ch 3, skip next 2 ch, [1 dc, ch 5, 1 Sl st] in last ch, turn.

Row 2: [1 sc, 2 hdc, 5 dc] in first ch-5 space, 1 dc in next dc, ch 5, skip next 2 ch-3 spaces, 1 dc in next dc, ch 5, skip next 4 dc, 1 dc in top of turn ch, turn.

Row 3: Ch 3 (counts as first dc), 4 dc in next ch-5 space, 1 dc in next dc, ch 3, 1 sc in next ch-5 space, ch 3, [1 dc, ch 5, 1 Sl st] in next dc, turn.

Rep Rows 2 and 3 for pattern.

NEAPOLITAN LACE

Skill Level: Intermediate

Note: Work from the narrow end.

Ch 5.

Row 1: [3 dc, ch 3, 3 dc] in 5th ch from hook (shell made), turn.

Row 2: Ch 3, shell in next ch-3 space of previous shell, turn.

Row 3: Rep Row 2.

Row 4: Ch 5, shell in next ch-3 space of previous shell, turn.

Row 5: Ch 3, shell in next ch-3 space of previous shell, [ch 2, 1 dc] 6 times in next ch-5 space, 1 sc in next ch-3 space, turn.

Row 6: Ch 3, 2 dc in next ch-2 space *Sl st, ch 3, 2 dc] in each of next 4 ch-2 spaces, 1 sc in next ch-2 space (before shell), ch 3, shell in ch-3 space of next shell, turn.

Row 7: Rep Row 2.

Rep Rows 4–7 for desired length, ending with Row 6 of pattern, end off.

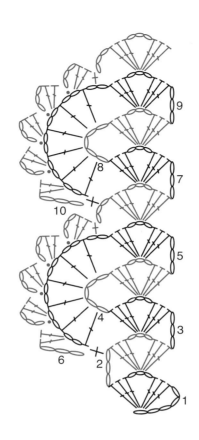

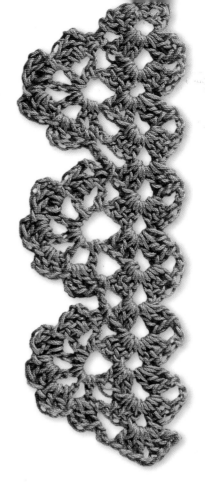

TREFOIL EDGE

Skill Level: Intermediate

Row 1 (WS): Ch 4 (counts as 1 dc, ch 1), [2 dc, ch 2, 3 dc] in 4th ch from hook, turn.

Row 2: Ch 8, Sl st in 6th ch from hook, ch 7, Sl st in same ch as last Sl st, ch 5, Sl st in same ch as last Sl st (trefoil completed), ch 2, [3 dc, ch 2, 3 dc] in next ch 2 space, turn.

Row 3: Sl st in each of first 3 dc, ch 3 (counts as a dc), [2 dc, ch 2, 3 dc] in next ch-2 space, turn.

Rep Rows 2 and 3 until edging is required length, ending with Row 2 of pattern, do not turn.

Edging: *Ch 3, 1 sc in top of row-end st, rep from * across, ending with 1 sc in the top of beg ch 4, end off.

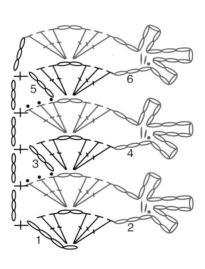

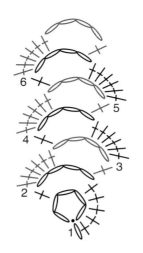

CRESCENT BRAID

Skill Level: Easy

Ch 5, join with a Sl st to form a ring.

Row 1: Ch 1, 6 sc in ring, ch 4, 1 sc in ring, turn.

Row 2: [6 sc, ch 4, 1 sc] in next ch-4 space, turn.

Rep Row 2 for desired length of trim.

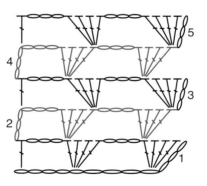

LITTLE BOWS

Skill Level: Easy

Note: Work from the narrow end.

Ch 12.

Row 1: 4 dc in 4th ch from hook, ch 3, skip next 3 ch, 4 dc in next ch (4-dc group made), ch 3, skip 3 ch, 1 dc in last ch, turn.

Row 2: Ch 6 (counts as dc, ch 3), skip next ch-3 space, 4 dc in first dc of next 4-dc group, ch 3, skip next ch-3 space, 4 dc in first dc of next 4-dc group, turn.

Row 3: Ch 3, 4 dc in first dc of first group, ch 3, skip next ch-3 space, 4 dc in first dc of next group, ch 3, 1 dc in 3rd ch of turning ch-6, turn.

Rep Rows 2 and 3 for desired length.

PRINCESS PICOTS

Skill Level: Intermediate

Ch a multiple of 4.

Row 1: 1 dc in 4th ch from hook, *ch 2, skip next 2 ch, 1 dc in each of next 2 ch, rep from * across, turn.

Row 2: Ch 4 (counts as dc, ch 1), *[1 dc, ch 1, 1 dc] in next ch-2 space (V-st made), ch 1, rep from * across, 1 dc in top of turning ch, turn.

Row 3: Ch 3 (counts as first dc), *skip next ch-1 space, 3 dc in ch-1 space of next V-st, rep from * across, 1 dc in 3rd ch of turning ch, turn.

Row 4: Ch 1, 1 sc in first dc, *, [1 sc, 1 dc, ch 4, Sl st in 4th ch from hook (picot made), 1 dc, 1 sc] in center dc of next 3-dc group, rep from * across, 1 sc in top of turning ch, end off.

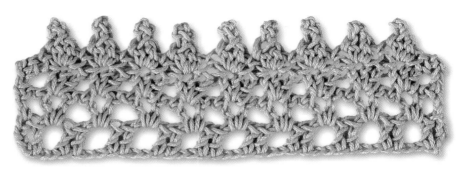

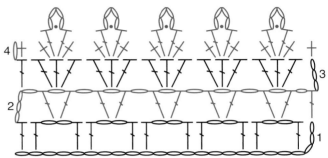

THREE-PETAL SCALLOP

Skill Level: Intermediate

*Tr3tog: *Yo twice, pick up a loop in designated stitch [yo, draw through 2 loops on hook] twice, rep from * twice in same stitch, yo, draw through all 4 loops on hook.*

Ch a multiple of 7 plus 3.

Row 1: 1 dc in 4th ch from hook, 1 dc in each ch across row, turn.

Row 2: Ch 1, 1 sc in first dc, *ch 8, Sl st in fourth ch from hook (picot made), ch 4, skip next 6 dc, 1 sc in next dc, rep from * across, ending with last sc in top of turning ch, turn.

Row 3: Ch 4, *[tr3tog, ch 5, tr3tog, ch 5, tr3tog] in next picot, 1 tr in next sc, rep from * across.

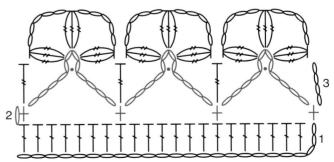

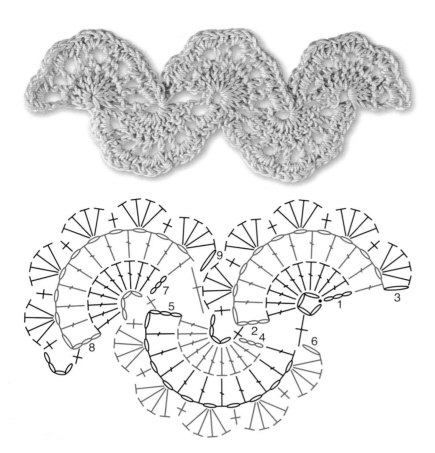

SURPRISING SHELLS

Skill Level: Experienced

Ch 4, join with a Sl st to form a ring.

Row 1: Ch 3 (counts as a dc), 10 dc in ring (11 dc), do not join, turn.

Row 2: Ch 4 (counts as dc, ch 1), skip first dc, *1 dc in next dc, ch 1, rep from * 8 times, 1 dc in top of turning ch (11 dc, 10 ch-1 spaces), turn.

Row 3: Ch 1, *4 hdc in next ch-1 space, 1 sc in next ch-1 space, rep from * 4 times, ch 4, 1 sc in turning ch, turn.

Row 4: Ch 3 (counts as a dc), 10 dc in next ch-4 space, turn.

Row 5: Ch 4 (counts as dc, ch 1), skip first dc, *1 dc in next dc, ch 1, rep from * 8 times, 1 dc in top of turning ch, do not turn, work 1 sc in the starting ring of the previous motif, turn.

Row 6: Rep Row 3.

Rep Rows 4–6 for shell pattern.

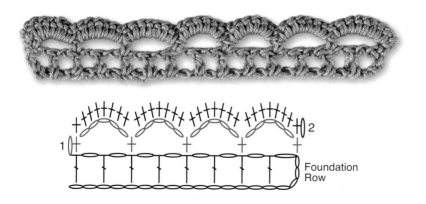

SIMPLE SCALLOP

Skill Level: Easy

Ch a multiple of 4.

Foundation Row: 1 dc in 6th ch from hook, *ch 1, skip next ch, 1 dc in next ch, rep from * across, turn.

Row 1: Ch 1, 1 sc in first dc, *ch 5, skip next dc, 1 sc in next dc, rep from * across to within last dc, ch 5, skip next dc, skip next ch, 1 sc in next ch, turn.

Row 2: Ch 1, 1 sc in first sc, * 7 sc in each ch-5 loop across, 1 sc in the last sc, end off.

SABRINA'S LACE

Skill Level: Experienced

*Dtr2tog: *Yo 3 times, pick up a loop in designated stitch, [yo, draw yarn through 2 loops on hook] 3 times, rep from * once, yo, draw through 3 loops on hook.*

Note: At the end of Row 1, the number of ch-1 spaces must be a multiple of 8 plus 1, in order for the pattern to work out correctly.

Ch a multiple of 16 plus 6.

Row 1: 1 dc in 6th ch from hook, *ch 1, skip next ch, 1 dc in next ch, rep from * across, turn.

Row 2: Ch 3 (counts as first dc now and throughout), [1 dc in next space, 1 dc in next dc] twice, *ch 5, skip next 2 ch-1 spaces, 1 tr in next ch-1 space, ch 5, skip 2 dc, 1 dc in next dc, [1 dc in next space, 1 dc in next dc] 3 times (7 dc in group), rep from * across to within last 2 ch-1 spaces, [1 dc in next dc, 1 dc in next ch-1 space] twice, 1 dc in 3rd ch of turn ch, turn.

Row 3: Ch 3, skip first dc, 1 dc in each of next 3 dc, *ch 7, 1 sc in next tr, ch 7, skip next dc**, 1 dc in each of next 5 dc, rep from * across, ending last rep at **, 1 dc in each of next 3 dc, 1 dc in top of turning ch, turn.

Row 4: Ch 3, skip first dc, 1 dc in each of next 2 dc, *ch 7, [1 sc, ch 5, 1 sc] in next sc, ch 7, skip next dc, 1 dc in each of next 3 dc, rep from * across, 1 dc in top of turn ch, turn.

Row 5: Ch 6 (counts as dc, ch 3), *[dtr2tog, ch 3] 5 times in next ch-5 space, skip next dc, dc in next dc, rep from * across, ending with last 1 dc in top of turning ch, turn.

Row 6: Sl st in first ch-3 space, ch 1, 1 sc in same space, *[ch 5, 1 sc] in each of next 5 spaces**, 1 sc in next space, rep from * across, ending last rep at **, Sl st in top of turning ch, end off.

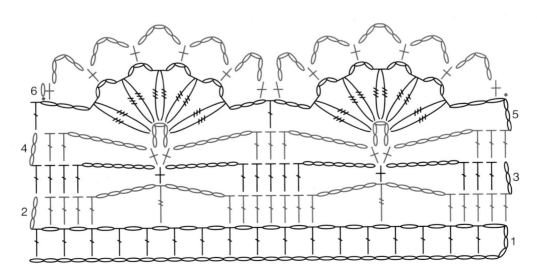

COLLEEN BORDER

Skill Level: Easy

Ch a multiple of 4 plus 2.

Foundation Row: 1 dc in 6th ch from hook, *ch 1, skip next ch, 1 dc in next ch, rep from * across, turn.

Row 1: Ch 1, 1 sc in first dc, *1 sc in next ch-1 space, 1 sc in next dc, rep from * across, working last sc in 3rd ch at beg ch, turn.

Row 2: Ch 3 (counts as first dc), skip first 3 sc, * 3 dc in next sc, skip next 3 sc, rep from * across to within last 3 sts, skip next 2 sc, 1 dc in last sc, turn.

Row 3: Ch 5 (counts as dc, ch 2), *[yo, pick up a loop in next dc, yo, draw through 2 loops on hook] 3 times, yo, draw through all 4 loops on hook (cluster made), ch 3, rep from * across to within last 4 sts, cluster in next 3 dc, ch 2, dc in top of turning ch, turn.

Row 4: Ch 1, 1 sc in first dc, 2 sc in next ch-2 space, 1 sc in top of cluster, *3 sc in next ch-3 space, 1 sc in next cluster, rep from * across, ending with 2 sc in next ch-2 space, 1 sc in top turning ch, turn.

Row 5: Ch 4 (counts as dc, ch 1), skip first 2 sc, *1 dc in next sc, ch 1, skip next sc, rep from * across, ending with 1 dc in last sc, end off.

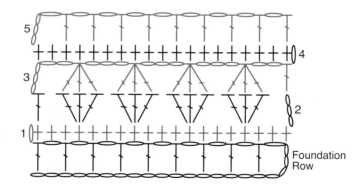

QUEEN'S LACE

Skill Level: Intermediate

*Tr3tog: *Yo twice, pick up a loop in designated space, [yo, draw through 2 loops] twice, rep from * 2 times, yo, draw through all 4 loops on hook.*

Ch a multiple of 16 plus 7.

Row 1: 1 dc in 7th ch from hook, *skip next 3 ch, [1 dc, ch 3, 1 dc] in next ch, rep from * across, turn.

Row 2: Ch 1, Sl st in first ch-3 space, ch 4 (counts as first tr), [3 tr, ch 3, 4 tr] in first ch-3 space, *1 dc in next ch-3 space, [4 tr, ch 3, 4 tr] in next ch-3 space, rep from * across, ending with last tr of last shell in top of turning ch, turn.

Row 3: Sl st across to next ch-3 space, ch 4, [yo twice, pick up a loop in same space, (yo, draw through 2 loops) twice] twice, yo hook through all 3 loops on hook, [ch 5, tr3tog] twice in same space, *[3 dc, ch 3, 3 dc] in next ch-3 space, [tr3tog, ch 5, tr3tog, ch 5, tr3tog] in next ch-3 space, rep from * across, turn.

Row 4: Sl st in first ch-5 space, ch 5 (counts as tr, ch 1), [1 tr, ch 1] 3 times in same space, *[1 tr, ch 3, 1 tr] in top of next cluster, [ch 1, 1 tr] 4 times in next ch-5 space**, [2 sc, ch 3, 2 sc] in next ch-3 space, [1 tr, ch 1] 4 times in next ch-5 space, rep from * across ending last rep at **, end off.

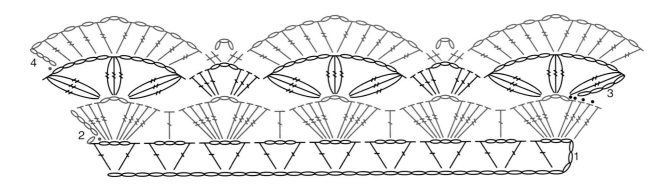

CIRCLES AND PICOTS

Skill Level: Intermediate

Ch a multiple of 5 plus 1.

Row 1: 1 sc in 2nd ch from hook, skip next ch, *5 hdc in next ch (shell made), skip next ch**, 1 sc in each of next 2 ch*, rep from * to * across, ending last rep at **, (1 sc, ch 1, 1 sc) in last ch, working across opposite side of foundation ch, skip next ch, rep from * to * across, ending last rep at **, sc in last ch, join with Sl st to first sc.

Row 2: Sl st in each of next 3 hdc, ch 1, sc in same st, *ch 7, 1 sc in third hdc of next shell, rep from * across, skip next hdc, 1 hdc in next hdc, turn.

Row 3: Ch 7 (counts as hdc, ch 5), *(1 sc, ch 2, 1 sc) in 4th ch of the next ch-7 loop (picot made), ch 5, rep from * across, ending with 1 hdc in last hdc of previous row, turn.

Row 4: Ch 5, *1 sc in 3rd ch of next ch 5, ch 7, rep from * across, ending with 1 sc in 3rd ch of last ch-7 space, skip next ch, 1 hdc in next ch, end off.

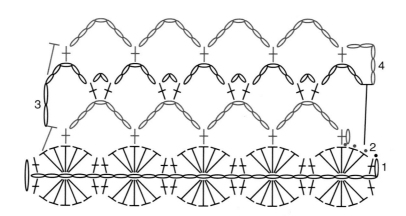

CRESCENT MOON

Skill Level: Experienced

First Crescent

Ch 6, join with a Sl st to form a ring.

Row 1: Ch 3 (counts as first dc) 13 dc in ring (14 dc), turn.

Row 2: Ch 1, 1 sc in first dc, 1 sc in next dc, [ch 5, 1 sc in each of next 2 dc] 6 times, ending with last sc in top of turning ch, turn.

Second Crescent

Row 3: Ch 6, Sl st in next ch-5 loop, turn.

Row 4: Ch 3 (counts as first dc), 13 dc in next ch-6 loop, Sl st to first sc of First Crescent, turn.

Row 5: Ch 1, 1 sc in first 2 dc, [ch 5, 1 sc in each of next 2 dc] 6 times, Sl st in the next ch-5 loop of previous crescent, turn.

Third Crescent

Row 6: Ch 6, Sl st in the first free ch-5 loop of last crescent, turn.

Row 7: Ch 3 (counts as first dc), 13 dc in the ch 6, Sl st in next free ch-5 loop of previous crescent, turn.

Row 8: Ch 1, 1 sc in first 2 dc, [ch 5, 1 sc in each of next 2 dc] 6 times, Sl st in the next ch-5 loop of previous crescent, turn.

Rep Third Crescent Rows 6–8 for pattern.

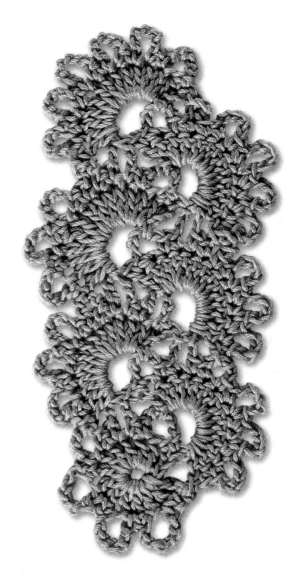

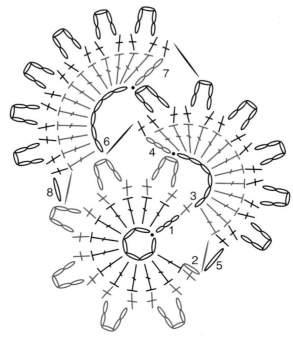

SWING SHELL

This summertime shell flares a bit toward the lower edge for comfort and easy wearing. For a feminine finish, the neckline and lower edges are trimmed with Neapolitan Lace (page 207).

YOU WILL NEED

Yarn

- Shown: Blue Heron Egyptian Mercerized Cotton, 8 oz (227 g)/1000 yd (914.4 m), Berry: 1 skein (all sizes)

Hook

- 5/F (3.75 mm)

Stitches used

- Chain
- Half double crochet
- Half double crochet decrease
- Double crochet

Gauge

- 18 hdc = 4" (10 cm); 16 rows hdc = 4" (10 cm)

Notions

- Tapestry needle

Finished size

- Small (Medium, Large, X-large)
- Finished chest size (after blocking): 36" (38", 40", 42") (91.5 [96.5, 101.5, 106.5] cm)

Notes:

Half Double Crochet Decrease (dec 1 hdc): At beg of row, ch 3, *yo, pick up a loop in next st, yo, draw through 2 loops on hook, yo, pick up a loop in next st, yo, draw through all 4 loops on hook*. To make hdc dec at end of row, work to within 3 sts of end, rep from * to *, 1 hdc in top of turning ch.

Back

Ch 90 (95, 100, 105).

Foundation Row: 1 sc in 2nd ch from hook, 1 sc in each ch across row, turn.

Row 1: Ch 3 (counts as first hdc, now and throughout) skip first st, 1 hdc in each st across, 1 hdc in top of turning ch, turn (89 [94, 99,104] sc).

Rep Row 1 until Back measures 2" (5 cm) from beg, then dec 1 hdc each end of next row (88 [93, 98,103] hdc); then dec 1 hdc each end of row every 2" (5 cm) 3 times more (82 [87, 92, 97] sts); work even for 1" (2.5 cm), dec 1 hdc at each end of next row (80 [85, 90, 95] sts). Work even in pattern until Back measures 9" (9½", 10", 10½") (23 [24, 25, 27] cm) from beg.

Armhole Shaping

Sl st over first 4 (5, 5, 6) sts, ch 3, work in hdc across to within last 4 (5, 5, 6) sts, turn, leaving these sts unworked (72 [75, 80, 83] hdc). Cont in pattern, dec 1 hdc at each end of every other row 4 (5, 6, 7) times (64 [65, 68, 69] hdc). Work even in pattern until armhole measures 5½" (6", 6½", 7") (14 [15, 16.5, 18] cm) from beg of armhole.

Neck Shaping

Cont in pattern, working across first 14 (15, 15, 16) sts, turn, leaving rem 50 (50, 53, 53) to be worked later. Keeping armhole edge even, dec 1 hdc at neck edge every other row 5 times, work even on rem 9 (10, 10, 11) sts until armhole measures 8" (8½", 9", 9½") (20.5 [21.5, 22, 24] cm) from beg, end off. Skip center 36 (35, 38, 37) sts, join yarn in next st and work in pattern across rem 14 (15, 15, 16) sts, turn. Work same as opposite side, reversing shaping, end off.

Front

Work same as Back until Armhole measures 4½" (5", 5½", 6") (11.5 [13, 14, 15.5] cm) from beg of armhole. Work Neck Shaping same as Back. Work each shoulder even until Front measures same as finished Back.

Trim

Follow instructions for Neapolitan Lace (page 207). Make 1 piece to fit around bottom edge and make 1 piece to fit around neckline when slightly stretched. Sew bottom trim right at edge. With tapestry needle, sew neck trim to overlap, allowing small scallop to show at top of neck.

Armhole Trim

Rnd 1: With right side facing, join yarn at center of one underarm, ch 1, sc evenly around armhole, join with Sl st in first sc.

Rnd 2: Ch 1, sc in each sc around, join with Sl st in first sc.

Rnd 3: Ch 1, working from left to right, reverse sc in each sc around, join with Sl st in first reverse sc.

Rep Armhole Trim around other armhole.

Tunisian Stitches

Tunisian crochet is also known as afghan stitch. Tunisian crochet is almost always worked from the right side, and almost all patterns done in Tunisian begin with the first row of basic Tunisian crochet. Each row of Tunisian consists of two parts, a forward and backward motion. In the forward part, all stitches are picked up and held on the hook; in the backward part, stitches are worked off, usually two at a time. Because all stitches are held on the hook, a special hook called an afghan hook is used for this method of crochet.

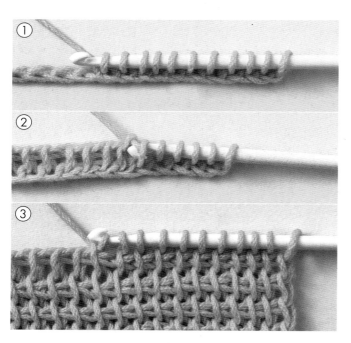

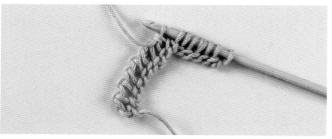

TUNISIAN SIMPLE STITCH

Skill Level: Easy

Ch any number of sts.

Foundation Row (first half): Keeping all loops on the hook, skip first ch from the hook (the loop on the hook is the first chain) and draw up a loop in each ch across, do not turn **(1)**.

Foundation Row (second half): Yo, draw it through the first loop on hook, *Yo, draw through next 2 loops, rep from * across until 1 loop remains. The loop that remains on the hook always counts as the first stitch of the next row **(2)**.

Row 1 (first half): Keeping all loops on the hook, skip the first vertical bar, draw up a loop under the next vertical bar and under each vertical bar across.

Row 1 (second half): Work the same as the second half of foundation row.

Rep Row 1 for Tunisian simple stitch **(3)**.

Last Row: Skip first st, insert hook in next vertical bar, yo, draw through 2 loops on hook (Sl st completed), Sl st in each vertical bar across row, end off.

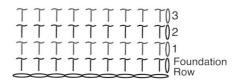

The foundation row of most Tunisian stitches is the same as the foundation row of Tunisian simple stitch (TSS). Another option for the foundation row is to cast stitches onto the hook as if to knit, and then work them off as for the second half of the TSS foundation row.

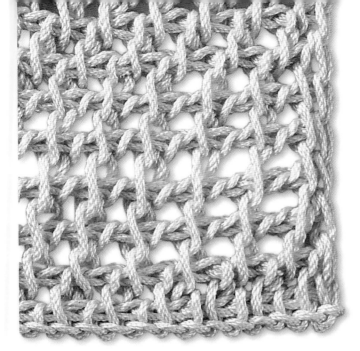

MESH STITCH

Skill Level: Experienced

Ch an even number of sts.

Foundation Row: Work forward and return halves same as for TSS.

Row 1 (forward half): Skip first st, TSS in next st, *yo, skip the next bar, pick up loop in next bar, rep from * across.

Row 1 (return half): Work off all loops as in TSS, counting each yo as a loop.

Row 2 (forward half): Skip first st, * yo, skip next bar, pick up a loop in next slanted st (yo of previous row), rep from * across, ending with TSS in last st.

Row 2 (return half): Work off all loops as in TSS, counting each yo as a loop.

Row 3 (forward half): Skip first st, pick up a loop in yo of previous row, *yo, skip next bar, pick up a loop in yo of previous row, rep from * across, ending yo, TSS in last st.

Row 3 (return half): Work off all loops as in TSS, counting each yo as a loop.

Rep Rows 2 and 3 for pattern.

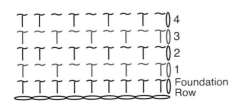

SEED STITCH

Skill Level: Experienced

Purl stitch: Bring yarn to front, insert hook in next vertical bar, bring yarn to back under hook, wrap around hook from back to front, draw yarn through st (Purl st made).

Ch an even number of sts.

Foundation Row: Work forward and return halves same as for TSS.

Row 1 (forward half): Skip first st, TSS in next st, *Purl st in next st, TSS in next st, rep from * across.

Row 1 (return half): Work off all loops as in TSS.

Row 2 (forward half): Skip first st, *Purl st in next st, TSS in next st, rep from * across, TSS in last st.

Row 2 (return half): Work off all loops as in TSS.

Rep Rows 1 and 2 for pattern.

Last Row: Skip first st, insert hook in next vertical bar, yo, draw through 2 loops on hook (Sl st completed), Sl st in each vertical bar across row, end off.

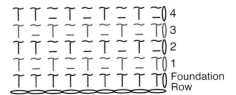

KNIT STITCH

Skill Level: Intermediate

Knit stitch: On forward half of row, insert hook from front to back through and between 2 vertical strands of next st, yo, draw yarn through st (Knit st made).

Ch any number of sts.

Foundation Row: Work forward and return halves same as for TSS.

Row 1 (forward half): Skip first st, Knit st in each st across, do not turn.

Row 1 (return half): Work off all loops as in TSS.

Rep Row 1 for pattern.

Last Row: Skip first st, insert hook in next vertical bar, yo, draw through 2 loops on hook (Sl st completed), Sl st in each vertical bar across row, end off.

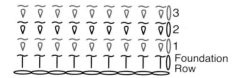

PURL STITCH

Skill Level: Intermediate

Purl stitch: On forward half of row, bring yarn to front, insert hook in next vertical bar, bring yarn to back under hook, wrap around hook from back to front, draw yarn through st (Purl st made).

Ch any number of sts.

Foundation Row: Work forward and return halves same as for TSS.

Row 1 (forward half): Skip first st, Purl st in each st across.

Row 1 (return half): Work off all loops as in TSS.

Rep Row 1 for pattern.

Last Row: Skip first st, insert hook in next vertical bar, yo, draw through 2 loops on hook (Sl st completed), Sl st in each vertical bar across row, end off.

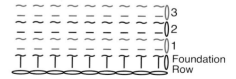

RIB STITCH

Skill Level: Intermediate

Ch a multiple of 4 plus 2.

Foundation Row: Work forward and return halves same as for TSS.

Row 1 (forward half): Skip first st, Knit st in next st, *Purl st in each of next 2 sts, Knit st in each of next 2 sts, rep from * across.

Row 1 (return half): Work off all loops as in TSS.

Rep Row 1 for pattern.

Last Row: Skip first st, insert hook in next vertical bar, yo, draw through 2 loops on hook (Sl st completed), Sl st in each vertical bar across row, end off.

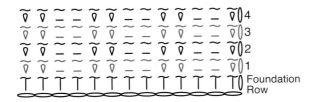

CLUSTERS STITCH

Skill Level: Intermediate

Notes:

1. Most Tunisian stitches begin with a basic row as in Tunisian Simple Stitch. The Cluster Stitch is unusual in that clusters are formed on the return half of first row.

2. When working ch 3, [yo, draw yarn through first loop on hook] 4 times before continuing on.

3. The ch 1 that forms the eye of the cluster is not counted as part of the ch 3.

Ch a multiple of 4 plus 1.

Row 1 (forward half): Work forward half of Row 1 of TSS.

Row 1 (return half): *Ch 3, yo, draw through 5 loops on hook (the loop at end of ch 3 just made, plus 4 more on hook), ch 1 (which forms the eye of the cluster), rep from * across.

Row 2 (forward half): *Draw up a loop in the eye of next cluster, draw up a loop in each of next 3 ch, rep from * across.

Row 2 (return half): Work off all loops as in TSS.

Rep Row 2 for pattern.

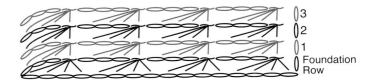

CABLE STITCH

Skill Level: Experienced

Tunisian Front Post Triple Crochet (FPtr): Yo twice, insert hook from front to back to front again around bar or post of designated st, yo, draw up a loop to height of current row (yo, draw through 2 loops on hook) twice, skip next vertical bar on last row behind FPtr.

Tunisian Front Post Double Triple Crochet (FPdtr): Yo 3 times, insert hook from front to back to front again around the post of designated st, yo, draw up a loop to height of current row (yo, draw through 2 loops on hook) 3 times, skip next vertical bar on last row behind FPdtr.

Ch a multiple of 7 plus 2.

Foundation Row: Work forward and return halves same as for TSS.

Rows 1–3: Rep Row 1 of TSS.

Row 4 (forward half): Skip first st, TSS in next 2 sts, *FPtr around next vertical bar 3 rows below, TSS in next st, FPtr around the next vertical bar 3 rows below, TSS in each of next 4 sts, rep from * across, ending with TSS in each of last 3 sts.

Row 4 (return half): Work off all loops as in TSS.

Row 5: Rep Row 1 of TSS.

Row 6 (forward half): Skip first st, TSS in next 2 sts, *skip next 2 sts, FPdtr, around the post of the second FPtr 2 rows below, working behind FPdtr just made, TSS in the second skipped st in current row, working in front of FPdtr, FPdtr around the post of first skipped FPtr 2 rows below, TSS in next 4 vertical bars on last row, rep from * across, ending with TSS in each of last 3 sts.

Row 6 (return half): Work off all loops as in TSS.

Row 7: Rep Row 1 of TSS.

Row 8 (forward half): Sk first st, TSS in next 2 sts, *FPtr around the post of next FPdtr 2 rows below, TSS in next st in current row, FPtr around the post of next FPdtr 2 rows below, TSS in next 4 sts, rep from * across, ending with TSS in each of last 3 sts.

Row 8 (return half): Work off all loops as in TSS.

Rep Rows 5–8 for pattern, ending with any return row.

Last Row: Skip first st, insert hook in next vertical bar, yo, draw through 2 loops on hook (Sl st completed), Sl st in each vertical bar across row, end off.

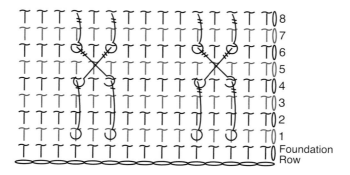

MOCK POPCORN STITCH

Skill Level: Experienced

Note: When working ch 4, [yo, draw yarn through first loop on hook] 4 times before continuing on.

Ch a multiple of 4.

Foundation Row: Work forward and return halves same as for TSS.

Row 1 (forward half): Work forward half of Row 1 of TSS.

Row 1 (return half): Yo, draw through 1 loop on hook, [yo, draw through first 2 loops on hook] 3 times, *ch 4, [yo, draw yarn through first 2 loops on hook] 4 times, rep from * across, 1 loop remains on hook.

Row 2 (forward half): Holding ch-4 loops to front of work rep Row 1 of TSS.

Row 2 (return half): Work off all loops as in TSS.

Row 3 (forward half): Work forward half of Row 1 of TSS.

Row 3 (return half): Yo, draw through 1 loop on hook, *yo, draw yarn through 2 loops on hook, *ch 4, [yo, draw yarn through first 2 loops on hook] 4 times, rep from * across until 3 loops rem on hook, ch 4, yo pull through first 2 loops on hook, 1 loop on hook.

Row 4: Rep Row 2.

Rep Rows 1–4 for pattern.

Last Row: Skip first st, insert hook in next vertical bar, yo, draw through 2 loops on hook (Sl st completed), Sl st in each vertical bar across row, end off.

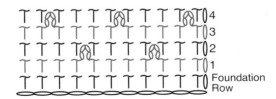

Cont in this manner, having 1 st more each row, until you have 7 loops on hook (Row 6), work off as before.

Bind off: Insert hook under next bar, draw yarn through bar and loop on hook (Sl st worked). Cont to work Sl st through each bar to end,* Sl st in same ch as last loop of Row 6. Do not fasten off, but cont to First Square, instructions below.

First Square

Row 1 (still working on first color strip): Draw up a loop in each of next 6 ch (7 loops on hook), [yo, draw through 2 loops] 6 times (1 loop left on hook). This loop is the first loop of the foll row.

Row 2: Insert hook under next bar, draw yarn through (2 loops on hook), draw up a loop in each of next 4 bars, draw up a loop in next ch (7 loops on hook), work off loops as for row 1 of square.

Rows 3–5: Rep row 2.

Bind Off: Sl st in each bar across, Sl st in same ch as last loop of row 5.

Next Squares: Work squares across strip in same manner as First Square (6 ch left at end of row).

End Triangle

Row 1 (end of first color strip): Draw up loop in each of 6 rem ch (7 loops on hook), work off as before.

Row 2: Draw up a loop in each of first 5 bars (6 loops on hook), work off as before.

Rows 3–6: Cont in this manner, always having 1 less loop for each row, until 1 rem, end off. This completes first color strip.

Strip 2

Begins and ends with a square. Each square has 5 rows.

First Square

Row 1: Join by drawing up a loop of B in top right corner of Strip 1. With B, pick up 1 loop in each of 5 Sl sts of beg triangle, pick up lp in end of first row of first square on Strip 1 (7 loops on hook), work off loops.

Complete Square as for rows 2–5 of First Square of Strip 1.

Bind Off: Sl st in each bar across, having last Sl st in last row (top point) of same square.

Next Squares: Work across strip in same manner as First Square, picking up first row of sts in Sl sts, then under bars in subsequent rows. End strip with complete square.

ENTRELAC PATTERN

Skill Level: Experienced

Note: This pattern is worked in Tunisian Simple Stitch, but a special hook is not required. Because of the pattern's uniqueness and since you will never have more than 7 stitches on the hook at one time, you can use a regular crochet hook.

Entrelac pattern is worked entirely from the right side. When one strip is completed, fasten off that yarn, join new yarn at beginning of row, and start again. To even out ends, every other color strip begins and ends with a half square (triangle). Each square or triangle in strip consists of 5 rows. Refer to page 216 for detailed instructions for Tunisian Simple Stitch.

For the sample shown, three colors of yarn are used (A, B, and C). Entrelac can also be done with just two colors, alternating strips.

Strip 1

Begins and ends with triangle.

With A, ch a multiple of 11 plus 2 loosely.

Beginning Triangle

Row 1: Draw up loop in 2nd ch from hook (2 loops on hook), yo, draw through both loops.

Row 2: Insert hook between first 2 vertical bars and pick up a loop (inc made), pick up a loop in next ch (3 loops on hook), [yo, draw through 2 loops] 2 times (1 loop left on hook).

Row 3: *Insert hook bet first 2 bars and pick up loop (inc made), draw up loop from under next bar and next ch (4 loops on hook), [yo, draw through 2 loops] 3 times (1 loop left on hook).

Strip 3

Begins and ends with a triangle.

Begining Triangle: Join by drawing up a loop of C in top right corner of last strip. With C, ch 2, draw up a loop in first ch from hook and pick up loop in side of first row of first square of strip 2 (3 loops on hook), [yo, draw through 2 loops] 2 times. Rep from * to * of Beg Triangle, Strip 1. Sl st in first bound off st of First Square, Strip 2.

Work Squares of Strip 3 same as Squares of Strip 2. End with a triangle, same as End Triangle, Strip 1.

Remaining Strips

Work same as Strips 2 and 3, ending with Strip 3, alternating colors until you have the desired number of full strips.

Closing Triangles

Work across top and bottom to even off edges.

Row 1: Join by drawing up a loop of A in top right corner of last Strip. With A, pick up 5 loops along bound off edge of first square, plus 1 lp in end of first row of second square (7 loops on hook), work off as before.

Row 2: Sk first bar, pick up 5 loops so you only have 6 loops on hook, work off as before.

Row 3: Sk first bar, pick up 4 loops (5 loops on hook), work off as before.

Row 4: Sk first bar, pick up 3 loops (4 loops on hook), work off as before.

Row 5: Sk first bar, pick up 2 loops (3 loops on hook), work off as before, 1 loop on hook, Sl st in next 2 bars, Sl st into last side st (at top).

Cont across top edge in this manner. Work same closing triangles across bottom edge.

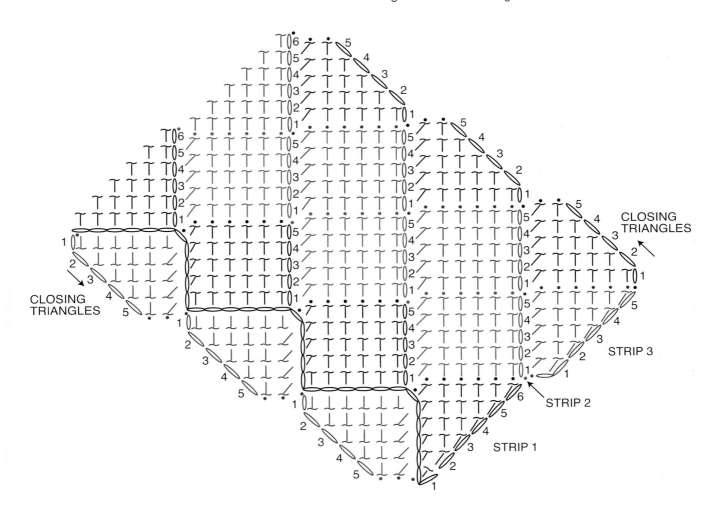

CHEVRON STITCH

Skill Level: Experienced

Ch a multiple of 12 plus 1.

Foundation Row: Work forward and return halves same as for TSS.

Row 1 (forward half): Sk first vertical bar, insert hook between strands of first vertical bar and next vertical bar (Tunisian increase made), *pick up a loop in each of next 7 vertical bars, yo and draw through 3 loops on hook (Tunisian decrease made)**, pick up a loop in each of next 4 vertical bars, inc 1, 1 TSS , inc 1, rep from * across, ending last repeat at **, pick up loop in each of next 4 vertical bars, inc 1, TSS in last st, do not turn.

Row 1 (return half): Work off all loops as in TSS.

Rep Row 1 for pattern.

Last Row: Skip first st, insert hook in next vertical bar, yo, draw through 2 loops on hook (Sl st completed), Sl st in each vertical bar across row, end off.

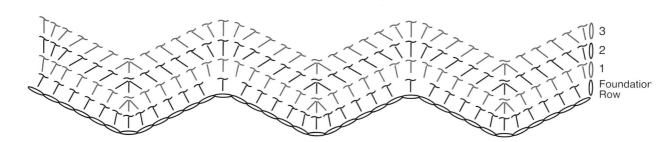

3
2
1
Foundation Row

BABY DIAMONDS BLANKET

This entrelac baby blanket is worked in adjoining strips of squares turned on their points. The pattern is a little challenging at first, but once mastered, it becomes quite easy. The blanket is worked in Tunisian crochet, but you can use a regular hook because there are never more than seven stitches on the hook at a time.

(continued)

YOU WILL NEED

Yarn

- Medium-weight acrylic yarn in 3 colors
- Shown: Canadiana by Patons, 100% acrylic, 3.5 oz (100 g)/201 yd (185 m): aqua #045 (MC), 4 balls; white #001 (A), 2 balls; light yellow #169 (B), 2 balls

Hook

- 9/I (5.5 mm)

Stitches used

- Tunisian
- Single crochet
- Double crochet

Gauge

- 1 square = 1½" (3.8 cm)

Notion

- Tapestry needle

Finished size

- 34" × 42" (86.5 × 107 cm)

Blanket

Entrelac patt is worked entirely from RS. When 1 strip is completed, fasten off that yarn, join new yarn at beg of row, and start again. To even out ends, every other color strip begins and ends with a half square (triangle). Each square or triangle in strip consists of 5 rows. Refer to page 216 for detailed instructions for Tunisian Simple Stitch.

Strip 1

Begins and ends with triangle.

With MC, ch 144 loosely.

Beg Triangle, Row 1: Draw up lp in second ch from hook (2 lps on hook), yo, draw through both lps.

Row 2: Insert hook bet first 2 vertical bars and pick up lp (inc made), pick up lp in next ch (3 lps on hook), [yo, draw through 2 lps] 2 times (1 lp left on hook).

*Row 3: Insert hook bet first 2 bars and pick up lp (inc made), draw up lp from under next bar and next ch (4 lps on hook), [yo, draw through 2 lps] 3 times (1 lp left on hook).

Cont in this manner, having 1 st more each row, until you have 7 lps on hook (row 5), work off as before.

Bind off: Insert hook under next bar, draw yarn through bar and lp on hook (Sl st worked). Cont to work Sl st through each bar to end.* Sl st in same ch as last lp of row 5. Do not fasten off, but cont to first square.

Square 1, Row 1 (still on first color strip): Draw up lp in each of next 6 ch (7 lps on hook), [yo, draw through 2 lps] 6 times (1 lp left on hook). This lp is the first lp of the foll row.

Row 2: Insert hook under next bar, draw yarn through (2 lps on hook), draw up lp in each of next 4 bars, draw up lp in next ch (7 lps on hook), work off lps as for row 1 of square.

Rows 3–5: Rep Row 2.

Bind off: Sl st in each bar to end, Sl st in same ch as last lp of row 5.

Squares 2–13: Work same as square 1 (6 ch left at end of row).

End Triangle, Row 1 (end of first color strip): Draw up lp in each of 6 rem ch (7 lps on hook), work off as before.

Row 2: Draw up 5 lps (6 lps on hook), work off as before.

Cont in this manner, always having 1 less lp each row, until 1 rem, fasten off. This completes first color strip.

Strip 2

Begins and ends with a square. Each square has 5 rows.

Square 1, Row 1: With A, pick up 1 lp in each of 6 Sl sts of beg triangle, pick up lp in end of first row of first square on strip 1 (7 lps on hook), work off lps.

Complete square as for Rows 2–5 of Square 1 of first strip.

Bind off: Sl st in each bar to end, having last Sl st in last row (top point) of same square.

Squares 2–14: Work same as Square 1, picking up first row of sts in slipped sts, then under bars in subsequent rows. End strip with completed square

Strip 3

Begins and ends with a triangle.

Beg Triangle: With MC, ch 2, draw up lp in first ch from hook and pick up lp in side of first row of first square of strip 2 (3 lps on hook), [yo, draw through 2 lps] 2 times. Rep from * to * of beg triangle, Strip 1. Sl st in first bound off st of Square 1, Strip 2.

Work squares of strip same as squares of strip 2. End with triangle, same as end triangle, Strip 1.

Remaining Strips

Work same as Strips 2 and 3 in this color sequence: B, MC, A, MC, ending with MC (39 strips).

Closing Triangles

Worked across top and bottom to even off edges.

Row 1: With MC, at top right corner, pick up 6 lps along bound off edge of first square, plus 1 lp in end of first row of second square (7 lps on hook), work off as before.

Row 2: Sk first bar, pick up 5 lps so you only have 6 lps on hook, work off as before.

Row 3: Sk first bar, pick up 4 lps (5 lps on hook), work off as before.

Row 4: Sk first bar, pick up 3 lps (4 lps on hook), work off as before.

Row 5: Sk first bar, pick up 2 lps (3 lps on hook), work off as before, 1 lp on hook, Sl st into last side st (at top).

Cont across top edge in this manner. Work same closing triangles across bottom edge.

Border

Row 1: Using MC, starting in top right corner, RS facing you, ch 1, work 1 sc in same st (half corner), * work sc along short edge, picking up 96 sts along this end, 3 sc in corner, sc along long end, picking up 126 sts along this end, 3 sc in corner, rep from * once, ending with 1 sc in same st as beg, join with Sl st to beg ch 1 (this forms last corner).

Row 2: Ch 3, work 2 dc in same st (half corner), * sk 2 sts, 1 sc in next st, sk 2 sts, [3 dc, ch 2, 3 dc] in next st, rep from * all around, ending with 3 dc in same st as beg ch 3, ch 2, join with Sl st to form last corner, fasten off.

Finishing

Weave in ends using tapestry needle.

Interlocking squares of Tunisian crochet are turned on their points. Peaks of the border echo the blanket's diamond motif.

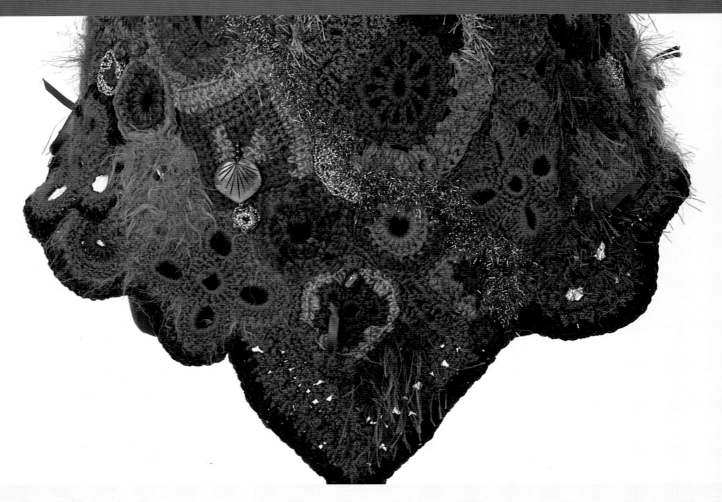

SPECIALTY CROCHET METHODS

Several unique crochet methods have evolved and become popular enough to carve their own niches. Some methods, like Polish star, intermeshing, and Bruges lace need no other tools than standard crochet hooks. Others, such as hairpin lace and broomstick lace, at first employed some common household items along with a crochet hook. Once these methods became mainstream, manufacturers designed specialty tools to replace the broomstick and hairpin.

Tapestry Tunisian

Tunisian crochet is a perfect canvas for imagery. There are two ways to work images in Tunisian crochet: by crocheting them in as you go or by embroidering them on afterward. Because basic Tunisian creates a fairly square grid, cross stitch is the perfect way to add detail.

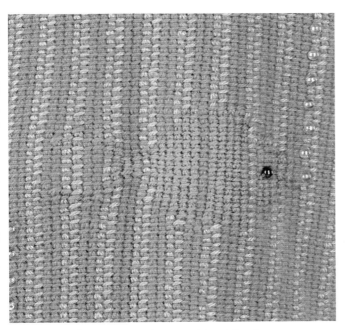

Fish image from a vest designed by Julia Bryant

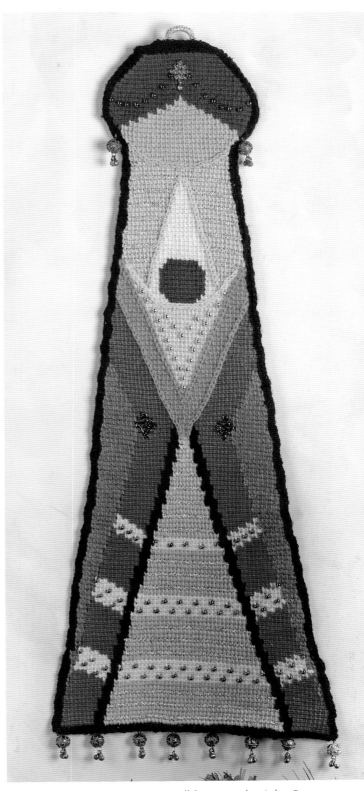

Madonna Tunisian tapestry wall hanging by Julia Bryant

VESTED INTEREST
by Julia Bryant

These playful child-size vests, designed by Julia Bryant, show two different ways to portray images in Tunisian crochet. Walter Whale was cross-stitched onto a solid ground of basic Tunisian Simple Stitch. Delilah Duck was worked into the fabric like knitted intarsia, changing yarn colors while crocheting, as indicated in the pattern grid (page 232). Either design can be worked in cross-stitch or inlaid into the fabric.

YOU WILL NEED

Yarn
- MC: two 50 g balls sport-weight yarn
- Color A: two 50 g balls sport-weight yarn
- small quantities of two contrast colors, B and C
- small amount of black yarn for eyes

Hooks
- 6/G (4 mm) afghan crochet hook
- 4/E (3.5 mm) crochet hook

Notions
- Tapestry needle

Gauge
- 24 sts and 20 rows = 4" (10 cm)

Size
- 2 years (4 years)
- Finished chest measurement: 26" (28") [66 (71) cm]
- Length from shoulder: 12" (13¾") [30.5 (35) cm]

Notes: For either design, the fabric may be worked plain and the design cross-stitched on the surface, or the design may be inlaid into the fabric as intarsia. One square on the graph (page 232) = 1 stitch, or 1 row of Tunisian Simple Stitch (forward and return passes)

Back

With afghan hook and MC chain 73 (79) sts.

Work 30 (35) rows in TSS, following chart for back for placement of stripes, using MC and color A. Continue in TSS following chart for armhole and neck shaping, binding off remaining 6 (7) sts. Fasten off

Left Front (Cross-stitch Version)

With afghan hook and MC chain 37 (40) sts.

Work 30 (35) rows in TSS. For Walter Whale do front in MC. For Delilah Duck follow chart for Left Front for placement of stripes, using MC and color A. Continue in TSS, following chart for neck and armhole shaping, binding off remaining 6 (7) sts. Fasten off.

Right Front

With afghan hook and MC chain 37 (40) sts.

Work 30 (35) rows in TSS, following chart for placement of stripes, using MC and color A. Continue in basic Tunisian crochet stitch, following chart for neck and armhole shaping, binding off remaining 6 (7) sts. Fasten off.

Finishing

With MC yarn and 4/E crochet hook, place pieces together with wrong sides facing, matching stitches and rows, single crochet through both thicknesses to join shoulder and side seams together.

Edging

Row 1: With right side facing, using 4/E hook attach MC to lower edge at right side seam. Single crochet around with 29 (31) sc along bottom right front, 3 sc in corner, 59 (68) sc up right front to shoulder, 30 (30) sc along neck edge, 59 (68) sc down left front to bottom corner, 3 sc in corner, 29 (31) sc across bottom of left front, 60 (65) sc along bottom of back. Join with Sl st to beginning sc. Fasten off.

Row 2: With right side facing, using 4/E hook, attach MC in joining of previous round; work 1 reverse single crochet in each sc around, placing two stitches in each corner st. Join with Sl st. Fasten off.

Armhole Edging

Row 1: With right side facing, using 4/E hook attach MC to underarm seam, ch 1, 1 sc in same place, work 68 (74) sc evenly spaced around armhole. Join with Sl st to first sc. Fasten off.

Row 2: With right side facing, using 4/E hook attach MC in joining chain. Ch 1, 1 sc in same place, 1 reverse sc in each sc around. Join with Sl st to first sc. Fasten off.

Embroidery

Following graph, cross-stitch design in colors A, B, and C on left front, using one square of the afghan stitch for each cross-stitch.

Make eye with a French knot, using black yarn.

Color Inlay Method

Make Back and Right Front same as cross-stitched vest.

Left Front

With afghan hook and MC, chain 37 (40) and using a bobbin for each color, complete the front working in the design of your choice and stripes as indicated.

(When changing colors be sure to cross yarns in the back to avoid a hole.)

Complete vest as for cross-stitched version.

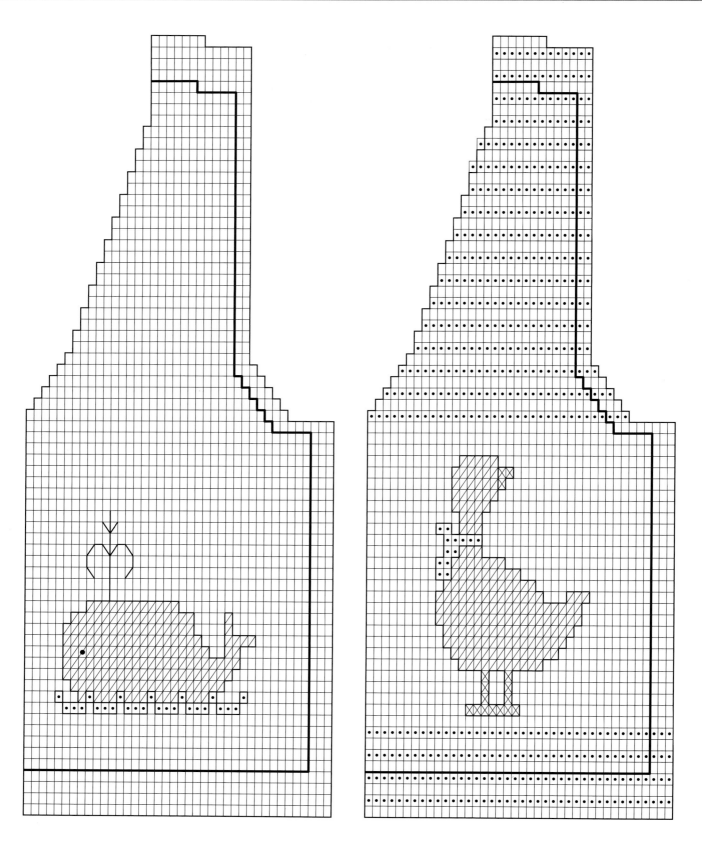

One Piece, Top Down

Most garment patterns begin at the lower edge and work toward the top. You make individual pieces for the fronts, back, and sleeves, and sew them together to finish. Another way to crochet is to work from the top down and crochet the entire garment in one piece, eliminating or greatly reducing the amount of finishing work needed.

TOP-DOWN CHILD'S PULLOVER

To make this child's pullover, you begin at the neck and work toward the bottom. Since it is crocheted all in one piece, there are no seams to sew. The neck and shoulders are worked in the round, going continuously in the same direction. Once you divide for the sleeves and body and begin the shell pattern, the rounds are worked differently. At the end of each round, you join to the beginning of the round with a slip stitch, and then turn and go back in the opposite direction to begin the next round. Each sleeve is worked in the round in this same manner.

(continued)

YOU WILL NEED

Yarn

- Medium-weight
- Shown: Lion Brand Cotton Ease, 50% cotton, 50% acrylic, 3.5 oz (100 g)/207 yd (189 m), #134 Terracotta: 3 (3, 4, 4) skeins

Hook

- 8/H (5 mm)

Stitches used

- Chain
- Double crochet
- V-stitch

Gauge

- 12 dc = 4" (10 cm)
- 4 clusters = 4" (10 cm)

Sizes

- 2 (4, 6, 8)
- Finished chest measurement 22" (25", 28", 30") (56 [63.5, 71, 76] cm)

Pullover

Notes:

1. When ch 3 to begin the round, work 1 linked dc (page 143) to avoid hole. Work 1 linked dc in seam stitch at end of round.

2. Each V-stitch increase adds 2 sts.

Starting at neck edge, ch 43 loosely (or use a larger hook to assure opening fits over child's head), being careful not to twist, join with a Sl st to form a ring.

Rnd 1: Ch 3 (counts as seam st at center back, now and throughout yoke), 1 dc in each of next 7 ch (Left Back section), [1 dc, ch 1, 1 dc] in next ch (V-st inc made), 1 dc in each of the next 5 ch (Left Sleeve section), [1 dc, ch 1, 1 dc] in next ch, 1 dc in each of the next 14 ch (Front section), [1 dc, ch 1, 1 dc] in next ch, 1 dc in each of the next 5 ch (Right Sleeve section) [1 dc, ch 1, 1 dc] in next ch, 1 dc in each of next 7 ch (Right Back section), join with a Sl st to top of beg ch-3.

There will be 14 dc in Front section, 5 dc in each Sleeve section, 14 dc plus seam st in Back section; sections will be divided by a V-st.

Rnd 2: Ch 3, 1 dc in each of next 8 dc, [1 dc, ch 1, 1 dc] in ch-1 space of next V-st, 1 dc in each of next 7 dc, [1 dc, ch 1, 1 dc] in ch-1 space of next V-st, 1 dc in each of next 16 dc, [1 dc, ch 1, 1 dc] in ch-1 space of next V-st, 1 dc in each of next 7 dc, [1 dc, ch 1, 1 dc] in ch-1 space of next V-st, 1 dc in each of next 8 dc, join with a Sl st to top of beg ch-3.

Rnd 3: Ch 3, 1 dc in each of next 9 dc, [1 dc, ch 1, 1 dc] in ch-1 space of next V-st, 1 dc in each of next 9 dc, [1 dc, ch 1, 1 dc] in ch-1 space of next V-st, 1 dc in each of next 18 dc, [1 dc, ch 1, 1 dc] in ch-1 space of next V-st, 1 dc in each of next 9 dc, [1 dc, ch 1, 1 dc] in ch-1 space of next V-st, 1 dc in each of next 9 dc, join with a Sl st to top of beg ch-3.

Rnd 4: Ch 3, 1 dc in each of next 10 dc, [1 dc, ch 1, 1 dc] in ch-1 space of next V-st, 1 dc in each of next 11 dc, [1 dc, ch 1, 1 dc] in ch-1 space of next V-st, 1 dc in each of next 20 dc, [1 dc, ch 1, 1 dc] in ch-1 space of next V-st, 1 dc in each of next 11 dc, [1 dc, ch 1, 1 dc] in ch-1 space of next V-st, 1 dc in each of next 10 dc, join with a Sl st to top of beg ch-3.

Cont in this manner, increasing 8 sts every round till you have 17 (19, 21, 23) sts on Left Back, 25 (29, 33, 37) sts on Left Sleeve, 34 (38, 42, 46) sts on Front, 25 (29, 33, 37) sts on Right Sleeve, 17 (19, 21, 23) sts on Right Back, 118 (134, 150, 166) dc plus seam st plus corner spaces.

Divide for Sleeves and Body

Due to the nature of the shell pattern, shell rnds will be joined at center back seam and then turned for next round.

Rnd 1: Ch 3, skip first dc, 1 dc in each of next 17 (19, 21, 23) sts of Left Back, ch 2 (2, 3, 3), skip next 25, (29, 33, 37) dc of Left Sleeve, 1 dc in each of next 34 (38, 42, 46) dc of Front, ch 2 (2, 3, 3), skip next 25, (29, 33, 37) dc of Right Sleeve, 1 dc in each of next 17 (19, 21, 23) dc of Right Back, join with a Sl st to beg ch-3, turn—68 (76, 84, 92) sts.

Rnd 2 (Shell Foundation Row): Ch 3, 2 dc in same dc, skip next 2 dc, 1 Sl st in next dc, *ch 3, 2 dc in the same dc, skip 2 dc, 1 Sl st next dc*, rep from * to * around to ch-space at armhole, work [1 Sl st, ch 3, 2 dc] in ch-space, 1 Sl st in next dc, rep from * to * to next ch-space at armhole, work [1 Sl st, ch 3, 2 dc] in ch-space, 1 Sl st in next dc, rep from * to * to end, join with 1 sc in beg ch-3, turn—24 (28, 30, 32) shells.

Rnd 3: Ch 3, 2 dc in same st, *[Sl st, ch 3, 2 dc] in next ch-3 space, rep from * around, join with 1 sc in top of turning ch, turn.

Rep Rnd 3 for pattern until body measures 7" (7½", 8", 8½") (18 [19, 20.5, 21.5] cm) from underarm, end off.

Sleeves (make 2)

You will be working Sleeves in rounds, joining and turning, same as Body. Join yarn in armhole opening, in ch-space at underarm, *ch 3, 2 dc in same space, skip next 2 dc, Sl st in next dc, *ch 3, 2 dc in the same dc, skip 2 dc, 1 Sl st next dc*, rep from * to * around Sleeve opening, ending last Sl st in the added ch-space at underarm, join with a Sl st to top of beg ch-3—9 (11, 12, 13) shells—turn.

Cont in shell pattern as established on Body until Sleeve measures 7½" (8", 8½", 9") (19 [20.5, 21.5, 23] cm) from underarm, end off.

Neck Trim

Join yarn at center back seam st, work shell pattern as follows all around neck edge, working in beg ch sts; join yarn at center back seam, *ch 3, 2 dc in same ch, skip 2 ch, 1 Sl st in next st, rep from * around, join with a Sl st in base of beg ch-3, end off.

Blocking

If needed, place on a padded surface, spritz with water, and pat into shape. Do not iron.

TOP-DOWN CHILD'S CARDIGAN

This easy-to-make child's cardigan is crocheted in one piece from the top down, just like the pullover on page 233. The biggest difference is that you will be going back and forth in rows, rather than crocheting continuously in rounds, thus creating the opening down the front. Likewise, the sleeves are worked in rows and seamed together at the underarm.

YOU WILL NEED

Yarn

- Medium-weight
- Shown: Lion Brand Cotton Ease, 50% cotton, 50% acrylic, 3.5 oz (100 g)/107 yd (189 m), #134 Terracotta: 3 (3, 4, 4) skeins

Hook

- 8/H (5 mm)

Stitches used

- Chain
- Slip stitch
- Single crochet
- Double crochet
- V-stitch

Gauge

- 12 dc = 4" (10 cm)
- 4 clusters = 4" (10 cm)

Notions

- Tapestry needle

Sizes

- 2 (4, 6, 8)
- Finished chest measurement 22" (25", 28", 30") (56 [63.5, 71, 76] cm)

Cardigan

Notes:

1. When ch 3 to begin the row, work 1 linked dc (page 143) to avoid hole. Work 1 linked dc in turning chain at end of row.

2. Each V-stitch increase adds 2 sts.

Starting at neck edge, ch 41.

Row 1: 1 dc in 4th ch from hook (counts as 2 dc), 1 dc in each of next 5 ch (Right Front section), [1 dc, ch 1, 1 dc] in next ch (V-st inc made), 1 dc in each of the next 5 chs (Right

Sleeve section), [1 dc, ch 1, 1 dc] in next ch, 1 dc in each of the next 12 chs (Back section), [1 dc, ch 1, 1 dc] in next ch, 1 dc in each of the next 5 chs (Left Sleeve section), [1 dc, ch 1, 1 dc] in next ch, 1 dc in each of rem 7 ch (Left Front section), turn.

There will be 7 dc in each Front section, 5 dc in each Sleeve section, 12 dc in Back section. Sections will be divided by a V-st.

Row 1: Ch 3 (counts as a dc, now and throughout), skip first dc, 1 dc in each of next 7 dc, [1 dc, ch 1, 1 dc] in ch-1 space of next V-st, 1 dc in each of next 7 dc, [1 dc, ch 1, 1 dc] in next ch-1 space, 1 dc in each of next 14 dc, [1 dc, ch 1, 1 dc] in next ch-1 space, 1 dc in each of next 7 dc, [1 dc, ch 1, 1 dc] in next ch-1 space, 1 dc in each of next 7 dc, 1 dc in top of turning ch.

Row 2: Ch 3, skip first dc, 1 dc in each of next 8 dc, [1 dc, ch 1, 1 dc] in ch-1 space of next V-st, 1 dc in each of next 9 dc, [1 dc, ch 1, 1 dc] in next ch-1 space, 1 dc in each of next 16 dc, [1 dc, ch 1, 1 dc] in next ch-1 space, 1 dc in each of next 9 dc, [1 dc, ch 1, 1 dc] in next ch-1 space, 1 dc in each of next 8 dc, 1 dc in top of turning ch.

Row 3: Ch 3, skip first dc, 1 dc in each of next 9 dc, [1 dc, ch 1, 1 dc] in ch-1 space of V-st, 1 dc in each of next 11 dc, [1 dc, ch 1, 1 dc] in next ch-1 space, 1 dc in each of next 18 dc, [1 dc, ch 1, 1 dc] in next ch-1 space, 1 dc in each of next 11 dc, [1 dc, ch 1, 1 dc] in next ch-1 space, 1 dc in each of next 9 dc, 1 dc in top of turning ch.

Cont in this manner, increasing 8 sts every row until you have 17 (19, 21, 23) sts on Right Front, 25 (29, 33, 37) sts on Right Sleeve, 32 (36, 40, 44) sts on Back, 25 (29, 33, 37) sts on Left Sleeve, 17 (19, 21, 23) sts on Left Front, turn (116 [132, 148, 164] dc).

Divide for Sleeves and Body

Row 1: Ch 3, skip first dc, 1 dc in next 16 (18, 20, 22) sts of Left Front, ch 2, (2, 3, 3), skip next 25 (29, 33, 37) dc of Left Sleeve, work 1 dc in each of next 32 (36, 40, 44) dc of Back, ch 2 (2, 3, 3), skip next 25 (29, 33, 37) dc of Right Sleeve, 1 dc in each of next 16 (18, 20, 22) dc of Right Front, 1 dc in top of turning ch, turn (66 [74, 82, 90] dc).

Row 2 (shell foundation row): Ch 3, 2 dc in same dc, skip 2 dc, 1 Sl st in next dc, *ch 3, 2 dc in same dc, skip 2 dc, 1 Sl st next dc*, rep from * to * to ch-space at armhole, work [1 Sl st, ch 3, 2 dc] in ch-space, 1 Sl st in next dc, rep from * to * across to next ch-space at armhole, work [1 Sl st, ch 3, 2 dc] in ch-space, 1 Sl st in next dc, rep from * to * across, ending with last Sl st in top of top of turning ch, turn (22 [25, 28, 31] shells).

Row 3: Ch 3, 2 dc in same st, *Sl st in next ch-3 space, ch 3, 2 dc in same space, rep from * across, ending with 1 Sl st in top of turning ch, turn.

Rep row 3 for pattern until Body measures 7" (7½", 8", 8½") (18 [19, 20.5, 21.5] cm) from underarm, ending at bottom right front, do not end off yarn.

Front and Neck Border

You will be working on the row ends of main body. Continuing along Right Front edge, work shell pattern as follows: *ch 3, 2 dc in same st, skip space made by turning ch, 1 Sl st in next nub*, rep from * to * to neck edge, working 1 shell in every other dc row edge, Working on other side of beginning ch, cont working shell pattern, skipping 2 sts between shells, rep from * to * across Left Front to bottom left corner, end off.

Sleeves (make 2)

You will be working sleeves back and forth; sew the underarm seam when finished.

Row 1: Join yarn in ch-space at underarm, *ch 3, 2 dc in same sp, skip 2 dc, Sl st in next dc, rep from * around sleeve, ending with last Sl st in added ch-space at underarm, turn (9 [11, 12, 13] shells).

Cont shell pattern as established on body until Sleeve measures 7½" (8", 8½", 9") (19 [20.5, 21.5, 23] cm) from underarm, end off, leaving a 24" (61 cm) length of yarn for sewing underarm seam.

Ties (make 2)

Ch 50, end off. Loop one tie in space between last front shell and first neck shell on each front corner, center, and tie in place. Repeat for second tie.

Blocking

If needed, place on a padded surface, spritz with water, and pat into shape. Do not iron.

Bruges Lace

Crocheted Bruges Lace is made by crocheting a straight tape using a few double crochet stitches with arches (or chain spaces) at each side of the tape. While the tape is crocheted, the arches are joined together to create the fabric's desired shape.

The creation of Bruges Lace offers advantages over crocheting other kinds of handmade lace. A large piece of Bruges Lace can be assembled out of small pieces, which can be made independently of one another. In-process projects are easy to carry around and can be worked on a little at a time.

SPARKLING WAVE SCARF
by Tatyana Mirer

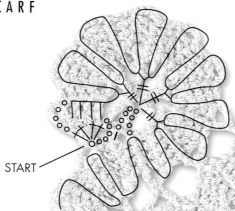

START

After making tape for 16 rows, join the arches to shape the scarf.

YOU WILL NEED

Yarn

- Patons Brilliant, 69% acrylic, 19% nylon, 12% polyester, 1.75 oz (50 g)/166 yd (152 m), 03005 White Twinkle: 2 skeins.

Hook

- 5/F (3.75 mm)

Stitches used

- Chain
- Double crochet
- Unfinished double crochet
- Unfinished triple crochet

Gauge

- 10 rows of Bruges tape = 4" (10 cm)
- 4 dc = ¾" (2 cm) but gauge is not important for this project

Finished size

- 5½" (14 cm) wide and 66" (167.5 cm) long

Unusual abbreviations

- Unf dc = unfinished double crochet
- Unf tr = unfinished triple crochet

TIP ✂

· ·

The pattern is created by joining the tape arches as you go. Do not twist the tape; your work should be flat at all times. Do not use fuzzy yarn.

· ·

Row 1: Ch 6, 4 dc into 6th ch from hook, turn.

Rows 2–16 (tape rows): Ch 5 (arch), dc in each of next 4 dc, turn (8 arches on each side of tape).

Row 17 (joining row): Ch 2, insert hook in adjacent arch, yo, draw through, yo 4 times, (insert hook in next arch, yo, draw through) 2 times, [yo, draw yarn through 2 loops] 3 times (unf tr made), *yo twice, [insert hook in next arch, yo, draw yarn through] twice, [yo, draw through 2 loops] 3 times (2nd unf tr made)*, rep from * to* once more, (7 loops on hook), yo, draw through only 3 loops on hook, [yo, draw through 2 loops] 2 times, yo, draw through last 3 loops, ch 2, turn, dc in each of next 4 dc, turn (4 joining made).

Rows 18, 20 (tape rows): Ch 5, dc in each of next 4 dc, turn.

Row 19: Ch 6, sc in center of previous joining (between 2nd tr and 3rd tr), ch 4, sc in next free arch, ch 1, turn, Sl st into 2nd ch of beg ch-6, ch 2, dc in each of next 4 dc, turn.

Row 21: Ch 2, work Sl st, inserting hook in 1st beg ch of Row 1 (starting ch), ch 2, turn, dc in each of next 4 dc.

Rows 22–33 (tape rows): Ch 5, dc in each of next 4 dc, turn (6 arches outside the tape from last joining).

Row 34: Rep Row 17.

Rows 35, 37, 39 (tape rows): Ch 5, dc in each of next 4 dc, turn.

Row 36: Ch 6, sc in center of previous joining (between 2nd tr and 3rd tr), ch 4, sc into next free arch, ch 3, turn, Sl st in 2nd ch of beg ch-6, ch 2, dc in each of next 4 dc.

Row 38: Ch 2, sc into opposite free arch, ch 2, turn, dc in each of next 4 dc.

Row 40: Ch 2, dc into opposite free arch, ch 2, turn, dc in each of next 4 dc.

Rows 41–50 (tape rows): Ch 5, dc in each of next 4 dc, turn (5 arches outside the tape from last joining).

Rep Rows 34–50 until piece measures 66" (167.5 cm) or desired length.

Finishing

Rep Rows 34 and 35.

Next row: Ch 6, sc into the center of previous joining (between 2nd tr and 3rd tr), ch 4, sc in next free arch, ch 1, turn, Sl st in 2nd ch of beg ch-6, ch 2, unf dc in each of next 4 dc, yo, draw through all 5 loops on hook, turn, Sl st into opposite free arch. Fasten off.

GALLERY OF BRUGES LACE
by Tatyana Mirer

Snowflakes

Pine tree

Butterflies

Intermeshing Crochet

Double filet intermeshing consists of two layers of traditional filet mesh that are crocheted at the same time, one row of each alternately. The stitches are intermeshed so that the two grids become woven together into one fabric.

BASIC INTERMESHING PATTERN

Notes:

The ch 4 always counts as a dc and ch 1.

You will always be removing the hook after chaining 4 at end of rows.

Foundation (takes 3 steps to complete):

Step 1: With MC, chain a multiple of 2 sts. Starting in 6th ch from hook work 1 dc, * ch 1, sk 1 ch, 1 dc in next ch, rep from * across to end, ch 4, drop loop off hook, lay piece aside **(1)**.

Step 2: With CC, chain 2 sts less than beg foundation ch .

Step 3: Join as follows: pick up and hold MC with the ch 4 to upper right corner, being careful not to twist CC chain, weave the CC chain in and out of the MC spaces, starting from right side and underneath MC, end with last ch off CC in center of last space in MC **(2)**.

Row 1: Pick up CC, starting in 6th ch from hook, working in back of work, work 1 dc in next ch, ch 1 skip 1, 1 dc next ch, rep from * across , ch 4, do NOT turn **(3)**.

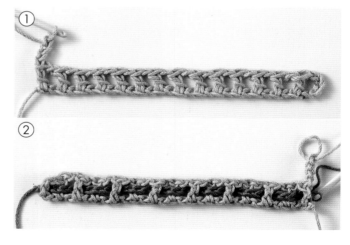

RS

WS

Row 2: Pick up MC, *work 1 dc from back in next MC dc, ch 1, 1 dc front in next MC dc, ch 1, rep from * across row, end last dc In the 3rd ch of the ch 4 (be sure that the last dc is behind the ch 4 of the CC), ch 4 turn **(4)**.

Row 3: Pick up CC, work in back of work, 1 dc first dc, * ch 1, sk 1, 1 dc next dc, rep from * to end , having last dc in the 3rd ch of the ch 4, ch 4, do NOT turn **(5)**.

Row 4: Pick up MC * 1 dc next dc from front, ch 1, 1 dc next dc from back, ch 1, rep from * having last dc in 3rd ch of the ch 4, behind the CC chain, ch 4 turn **(6)**.

Row 5: Pick up CC, same as Row 3.

Row 6: Pick up MC, *1 dc next dc from back, ch 1, 1 dc from front, ch 1, rep from * having last dc in 3rd ch of the ch 4, behind the CC chain, ch 4 turn.

Rep Rows 3, 4, 5, 6 for Basic Intermeshing Pattern

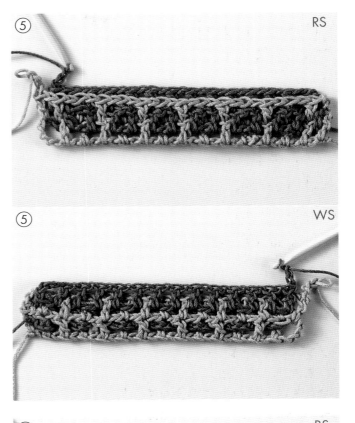

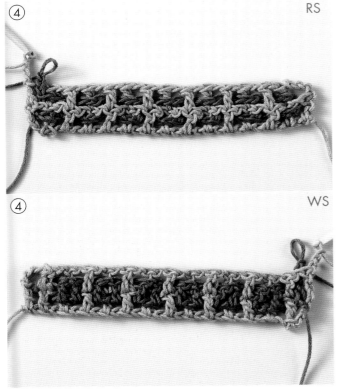

Handbag

Foundation A

Row 1: With MC, ch 32, dc in 6th ch from hook, *ch 1, skip next ch, dc in next ch, rep from * across, ch 4 (counts as first dc, ch 1 of Row 3). Drop loop off hook and lay foundation aside (14 spaces make up the foundation).

Foundation B

With CC ch 30.

Join 2 foundation pieces as follows:

Pick up and hold Foundation A (MC) with ch 4 in upper right; weave Foundation B (CC), taking care not to twist, in and out starting from right side and underneath MC Foundation, end with last ch of CC in middle of last space in MC Foundation A.

INTERMESHING HANDBAG

Try your hand at intermeshing by making this easy-to-stitch rectangular handbag. For the yarn, choose two related colors that have enough contrast to make the pattern stand out. Once you get the rhythm of intermeshing, use the stitch method to create a scarf, blanket, or any other project that can be made from a crocheted rectangle.

Row 2: Pick up CC, working back (other side of next MC dc), work 1 dc in 6th ch from hook, *ch 1, skip next ch, 1 dc in next ch, rep from * across, ch 4 (counts as first dc, ch 1 of Row 4), do not turn. Drop CC.

Row 3: Pick up MC, *working behind last row, 1 dc in next MC dc, ch 1, working in front of last row, 1 dc in next MC dc, ch 1, rep * across, ending with last dc in 3rd ch of the ch-4 turning ch (last dc is behind the ch of CC), turn, ch 4 (counts as first dc, ch 1 of Row 5). Drop MC.

Row 4: Pick up CC, working in back of Row 3, 1 dc in next CC dc, *ch 1, 1 dc next CC dc, rep from * across, ending with last dc in 3rd ch of ch-4 turning ch, ch 4 (counts as first dc, ch 1 of Row 6), do not turn. Drop CC.

Row 5: Pick up MC, *working in front of last row, 1 dc in next MC dc, ch 1, working in back of last row, 1 dc next MC dc, ch 1, rep from * across, ending with last dc in 3rd ch of ch 4, behind CC, ch 4 (counts as first dc, ch 1 of Row 7), turn. Drop MC.

Row 6: With CC, rep Row 4.

Row 7: With MC, rep Row 3.

Rows 8–24: Rep Rows 4–7 (4 times); rep Row 4. End off.

Finishing

1. If desired, line bag before sewing.

2. Fold in an envelope shape, leaving 4 blocks for front flap.

3. With right side facing work a row of sc on edge of flap for buttonhole row as follows:

Work sc over 3 blocks, next block work 1 sc in next st, ch 10, skip next st, 1 sc in next st, sc across remainder of row, end off.

4. Make a twisted cord for strap; sew to inside as follows:

To make twisted cord, cut 6 pieces of yarn each 5 yd (4.6 m) long. Holding these strands together, fold in half and knot the ends together. Pin the knot to a padded stationary surface and twist the yarns until they become tightly twisted and begin to crimp. Pinch the yarns at the center and bring the fold to the knot. Holding the twisted halves next to each other, release the center and allow the halves to twist together. Tie at loose end.

More Intermeshing Ideas

Handbag in high contrast colors

Warm, colorful scarf

Cozy blanket

Polish Star

British-born Mary Davies had won a prestigious business award enabling her to go to Poland prior to the removal of the Iron Curtain. She was closely guarded, but her ability to speak Esperanto and find a home in which to reside through global Esperanto networking meant she could stay an additional week in Poland. While there, Mary admired some crocheted pillows, made by a neighbor. Although Mary did not crochet, the Polish-speaking neighbor helped her to master the technique while the man of the house translated it into Esperanto.

Mary brought the stitch pattern to England and challenged Pauline Turner to work it out. Having done so, Pauline felt its origin deserved recognition and named it the Polish Star Stitch. She designed patterns using this crochet fabric in two books before offering it at a Crochet Guild of America conference. Since then designers have found the Polish Star fabric a fascinating study.

POLISH STAR PILLOW
by Pauline Turner

YOU WILL NEED

Yarn

- Worsted yarn [medium (4)] in two complementary colors, 6 oz (170 g) each

Hooks

- 9/I (5.5 mm)

Notions

- stitch holder such as a safety pin
- tapestry needle
- 18" (45.5 cm) square pillow form

Gauge

- 12 sts = 4" (10 cm) and 6 rows = 4" (10 cm) measured over the stitch pattern given for the back of the pillow

Finished size

- Approximately 17½" (44.5 cm) square

Notes:

Edc: Extended double crochet is the height of a triple but without the extra twist, giving a softer effect to the stitch.

To work Edc: yo, insert hook as for a normal double crochet, yo and bring yarn to the front (3 loops on hook), yo and pull through just the first loop on the hook which extends the height of the stitch, (yo, pull through two loops) twice. One Edc made.

C1: The first color worked and places 4Edc between each 10 ch loop

C2: The contrast color worked on alternate rows using a group of 2Edc followed by a group of 6Edc.

Front

In C1, ch 51.

Row 1: 1Edc in 4th ch from hook, ch10, *skip 1ch, work 1Edc in each of next 4ch, ch10, repeat from * to last 3ch, skip 1ch, 1Edc in next ch, 1Edc in last ch, changing to C2 when there are two loops left on the hook, turn work—11 groups of 4Edc plus 2 halves = 48Edc including the turning ch **(1)**.

Row 2: Ch4, 2Edc in next st, ch10, * skip 1st, 1Edc in next 2sts, ch10, skip 1st, (2Edc in next st) twice, ch10, rep from * to end, placing only 1Edc in last st. Put the loop on the hook into a stitch holder. DO NOT TURN THE WORK **(2)**.

Row 3: Go back to the start of row 2 and pull the C1 yarn through the top turning ch of Row 2, ch3, 1Edc in next st, skip 1st, *ch10, (2Edc in next st) twice, ch10, skip 1st, 1Edc in next 4sts, skip 1st, rep from * to last 2-st group, ch10, (2Edc in next st) twice, ch10, skip 1st, 1Edc in next st, 1Edc in the last stitch working the last stitch as follows: insert the hook into the stitch as normal and at the same time collect the loop from the holder, yo, bring through both the loop and the stitch securing the C2 loop from the previous row, complete the st changing to C2 when there are only 2 loops of C1 remaining, turn work **(3)**.

Row 4: Ch13 (to count as first Edc and ch10), skip 1st, *2Edc in first st of next group, 2Edc in next 2sts, 2Edc in last st of group, ch10, skip 1st, 1Edc in next 2sts, skip 1st, rep from * to last group of 4sts, 2Edc in first st of next group, 2Edc in next 2sts, 2Edc in last st of group, ch10, skip 1st, 1Edc in last st placing loop in a stitch holder.

Row 5: Go back to the start of previous row and work with C1 bringing through the third of the turning ch of previous row, ch3, 1Edc in same place as the turning ch, *ch10, skip 1st, 1Edc in next 4sts, skip 1st, ch10, (2Edc in next st) twice, rep from * to last 6-st group, ch10, skip 1st, 1Edc in next 4sts,

skip 1st, ch10, 2Edc in last st securing the loop in the holder as described at the end of Row 3.

Rows 2–5 inclusive form the pattern. Repeat these rows 4 times and rows 2 and 3 once more.

Before working the final row, link the 10-ch loops to form the pattern. Fasten off C2.

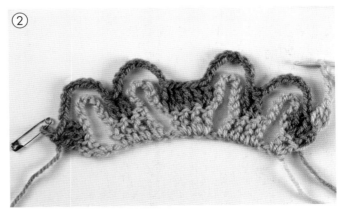

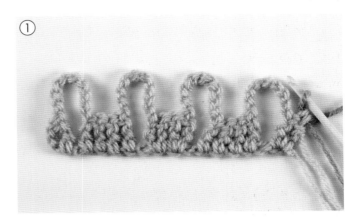

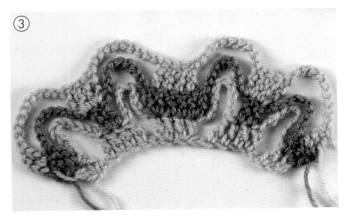

(continued)

Polish Star Pillow (continued)

Linking the loops

1. Always begin with the 10-ch loops of the odd numbered rows (C1), lying either side of the 2st group on the even numbered rows. Cross these over. Repeat along the row.

2. Link the 10-ch loops from the even numbered row (C2) through each of the crossed loops to anchor them in place as these form the 'star' effect.

3. Link the 10-ch loops in C1 through those lying exactly above the C2 loops just connected.

4. Once the C1 loops are through the C2 loops repeat stages 1–3 until all the 10-ch loops have been linked.

Note: Ensure you link the C1 loops over the 2st group to ensure an all over pattern. It prevents the 'stars' from forming columns.

Final Row: ch3, 1dc in next st, 1dc in next two sts, *(1dc through 10-ch loop and the next st) twice making sure the C2 yarn is following the linking pattern as closely as possible, 1dc in next 6sts, rep from * to last 4sts, 1dc in each of the remaining 4sts. Fasten off C1 yarn. Sew in all ends securely.

④

Back

There is no reason why you cannot make the back and the front of the pillow the same. However you may prefer to have a flatter fabric on the side least likely to be seen.

In C1 ch51.

Row 1: 1dc in 4th ch from the hook, 1dc in each ch to last ch, 2dc in last ch—49sts.

Row 2: Ch1, *ch1, skip 1st, 1sc, rep from * to end changing to C2 in last st.

Row 3: Ch2, *1dc worked in the stitch of row 1 directly below the ch-1 of row 2, 1hdc in next sc, rep from * to end

Row 4: Ch1, 1sc in next st * ch1, skip 1st, 1sc, rep from * to last 2sts, 1sc in each of last 2 sts changing to C1 in last st.

Row 5: Ch2, 1hdc in next st, *1dc worked in the stitch of the row directly below the ch-1 of previous row, 1hdc in next sc, rep from * to last st, 1hdc in last st

Row 6: Ch1, *ch1, skip 1st, 1sc, rep from * to end changing to C2 in last st.

Row 7: Ch2, *1dc worked in the stitch directly below the 1ch, 1hdc in next sc, rep from * to end

Row 8: Ch1, 1sc in next st * ch1, skip 1st, 1sc, rep from * to last 2sts, 1sc in each of last 2 sts changing to C1 in last st.

Repeat rows 5–8 inclusive 10 times and row 5 once more.

Final row: Ch1, 1sc in each st to end. Fasten off both yarns. Sew in the ends securely.

Optional Extra

Sometimes after linking the loops in the Polish Star Stitch fabric, the sides may gape should it be added to another piece of crochet or fabric. It is particularly noticeable where it is necessary to stretch the Polish Star Stitch crochet, as in the case of a cover for a pillow where the pillow casing is smaller than its inner pad.

The following two-color ribbon fits in with the two color bands of both the Polish Star Stitch and the two color bands on the back.

In C1 ch 6.

Row 1: 1sc in 3rd ch from hook, 1sc in each of the remaining 3ch.

Row 2: Ch2, 1hdc in next st, 1 FPdc in next st, 1hdc in 2 rem sts.

Row 3: Ch2, 1hdc in each st to end changing color to C2 in last st.

Row 4: Rep Row 2.

Row 5: Rep Row 3 but change to C1.

Repeat Rows 2 to 5 inclusive 5 times and Rows 2 and 3 once. Fasten off both yarns. Sew in the ends securely.

Make two identical braids and thread them through the sides of the Polish Star Stitch fabric crocheted for the front of the pillow. The best way is to thread them under C1 chain loops and over the C2 chain loops so the braid fills in any gaps. The color bands should match with both the back and the front bands of color, which means the chains worked in C1 need to lie over the C1 band of the braid, while the chain loops of C2 are hidden under the braid.

To Complete

1. Should optional braids have been made and threaded through the sides of the Polish Star Stitch panel, invisibly attach them using C1 and a large-eyed sewing needle.

2. Attach the back to the top of the pillow and also to the sides of the braids, to form a pouch.

3. Insert the pillow pad and close the base of the crochet pillow cover with single crochet.

Overlay Crochet

Overlay Crochet was inspired by stained-glass rose windows, Buddhist sand mandalas, and Mexican and Islamic tile patterns. It involves creating a background fabric of single crochet stitches while simultaneously working a variety of long, often highly complex stitches and clusters of stitches that "overlay" the base fabric. When this stitch technique is combined with frequent color changes, a vibrant, densely textured fabric gradually emerges. The fabric is typically characterized by richly varied linear, floral, and geometric design elements that obscure the horizontal rows or concentric rounds of the base fabric.

YOU WILL NEED

Yarn

- Shown: Size 10 Cotton Crochet Thread, 100% cotton, 1 ball each in Dark Brown, Tan, Yellow, Orange, Cappuccino, Red, and Burgundy

Hook

- 6/G (4 mm)

Stitches used

- Chain
- Single crochet
- Half double crochet
- Double crochet
- Triple crochet
- Double treble crochet
- Triple treble crochet
- Sc2tog
- Hdc2tog
- Dc2tog
- Tr2tog

Unusual abbreviations

- BLO: back loop only
- FLO: front loop only
- AP: around the post

Finished size

- 10" × 16" (25.4 × 40.6 cm)

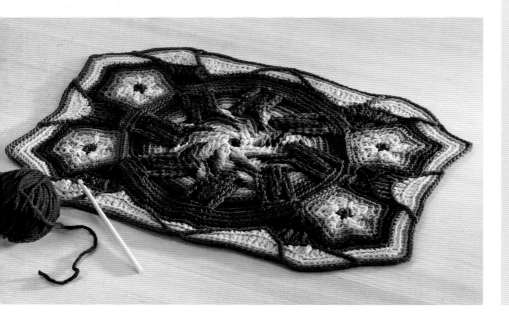

OVERLAY PLACEMAT
by Melody MacDuffee

Special Stitches:

Triple treble crochet (trtr): Yo 4 times, insert hook in designated st, yo, draw yarn through st, [yo, draw through 2 loops on hook] 5 times.

Quadruple treble crochet (qutr): Yo 5 times, insert hook in next st, yo, draw through st, (yo, draw through 2 loops on hook) 6 times.

Single crochet 2 together (sc2tog): [Insert hook in next st, yo, draw yarn through st] twice, yo, draw through all 3 loops on hook.

Half double crochet 2 together (hdc2tog): [Yo, insert hook in next st, yo, draw through st] twice, yo, draw through all loops on hook.

Double crochet 2 together (dc2tog): [Yo, insert hook in next st, yo, draw through st, yo, draw through 2 loops] twice, yo, draw through all 3 loops on hook.

Notes:

1. Use four strands of thread throughout.

2. Work stitches in back loops throughout unless otherwise instructed.

3. If you have elected to use colors other than those indicated, make a color key to refer to as you work. The following instructions frequently refer to specific colors when describing where to anchor your Overlay stitches.

Placemat

With Dark Brown, ch 5, join with Sl st to form ring.

Rnd 1 (Dark Brown): Work 8 sc in ring, join with Sl st in beg sc.

Rnd 2 (Dark Brown): 2 sc in next st and in each st around (don't forget to always work in back loops unless otherwise instructed!), join with Sl st in beg sc (16 sts).

Rnd 3 (Dark Brown): [2 sc in next st, sc in next st] 8 times, join with Sl st in beg sc (24 sts).

Rnd 4 (Dark Brown): [2 sc in next st, sc in next 2 st] 8 times, join with Sl st in beg sc (32 sts), end off.

Note: To join a new color, pull up a loop in indicated stitch and then work your first stitch in the following stitch.

Rnd 5 (Tan): Join Tan in any st, [sc in next st, holding work with this first st at top, locate the front loop of the st on Rnd 1 most directly below it, count back 2 sts on Rnd 1 and work a dtr in the front loop only (FLO) of that st, sc in next 3 sts on Rnd 4] 8 times, join with Sl st in beg sc (40 sts), end off.

Rnd 6 (Yellow): Join Yellow 2 sts prior to any dtr, [sc in next st, dtr in st on Rnd 2 just after the one where you placed next Tan dtr, sc in top of the same Tan dtr and in next 3 sc], join with Sl st in beg sc (48 sts), end off.

Rnd 7 (Orange): Join Orange 2 sts prior to any Yellow dtr, [sc in next st, dtr in st on Rnd 3 just after the one where you placed next Yellow dtr, sc in top of the same Yellow dtr and in next 4 sts] 8 times, join with Sl st in beg sc (56 sts), end off.

Rnd 8 (Cappuccino): Join Cappuccino 2 sts prior to any Orange dtr, [sc in next st, dtr in st on Rnd 4 just after the one where you placed next Orange dtr, sc in top of the same Orange dtr and in next 5 sts] 8 times, join with Sl st in beg sc (64 sts), end off.

Rnd 9 (Red): Join Red in st just prior to any Cappuccino dtr, [sc in next st, dtr in st on Rnd 5 just after the one where you placed next Cappuccino dtr, sc in next 7 sts] 8 times, join with Sl st in beg sc (72 sts), end off.

Rnd 10 (Burgundy): Join Burgundy in st just prior to any Red dtr, [sc in next st, dtr in st on Rnd 6 just after the one where you placed next Red dtr, sc in next 8 sts] 8 times, join with Sl st in beg sc (80 sts), end off.

Rnd 11 (Dark Brown): Join Dark Brown in st just prior to any Burgundy dtr, [sc in next st, dtr in st on Rnd 7 just after the one where you placed next Burgundy dtr, sc in next 8 sts] 9 times, join with Sl st in beg sc (88 sts), end off.

Rnd 12 (Tan): Join Tan in st just prior to any Dark Brown dtr, [sc in next st, dtr in st on Rnd 8 just after the one where you placed next Dark Brown dtr, sc in next 10 sts] 8 times, join with Sl st in beg sc (96 sts), end off.

Rnd 13 (Yellow): Join Yellow in st just prior to any Tan dtr, [sc in next st, dtr in st on Rnd 9 just after the one where you placed next Tan dtr, sc in next 11 sts] 8 times, join with Sl st in beg sc (104 sts), end off.

Rnd 14 (Orange): Join Orange in st just prior to any Yellow dtr, [sc in next st, dtr in st on Rnd 10 just after the one where you placed next Yellow dtr, sc in next 12 sts] 8 times, join with Sl st in beg sc (112 sts), end off.

Rnd 15 (Cappuccino): Join Cappuccino in st just prior to any Orange dtr, [sc in next st, dtr in st on Rnd 11 just after the one where you placed next Orange dtr, sc in next 13 sts] 8 times, join with Sl st in beg sc (120 sts), end off.

Rnd 16 (Red): Join Red in st just prior to any Cappuccino dtr, [sc in next 12 sts, trtr in the third Red sc on Rnd 9 after the next Red dtr, trtr in next Red sc on Rnd 9, skip one sc on Rnd 15, sc in next 2 sts] 8 times, end with Sl st in beg st (128 sts), end off.

Rnd 17 (Burgundy): Join Burgundy in first of any pair of 2 Red trtr, [sc in next trtr, sc in next 13 sts, trtr in st on Rnd 10 after next Burgundy trtr, trtr in next st on Rnd 10, skip one st on Rnd 16, sc in next trtr] 8 times, end with Sl st in beg st (136 sts), end off.

Rnd 18 (Dark Brown): Join Dark Brown in first of any pair of 2 Burgundy trtr, [sc in next 15 sts, work 2 trtr around the post of the Dark Brown dtr on Rnd 11 directly below, skip one Burgundy st on Rnd 17, sc in next trtr] 8 times, end with Sl st in beg st (144 sts). Do not end off.

Rnd 19 (Dark Brown): [Sc in next 5 sts, qutr in each of last 2 visible (not hidden behind long stitches) Dark Brown sc on Rnd 11 directly below (these will be the 2 Dark Brown sc just prior to the one where you placed the Cappuccino dtr), skip one Dark Brown st on Rnd 18, sc in next 12 sts] 8 times, end with Sl st in beg st (152 sts), end off.

Flowers (Make 4)

Using Dark Brown, ch 4, join with Sl st to form ring.

Rnd 1F (Dark Brown): Work 5 sc into center ring, join with Sl st in beg sc (5 sts in all), end off.

Rnd 2F (Tan): Join Tan in any st, [sc, hdc, dc, hdc, sc, Sl st] in each sc around, join with Sl st in beg sc (30 sts), end off.

Rnd 3F (Yellow): Join Yellow in any dc, [sc in next hdc, sc in next sc, Sl st in Dark Brown sc directly below on Rnd 1 FL, sc in next sc, sc in next hdc, 3 sc in next dc] 5 times, join with Sl st in beg sc (30 sts), end off.

Rnd 4F (Orange): Join Orange in first of 3 sc in any petal tip, [3 sc in next st, sc in next 2 sts, Sl st AP of next Yellow Sl st, sc in next 2 sts] 5 times, join with Sl st in beg sc (40 sts), end off.

Rnd 5F (Cappuccino): Join Cappuccino in first of 3 sc in any petal tip, [3 sc in next st, sc in next 3 sts, sc in next 3 sts] 5 times, join with Sl st in beg sc (40 sts), end off.

Continue Placemat

Rnd 20 (Red): Join Red in the first of any 2 qutr in Rnd 19 of Placemat, *[sc in next st, holding flower with wrong side against wrong side of work, Sl st through next st and through the center of any 3 tip sc on flower at the same time, (matching sts, Sl st in next st of Mat and Flower) 4 times, skip one st on Rnd 19, (matching sts, Sl st in next st of Mat and Flower) 5 times, sc in next 7 sts*, rep from * to * once, sc in next 38 sts] twice, join with Sl st in beg sc (150 sts). Do not end off.

Rnd 21 (Red): *Working up the side of the flower, [sc in next 4 sts, skip 1 st, sc in next 3 sts, 3 sc in next st] twice, sc in next 3 sts, skip 1 st, sc in next 4 sts, 3 sc in next st, sc in next 3 sts, skip 1 st, sc in next 4 sts, sc in next 8 sts*, rep from * to * once, 2 sc in next st, sc in next 9 sts, 2 sc in next st, sc in next 5 sts, [2 sc in next st, sc in next 9 sts] 3 times*, rep from * to * once, join with Sl st in beg sc (266 sts), end off.

Rnd 22 (Burgundy): Join Burgundy in first of next 3-sc group in tip of next petal, *(3 sc in next st, sc in next 4 sts, skip 1 st, sc in next 4 sts) twice, 3 sc in next st, sc in next 4 sts, skip 3 sts, 2 tr in each of next 2 sts, skip 3 sts, sc in next st, skip 3 sts, 2 tr in each of next 2 sts, sc in each of next 4 sts, (3 sc in next st, sc in next 4 sts, skip 1 st, sc in next 4 sts) twice, 3 sc in next st, sc in next 4 sts, skip 3 sts, 2 tr in next st, 3 dtr in next st, skip 4 sts, sc in next 10 sts, 2 sc in next st, sc in next 6 sts, 2 sc in next st, sc in next 4 sts, 2 sc in next st, sc in next 6 sts, 2 sc in next st, sc in next 10 sts, skip next 4 sts, 3 dtr in next st, 2 tr in next st, skip 3 sts, sc in next st *, rep from * to * once, join with Sl st in beg sc (258 sts), end off.

Rnd 23 (Dark Brown): Join Dark Brown in first of 3-sc group in same tip of same petal, [*3 sc in next (tip) st, sc in next 4 sts, skip 1 st, sc in next 5 sts, 3 sc in next st, sc in next 4 sts, skip 1 st, sc in next 5 sts, 3 sc in next st, sc in next st*, skip 3 sts, tr in next st, (tr2tog over next 2 sts) twice, tr in next st, (tr2tog over next 2 sts) twice, tr in next st, skip 3 sts, sc in next st, rep from * to * once, skip 3 sts, tr in next st, 2 tr in each of next 5 sts, skip 3 sts, sc in next 5 sts, 2 sc in next st, sc in next 8 sts, 2 sc in next st, sc in next 8 sts, 2 sc in next st, sc in next 8 sts, 2 sc in next st, sc in next 5 sts, skip 3 sts, 2 tr in each of next 5 sts, tr in next st, skip 3 sts, sc in next st] twice, join with Sl st in beg sc (266 sts), end off.

Rnd 24 (Tan): Join Tan in first of next 3-sc group in tip above top of flower, [3 sc in next st, sc in next 5 sts, skip 1 st, sc in next 5 sts, 2 sc in next st, sc in next st, hdc in next 2 st, dc2tog over next 2 sts, dc in next st, dc2tog over next 2 sts, hdc in next 2 st, sc in next st, 2 sc in next st, sc in next 5 sts, skip 1 st, sc in next 5 sts, 3 sc in tip st, sc in next 5 sts, skip 1 st, sc in next 5 sts, 2 sc in next st, hdc in next st, dc in next st, 3 tr in next st, dc in next 2 sts, hdc in next st, sc in next 5 sts, hdc2tog over next 2 sts, dc2tog over next 2 sts, (hdc2tog over next 2 sts) twice, sc in next 11 sts, (sc2tog over next 2 sts) 4 times, sc in next 11 sts, (hdc2tog over next 2 sts) twice, dc2tog over next 2 sts, hdc2tog over next 2 sts, sc in next 5 sts, hdc in next st, dc in next 2 sts, 3 tr in next st, dc in next st, hdc in next st, 2 sc in next st, sc in next 5 sts, skip 1 st, sc in next 5 sts] twice, end with Sl st in beg st (246 sts), end off.

Rnd 25 (Yellow): Join Yellow in first of next 3-sc group in tip above top of flower, [3 sc in next st, sc in next 5 sts, skip 1 st, sc in next 7 sts, hdc in next st, hdc2tog over next 2 sts, dc in next 3 sts, hdc2tog over next 2 sts, hdc in next st, sc in next 7 sts, skip 1 st, sc in next 5 sts, 3 sc in next st, sc in next 5 sts, skip 1 st, sc in next 10 sts, 2 sc in next st, hdc in next 2 sts, hdc2tog over next 2 sts, dc in next 2 sts, dc2tog over next 2 sts, tr in next 2 sts, tr2tog over next 2 sts, dc in next 2 sts, dc2tog over next 2 sts, hdc in next 2 sts, hdc2tog over next 2 sts, sc in next 12 sts, hdc2tog over next 2 sts, hdc in next 2 sts, dc2tog over next 2 sts, dc in next 2 sts, tr2tog over next

2 sts, tr in next 2 sts, dc2tog over next 2 sts, dc in next 2 sts, hdc2tog over next 2 sts, hdc in next 2 sts, 2 sc in next st, sc in next 10 sts, skip 1 st, sc in next 5 sts] twice, end with Sl st in beg st (226 sts), end off.

Rnd 26 (Orange): Join Orange in first of next 3-sc group in tip above top of flower, [3 sc in next st, sc in next 33 sts, 3 sc in corner tip st, sc in next 17 sts, 2 sc in next st, sc in next 21 sts, sc2tog over same st and next st, sc in same st as last, sc in next 20 sts, 2 sc in next st, sc in next 17 sts] twice, end with Sl st in beg st (240 sts), end off.

Rnd 27 (Dark Brown): Join Dark Brown in first of next 3-sc group in tip above top of flower, [3 sc in next st, sc in next 9 sts, trtr in FLO of center Dark Brown st in next 3-sc group on Dark Brown Rnd 23, skip 1 st on Rnd 26, sc in next 15 sts, trtr in FLO of center Dark Brown st in 3-sc group on Dark Brown Rnd 23 just passed, skip 1 st on Rnd 26, sc in next 9 sts, 3 sc in corner tip st, sc in next 7 sts, qutr in FLO of third Dark Brown st in next 3-sc group on Dark Brown Rnd 23, skip 1 st on Rnd 26, sc in next 14 sts, qutr in FLO of eighth tr on Dark Brown Rnd 23, skip 1 st on Rnd 26, sc in next 18 sts, find the st on Dark Brown Rnd 23 directly below next st and work 1 qutr in 10th st prior to that one and another qutr in the 10th st after that one, skip 1 st on Rnd 23, sc in next 18 sts, qutr in FLO of fourth tr on Dark Brown Rnd 23, skip 1 st on Rnd 26, sc in next 14 sts, qutr in FLO of first Dark Brown st in next 3-sc group on Dark Brown Rnd 23, skip 1 st on Rnd 26, sc in next 7 sts] twice, end with Sl st in beg st (250 sts), end off.

GALLERY OF OVERLAY CROCHET BY MELODY MACDUFFEE

Melody MacDuffee created her "Kaleidoscope Necklace" from colorful scraps of sewing thread. She doubled the threads and used a size 14 metal hook and her Overlay Crochet technique to crochet the threads around wooden balls.

Melody MacDuffee created this "Eye of the Tiger" bracelet using doubled silk sewing thread and a size 14 metal hook. The shapes and motifs result from "overlaying" a background fabric of single crochet stitches with longer stitches and clusters of stitches in contrasting shades of brown and gold. The cabochons are made of tiger eye gemstones.

"Splendor" is an example of Melody MacDuffee's Overlay Crochet technique. The plume agate cabochon is inset in a bezel-like rim of double strands of Japanese silk sewing thread worked with a size 14 steel hook. The necklace is crocheted with matte ivory seed beads, and the fringe is a fall of freshwater pearls, gemstones, and glass and metal beads strung on Nymo beading thread.

Freeform Crochet

In the 1970s, there was a movement toward a form of crochet that has become known as Freeform Crochet. Freeformers did not want to follow patterns; they liked to do their own thing. Some did a whole garment in one piece, randomly using different yarns and different stitches. One of the methods from that era was the making of many smaller pieces from many yarns and stitches, much like the pioneers. The small pieces were then combined into a garment that became a one-of-a-kind artwork.

Traditional Irish crochet is believed to be the original freeform crochet method. The beautiful leaves and flowers, joined with lovely mesh stitches and Clones knots, worked in tiny stitches and fine cotton, were works of art worn by royalty and the very wealthy.

Two of the early movers and shakers of the freeform movement, James Walters and Sylvia Cosh, coined a word for the small pieces used in making a freeform garment; they named them "scrumbles." Freeform crochet, by some definitions, is a combination of stitches and colors, worked in a multidirectional way. For years, I did all my freeform crochet in neutral colors, with a variety of highly textured stitches in shades of white, beige, and tan. I loved the look. It was not until much later that I began experimenting with more color. Lately, I have tried using one color in different yarns. I have seen gorgeous examples of freeform, using one yarn, one color, many different stitches. Whatever your preference, don't be afraid to experiment. Freeform crochet is not a weekend project, not meant for instant gratification. Allow yourself the time to experiment, play, and get creative. The results are worth it.

Mesh Method

I use several methods to create freeform crochet. The one I find most resembling Irish Crochet, with less work, is embellishing a mesh background. The jacket on page 112 is worked in a mesh stitch with some puff stitches to imitate Clones Knots. You can wear the jacket without further embellishment. To transform it with freeform crochet, I embellished it with some traditional flowers and leaves from old Irish Crochet patterns.

When I first started writing instructions for freeform crochet, I received a lot of notes from fellow freeformers who thought that writing instructions took the "free" out the equation. They felt that the whole idea behind freeform is that one does not use patterns but lets their imagination guide them. While I agree with that wholeheartedly, some people need a little head start to get motivated. Students love to have something written down. They feel more comfortable taking that first step with some guidance. Once they understand the process, their imagination does takes over and their creativity soars. If you love the look of the freeform jacket but you rely on written instructions, follow the instructions to the letter. Once you understand the process, feel free to design your own embellishments.

Template Method

You can also work freeform crochet using a template, such as a piece of paper cut to the shape of the finished piece. This could also be a commercial sewing pattern. Then place small pieces of crochet (scrumbles), like a puzzle, all over your template and sew them together.

Lining Method

Similar to the template method is the lining method. In this case, your template is a piece of lining or other fabric cut to the finished shape of the garment or accessory. The scrumbles are then sewn, or appliquéd, to the fabric. The underlying fabric provides support and you don't have to cover it completely if you don't want to. In essence, the scrumbles can be used like appliqués. I have appliquéd scrumbles to gloves and mittens, sock cuffs, cloth slippers, pillows, and even purchased garments, such as sweatshirts.

A sweatshirt can become the lining for a warm freeform jacket. First, cut off all the ribbing at the neck, cuffs, and bottom. Then cut the sweatshirt down center front, creating a cardigan. Pin your scrumbles in place, working from the top down, then hand-sew them to the sweatshirt and to each other as you work. The result is a fairly heavy, lined jacket.

If you would like a lighter-weight jacket, use the sweatshirt as a template only. After pinning your scrumbles in place, sew them to each other, but not to the sweatshirt. The sweatshirt can then be removed, and you will have a lovely shaped garment. Add borders, buttonholes, and edges if you want, or leave as is with asymmetrical edges.

TIP

When pinning your scrumbles to the template or lining, do not be afraid to occasionally overlap pieces, or stretch them a little, to fit in a certain space. Where pieces do not exactly meet, use a small flower or little circle to fill in the space.

Beyond the Freeform Fabric

A freeform crochet project isn't finished until you are happy with your results. Surface crochet can be used to "correct" a section that you are not fond of, to connect two adjoining scrumbles, to give some conformity, or to fill in a little space. Surface crochet is working over existing stitches from the right side of the work, picking up a loop and working off as usual. Surface crochet also adds dimension and texture to your work.

Embellishing with beads is fun. Sewing a bead in a flower center, or adding a group of beads to fill in an area adds a bit of whimsy or glamour to your work.

The possibilities are endless. Take the first step with instructions, then let yourself have fun and experiment.

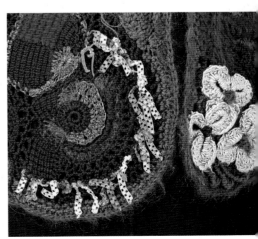

FREEFORM HANDBAG

Clutch-style freeform crochet handbags are fun and easy to make, and they are an interesting way to use some of your scrumbles. This bag is made using the lining method of freeforming.

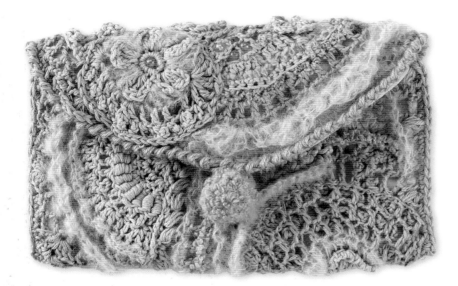

YOU WILL NEED

- Scrumbles
- ⅜ yd (0.35 m) synthetic fleece for interlining
- ⅜ yd (0.35 m) lining
- Needle and thread
- Yarn to coordinate with scrumbles
- Button

1. Cut interlining to the desired shape. For the handbag shown, cut a 9" × 15" (23 × 38 cm) piece and round one end. Cut a piece of lining, using the interlining as a guide and leaving ½" (1.3 cm) extra on the edge.

2. Arrange the scrumbles on the interlining with their edges touching. Leave as little open space as possible. Open spaces can be filled with additional crochet stitches later. Pin the scrumbles to the interlining.

3. Sew the scrumbles to each other using coordinating lightweight yarn or sew them to the interlining using needle and thread. Fill in any spaces with additional crochet stitches.

4. Work one row sc around entire outside edge. At the center of the rounded end, make a button loop.

5. Place the lining, right side up over the wrong side of the bag piece. Turn under the edge all around so that it just covers the interlining. Pin the lining in place. Stitch the lining to the bag.

6. Fold the bag into an envelope shape and sew the side seams. Add a button. Add a shoulder strap it desired.

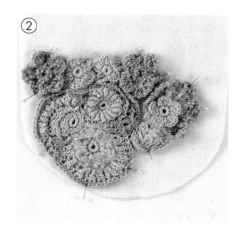

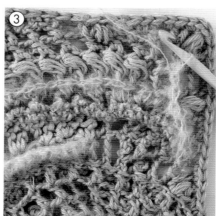

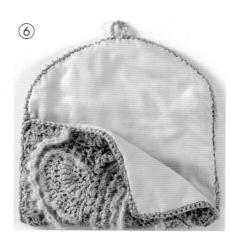

FREEFORM MESH JACKET

Follow the directions for the Mesh Jacket (page 112). Then crochet several embellishments from the Motifs Section (page 164) and arrange them on the jacket wherever you like. Freeform means following your own muse, so embellish your jacket however you wish. The following instructions detail how I embellished my jacket.

Embellishments

All Plymouth Yarns, 1 skein each: Yardley, #9210; King George, #9210; Imperiale Super Kid Mohair, #4107; Royal Bamboo, #4

Crochet the following embellishments, leaving an 18" (45.5 cm) tail of yarn on each embellishment for sewing motif to garment:

1 Butterfly (page 181) in Royal Bamboo

10 Flowers (page 186) in Royal Bamboo

14 Broad Leaves (page 191) in King George

10 Broad Leaves (page 191) in Yardley Yarn

10 Flowers (page 186) in Imperiale

Using photos as guides, pin motifs in place, then sew to both the mesh base and to each other.

This freeform vest was designed by Myra Wood. She incorporated freeform knitting with her freeform crochet. The garment is accented with bead drops and a feathered freeform brooch.

Prudence Mapstone designed this asymmetric freeform vest. The wild mix of yarns includes metallics, ribbon yarns, bouclés, eyelashes, and tubular yarns.

These detail shots are from another incredible garment designed by Prudence Mapstone. The amazing texture is the result of a wide variety of different yarns as well many different stitches.

Freeformers are a very innovative group, and they will crochet with just about anything. Pamela Shore created this lovely jacket using kite string.

Hairpin Lace

Hairpin lace is worked with an ordinary crochet hook on a tool referred to as a loom, frame, or fork. The sides, or prongs, of the loom fit into holes in the top and bottom bars of the tool.

Hairpin lace work is created by first making strips (also called braids) and then joining them together. Each strip is a series of side loops that form around the prongs, joined by a center row of single crochet stitches. The prongs can be positioned at different widths apart to make hairpin lace strips of different widths.

Most designs do not differ in the way the basic strip is made, rather it is the technique used for joining the strips that truly differentiates a hairpin lace pattern. Consider the basic strip as the universal building block of hairpin lace and the joining techniques are where the creativity comes into play!

When working a hairpin lace strip, mark the starting end of the strip. When joining strips, begin at the starting ends, working to the tied-off ends. In this way, you can "even out" your strips by unraveling the longer one at the end of the joining process.

To measure the gauge of hairpin lace, create a strip of 4" (10 cm) or more, take the strip off of the loom and lay the strip down without stretching. Mark off 4" (10 cm) and count the total number of loops (on both sides) between the marks.

Making a Hairpin Lace Strip

1. Set up the loom by setting the prongs to the width for which the pattern calls. Orient the loom so that the bar that can be removed the most easily (for slipping off the work) is at the bottom. Cut two lengths of waste yarn slightly longer than the desired finished length of the strip, and loosely tie them to the bars, allowing them to trail along each prong. You will work the loops over the prongs and waste yarn; the waste yarn will keep the loops in order and untangled as they slide off the loom.

2. Secure working yarn with a slip knot to the left-hand prong of the loom. Ease the knot to the center of the loom; tape the tail to the back of the bottom bar to hold it in place, if desired. Wrap yarn from front to back over the right prong and bring yarn back to the left side.

3. Tension the working yarn in your fingers as you would for regular crochet. Insert the hook from bottom to top through loop on the left-hand prong, wrap the yarn over the hook, and draw it through the loop. Wrap the yarn over the hook again and draw it through, completing a single crochet.

4. Prepare to turn the loom by twisting the hook so that handle side faces up and insert the handle end of the hook through the loom above the work. Keep the loop on the hook, keep the yarn tensioned in your fingers. Grab the hook from opposite side of loom, still keeping the loop on the hook.

5. Turn the loom 180 degrees clockwise, allowing the yarn to wrap around the left prong as you turn. The back will now be facing you, and the prongs will have switched positions, and the hook will again be in front.

6. Insert hook under the loop of the front strand of the loop on the left prong, pull through a loop (there are now two loops on the hook), pick up a loop and complete a single crochet.

7. Repeat steps 5 and 6, filling the loom with loops. Always turn the loom in the same direction and work loops on the same side of the loom. Keep the single crochet stitches centered.

TIP

• •

The side to which your starting loop was attached is your "home prong." When working the strip, consistently work the upper loop on the "home prong." Most right-handers find it easier to attach the loop to the left-side prong, while left-handers prefer the right.

• •

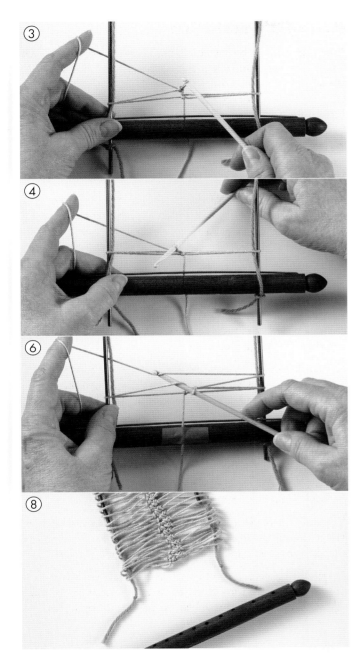

8. Most projects will require that you create a strip with more loops than can fit on the loom so you will need to move loops off of the loom as you work. When you feel you no longer have enough room to work comfortably, remove the bottom bar and slide most of the loops from the loom.

9. Reassemble the loom and continue. When your strip is the desired length, tie off the last loop: Insert the hook from top to bottom through the back of the loop on the right prong, yarn over and pull loop through the loop on the hook. Tie off.

Cable Join

An easy way to join strips that requires no extra yarn is with a cable join. This method entails slip stitching the loops of two strip through each other.

1. Place the strips side by side, with the starting slipknots at the same end. In the photo, the waste yarn is still in place, holding the loops in position as they came off the loom.

2. Insert the hook into the first loop of the right strip and then into the first loop of the left strip. Draw the loop of the left strip through the loop of the right strip, thus slipstitching one loop through the other.

3. Insert the hook into the second loop of the right strip and draw it through the loop on your hook, completing another slipstitch. Continue working from one strip to the other to the end of the strips.

4. At the end, if one strip has more loops than the other, loosen the last stitch of that strip, remove the extra loops, and tie off the strip again. After the last slipstitch, pull up a loop from the yarn tail from one of the strips, and pull the tail through the last loop on the hook. Tie off the yarn.

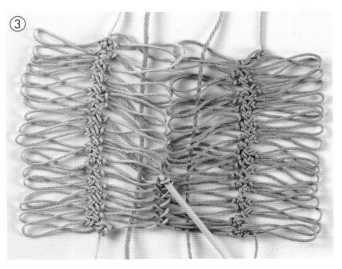

TIP ✂

Keep the work as low as possible on the loom to allow room to pass the crochet hook from front to back. Maintain tension on the yarn with your non-hook hand to control placement of the loops on the loom.

HAIRPIN LACE NECK SCARF

By Jennifer Hansen

Six short strips of hairpin lace are simply joined using a cable join and then edged using an ornate crochet stitch. The results of this quick project are enough to spice up any outfit. And better yet, this project is fast enough to make a gorgeous last-minute gift. One of the advantages of working this design in hairpin lace is that it behaves like a keyhole scarf: it can either be tied at the throat, or one end of the scarf can be brought through the stitches at the opposite side of the scarf to affix it around the neck.

YOU WILL NEED

Yarn

- 95 yd (86 m) double knitting weight yarn

- Shown: Tilli Tomas Plie, 100% silk, 50 g/140 yd, Gloxinia: 1 skein

Hooks/Tools

- G/4 mm crochet hook or size needed to obtain gauge

- H/5 mm cochet hook or size needed to obtain gauge

- Hairpin lace loom that will adjust to 4½" (11.5 cm)

- 5 clip on markers

- Tapestry needle

Gauge

- 36 lps = 4" (10 cm) with 2 strands yarn and larger hook

- 16 sc = 4" (10 cm) with 1 strand yarn and smaller hook

Skill level

- Intermediate

Strips

Notes:

Six short strands of hairpin lace are created using two strands of yarn held together and then joined using a 1 × 1 cable join. A single strand of yarn is then joined at one of the short ends to create an ornate crochet edging. The edging is continued without cutting along the entire perimeter of the scarf.

Set up loom so prongs are 4½" (11.5 cm) apart. Using yarn double-stranded, make six strips that have 28 loops each. Leave 8" (20.3 cm) starting and ending tails.

Work Cable Joins

Following steps 1 to 3 on page 261, join two strips. Treat both strands of each loop as one. End the join with the last loop on your hook. Temporarily secure this loop with a clip-on marker. The side of the fabric facing you now is the RS.

Keeping RS facing, join each of the next 5 strips to one of the free sides of the joined work. Join these strips in exactly the same way as the first join, securing the last loop on the hook temporarily with a clip on marker.

Short Side Edging

With RS facing and smaller hook, take a single strand of yarn and join with Sl st through right-most loop (remember, each loop has 2 strands!) on shorter side.

Working into untwisted loops throughout:

Row 1: Ch 4, tr in first 2-lp-grp, ch 2, 2 tr in same 2-lp-grp, [(2 tr, ch 2, 2 tr) in next 2-loop-group] 5 times, (2 tr, ch 2, 2 tr) in last 2-lp-grp, turn. (7 groups of loops worked)

Row 2: Sl st in each of first 2 trs and in first ch-2 sp. Ch1, sc in same ch-2 sp, [ch 2, (tr, ch 1) 3 times in next ch-2 sp, ch 2, (tr, ch 1) 3 times in same ch-2 sp, ch 2, sc in next ch-2 sp] 3 times, turn.

Row 3: Ch 3, [ch 3, (dc, ch 2, sc in last dc) 5 times in ch-3 sp, ch 3, dc in next sc] 3 times.

Work ch 2, 3 sc in edge tr of Row 1, then continue to Edge Long Side.

Edge Long Side

The long side is edged with a simple pattern of [ch-5, sc around one side (2 strands) of edge loop] evenly across. Sc into the center stitches of each strip and also into each join. When doing so, stop and pull the chain tightly to make sure it lies evenly along the edge of the strips. Adjust the number of chains before working a sc into the center of the strip or the joins so that the chain edging does not ruffle or pucker. Work the last sc so that it is even with the top of the strip at the opposite side of the neck scarf.

To edge the opposite short side of the strip, repeat Short Side Edging instructions, then repeat Edge Long Side. End this long side edging by working a chain and then a Sl st to the 3rd ch at the start of Row 3 on the Short Side Edging. Tie off.

Finishing: Use tails to secure the last loops of each join to the first loops of each join so as to mimic the join pattern. Weave in and trim all ends.

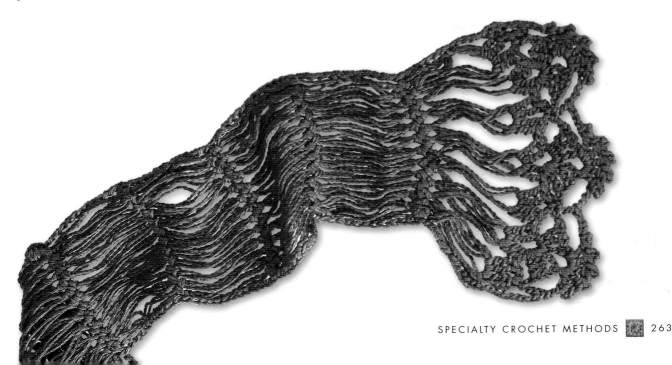

Broomstick Lace

Broomstick lace is worked with one large knitting needle (about the size of a broom handle) and a crochet hook.

Each row is worked in two stages. In the first stage, loops are pulled up with the hook along a foundation chain or previous row of stitches and slipped onto the large needle. In the second stage, the loops are worked off the needle, usually in groups to form clusters. The clusters can be worked with single, double, or even triple crochet stitches, depending on the look you want. When working broomstick lace, the right side of the work is always facing—you do not turn the work from stage to stage or row to row.

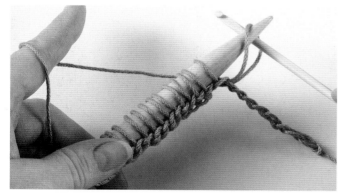

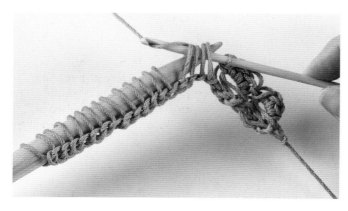

Broomstick Lace Stitch Pattern

Chain the designated number of stitches.

Stage 1, Row 1: Without turning the work, extend the loop that is on the hook and slip it onto the knitting needle. Insert the crochet hook into each chain, pull up a loop, and transfer the loop to the knitting needle without twisting the loop.

Stage 2, Row 1: Without turning the work, work crochet stitches as indicated by the broomstick pattern. Shown here: Insert hook into first 4 lps, yo, pull yarn through all 4 lps, ch 1 (counts as first sc), work 3 more sc in same lps, [4 sc in next group of 4 lps] until end of row. Do not turn.

Stage 1, Row 2: Without turning the work, extend the loop that is on the hook and slip it onto the knitting needle. Insert the crochet hook into each sc in the previous row, pull up a loop, and transfer the loop to the knitting needle without twisting the loop. For the last loop, pull up a loop in the ch-1.

Stage 2, Row 2: Same as Stage 2, Row 1.

Repeat Stages 1 and 2 of Row 2 for the desired number of rows. Tie off.

To stagger the clusters from row to row, begin and end every other row by joining only two loops together.

For a more substantial foundation, work a row of single crochet into the foundation chain before beginning Stage 1 of Row 1. Then pull up loops in each of the single crochets.

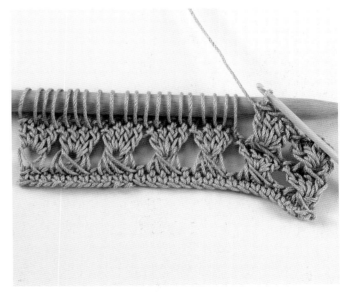

Try other variations by working off the clusters in double crochets (shown here) or triple crochets. Just remember to use the appropriate number of chain stitches to begin the first cluster of Stage 2. Always work the same number of stitches into the loops as the number of loops in the cluster.

BROOMSTICK LACE JEWELRY FRAME
by Jennifer Hansen

What girl doesn't need a pretty way to organize her jewelry? Featuring a simple Broomstick Lace stitch that is as beautiful as it is quick to work up, this pattern provides a "recipe" so you can fit any size frame and crochet a pretty way to display your shawl pins or earrings as works of art!

YOU WILL NEED

Yarn

- Dk-weight yarn, 140 yd (129 m)
- Shown: Tilli Tomas Plie, 100% silk with beads, 50 g/140 yd (129 m), Jade: 1 skein

Hooks/Tools

- 3/D (3.25 mm) crochet hook or size needed to obtain gauge
- US #19 (15mm) straight knitting needle
- Tapestry needle

Materials

- 11" x 14" frame or size frame desired
- Coordinating fabric
- Cardboard cut to fit frame
- Stapler

Gauge

- 25 sc = 4" (10 cm) (unstretched)
- Approx 20 sts = 4" (10 cm) in Broomstick Lace Pattern (stretched)

Jewelry Frame

Notes:

This project requires a frame with the glass removed, one that can accommodate the thickness of knitted or crocheted fabric.

This broomstick lace pattern uses double crochet stitches for Stage 2 of each row.

Ch 57, turn.

Foundation (RS): Sc into 2nd ch from hook and into each ch until end—56 sts.

Stage 1, Row 1: Without turning the work, extend the loop that is on the hook and slip it onto the knitting needle. Insert the crochet hook into each sc, pull up a loop, and transfer the loop to the knitting needle without twisting the loop—56 loops.

Stage 2, Row 1: Insert hook into first 4 lps, yo, pull yarn through all 4 lps, ch 3 (counts as first dc), work 3 more dc in same lps, [4 dc in next group of 4 lps] until end of row—14 clusters. Do not turn.

Stage 1, Row 2: Without turning the work, extend the loop that is on the hook and slip it onto the knitting needle. Insert the crochet hook into each dc in the previous row, pull up a loop, and transfer the loop to the knitting needle without twisting the loop. For the last loop, pull up a loop in the top of the ch-3.

Stage 2, Row 2: Repeat Stage2, Row 1.

Repeat Stages 1 and 2 of Row 2 twelve times, or until the work is long enough to stretch across the length of the frame. Tie off. Weave in ends.

Assemble Frame

Many frames come with a cardboard insert cut to the size of the frame opening. If yours doesn't, make one out of thin cardboard. Then cut your fabric about 1" (2.5 cm) wider on all sides than the cardboard insert and staple it as close as possible to the edges of the cardboard around the perimeter. The staples should be covered by the frame itself. Note the position of the staples, as you will also be stapling your knit or crochet work in the same way and do not want to hit the same staples.

Variations

Make a broomstick lace panel for any size frame, with any yarn! Make a 4" (10 cm) square gauge swatch and stretch the swatch tightly both vertically and horizontally to figure out the stretched gauge. Note the horizontal measurement. Use your stretched gauge swatch to determine the correct number of stitches to fit your desired frame dimensions based on the pattern stitch multiple:

Number of pattern repeats in a 4" (10 cm) width = _____ (A)

Width of frame opening = _____ (inches) (B)

Number of sts in a pattern repeat (see pattern) = _____(C)

Figure out the number of pattern repeats for best fit = (A x B)/4 = Pattern Repeats = _____ (D). Round to the nearest whole number.

Fit for length as you work: Your stitch gauge should ensure that the width of your project is a near perfect fit to the width of the frame. To ensure a perfect height, stop stitching from time to time to fit the work over the frame insert to determine when enough rows have been completed to fill the height of the frame opening. Stop when you reach the desired length.

About the Author

Margaret Hubert of Pawling, New York, is the author of 14 other books including *Hooked Hats, Hooked Bags, Hooked Scarves, Hooked Throws, Hooked for Toddlers, Plus Size Crochet, Knits for Men,* and *Knit or Crochet—Have It Your Way.* She has enjoyed a life-long career designing both crochet and knit patterns for yarn companies and book and magazine publishers. Margaret also teaches at yarn shops, retreats, and national gatherings, and rarely misses a national conference in the needle arts field. A world traveler, Margaret pays close attention to the fashions in Europe and spots style trends as they hit New York. She is equally as passionate about knitting and crochet, and can design patterns for either, in any size or shape. Among her specialties, she is a master at freeform crochet.

Contributors

Julia Bryant

Julia Bryant is a textile artist whose crafts include crochet, knitting, tapestry weaving, and counted cross-stitch embroidery. She became fascinated with Tunisian/afghan crochet more than 25 years ago, and has been developing and perfecting her skills using the color inlay technique ever since. She creates all her own designs, and her work is often embellished with beads, bobbles, and embroidery. In 2008 Julia co-led a craft tour to Morocco, teaching Tunisian crochet and filet crochet. In the summer of 2008, Julia was awarded first prize in a design contest held by the Crochet Guild of America for one of her wall hangings. She has had several exhibitions of her work in Toronto and has taught at weekend craft seminars, the Creative Needlework Festival, Crochet Guild of America/Knitters' Guild of America conferences, and at Knitters' Guilds across Canada. Julia is a founding member and co-president of a Toronto Knitters' Guild, a member of the Downtown Knit Collective, the Toronto Hook-ups, and the Knitters' Guild of America, and a professional member of the Crochet Guild of America. She has a passion for color and loves to teach!

Jennifer Hansen

Jennifer Hansen lives in Fremont, California, where she is a full-time crochet and knit designer, teacher, and writer. Her innovative crochet work has been featured in various books, magazines, and television shows, including *Vogue Knitting, Interweave Crochet, The Happy Hooker, The Encyclopedia of* *Crochet* and *Knitty Gritty.* She has been described as "One of the names that immediately comes to mind when thinking of the creative forces that have helped transport crochet from the realm of acrylic afghans to the sexy world of figure-flattering fashions." *(Yarn Market News)* Her professional background is in architecture and information technology. Jennifer is passionate about the craft and wants to contribute to the joy you'll find in creating beautiful things.

Melody MacDuffee

A true lover of the art of crochet, Melody MacDuffee has been publishing her work since 1989. Some 2000 of her designs have been published over the years, and examples of her work have been exhibited in juried shows in several states, and have toured the country in the 2003/2004 "Rhythm of Crochet" traveling exhibit. Her art jewelry and wall hangings are examples of her overlay crochet technique, on the basis of which she was selected by the Crochet Guild of America to be its first traveling crochet instructor. The author of three books, with a fourth in the works, Melody has taught various crochet and jewelry-making techniques all around the country and as far away as Morocco and West Africa.

Prudence Mapstone

Prudence Mapstone is an Australian textile artist whose chosen medium is freeform knitting and crochet. She is passionate about color and loves to create tactile fabrics from multi-directional patches that often combine both crafts. She also loves to travel and has exhibited her work and demonstrated her methods in many different parts of the world. She first met Margaret Hubert over the internet, then in person, and they discovered that they have so much in common that they have become firm friends. Prudence is the author of five books that outline her free-form techniques, and you can see further examples of her creations at http://www.knotjustknitting.com

Tatyana Mirer

Tatyana Mirer is a knitwear and crochet designer and teacher. Her works and designs have been published in various magazines and books. Having a bachelor's degree in ladies wear fashion design from the Moscow Design Institute, Russia, Tatyana has studied specialized knitting and crochet to improve her craft knowledge and skills. Tatyana is a recognized Craft Yarn Council certified teacher and conducts workshops for beginners and advanced students at yarn shops, guilds, and knitting retreats. She translated *The Sweater Book* and *Big and Little Sweaters* by English designer Sasha Kagan for Mir, a Moscow publishing house. Her crochet cardigan won the "Honorable Mention" in CGOA Design Contest/2008. Her crochet designs have been published in *Family Circle Easy Crochet Book* (Sixth & Spring Books, New York) and in magazines, including *Crochet!* (July/2008; May/2009) and *Crochet Today!* (March/April, 2009).

Nancy Nehring

Nancy Nehring is a nationally recognized author, designer, and teacher in the needle-arts field. She is the author of several books including *The Lacy Knitting of Mary Schiffmann, 50 Heirloom Buttons to Make,* and *Embellishing with Beads.* Numerous needle-art magazines, including *Threads, PieceWork, and Crochet!,* have published her work. She has designed for DMC, Coats and Clark, and Dynamic Resources Group, among others. Her Irish crochet doll dress was awarded first place in crochet in the 2003 PieceWork Needleworker of the Year contest. She lectures and teaches locally, regionally, and nationally at events that include Embroiderers' Guild of America Seminar, Crochet Guild of America Chain Link, and Stitches.

Pam Shore

Crocheting for 50 years, Pam Shore is a member of the Crochet Guild of America and has attended their annual conferences since 1995. She is also a member of the International Free Form Crochet Guild where her work may be seen on www.freeformcrochet.com. Her designs have been published by Lark Books in *Kooky Crochet* and *Jewelry with a Hook.* The Ravelry name of "uncommoncrochet," aptly describes what she loves to do.

Pauline Turner

Pauline Turner has been a recognized crochet authority for many years. She was the first editor of *SlipKnot,* the Knitting and Crochet Guild magazine; she is the founder and instigator of the International Diploma in Crochet distance learning course; she served as international liaison chairperson of the Crochet Guild of America; she is a prolific author of books and magazine articles; has produced innumerable designs exploring the unexpected aspects of crochet; lectures in many countries and runs her own business.

Myra Wood

Myra Wood is an internationally known teacher, fiber and bead artist, designer, and author. Specializing in all things freeform, she teaches workshops and lectures on crochet, knitting, beading, and embroidery at national retreats, conventions, and yarn shops across the country. She was a regular guest on *Knitty Gritty* and *Uncommon Threads* for the DIY and HGTV networks and has published a number of beaded jewelry and knit/crochet clothing patterns in a wide range of books and magazines. Her own book, *Creative Crochet Lace,* is available online and through local yarn and book stores. Myra has been crocheting, sewing, and crafting since she was young and is passionate about any opportunity to inspire others creatively. She is also the moderator for the 1600-member International Freeform Guild and is the coordinator for their annual international shows. Go to www.myrawood.com to see galleries of her work.

Index